Fraud

THE AMAZING CAREER OF DR. SAVUNDRA

Fraud

THE AMAZING CAREER OF DR. SAVUNDRA

Jon Connell and Douglas Sutherland

STEIN AND DAY/*Publishers*/New York

First published in the United States of America in 1979
Copyright © 1978 by Jon Connell and Douglas Sutherland
All rights reserved
Printed in the United States of America
Stein and Day/*Publishers*/Scarborough House
Briarcliff Manor, N.Y. 10510

Library of Congress Cataloging in Publication Data

Connell, Jon.
  Fraud: the amazing career of Dr. Savundra.

  1. Savundra, Emil.   2. Crime and criminals—Great
Britain—Biography.   3. Swindlers and swindling—Great
Britain—Biography.   4. Fraud.   I. Sutherland, Douglas
joint author.   II. Title.
HV6248.S365C65   1979   364.1'63'0924 [B]   78-66247
ISBN 0-8128-2602-7

To Jeremy and Fiona

Contents

Acknowledgments

OUR THANKS TO ALL who helped us write this book. Among the journalists who worked on the story in the sixties, Kenneth Clark, Len Adams, Roy East, Colin Simpson, Lewis Chester, Brian McConnell, Jack Knights, Peter Earle, Don Cassell and Alex Hendry were particularly helpful. The cuttings libraries of the *Daily Express* and the *Daily Telegraph* proved a valuable starting point. So did INSIDE INTERPOL by Tom Tullett and THE GNOMES OF ZÜRICH by T. H. Fehrenbach, which helped us to untangle the intricacies of the Belgian saga. Willie Frischauer's biography of David Frost and his study of the London Clinic (THE CLINIC) also yielded useful material.

Some of the original research for the book involved studying lengthy trial transcripts and a mass of memos, letters and other documents. But much of it came from talking to dozens of people who once knew Savundra well. We are grateful to ex-members of the staff of Fire, Auto and Marine whom we were able to interview, and who were almost without exception extremely helpful. Stuart de Quincey Walker was always prepared to talk to us, even though he knew our attitude was a critical one.

Ceylonese journalist Nihal Corea helped us with background information; John Fleming gave us a graphic account of Savundra's early power-boating adventures; various members of David Frost's sixties production team reminded us of a remarkable interview; and many others, whom space prevents us from naming, patiently submitted to our enquiries and helped to build up the picture. Norman Nail of the Board of Trade deserves special mention—not only for his information, but for his many suggestions about the final manuscript.

We are also grateful to a variety of people—from underworld acquaintances of Savundra to those who knew him as a young man—who filled in details during unattributable conversations; and to all others who wrote to us or answered our questions. Thanks are due to Peter Watson, editor of *The Press* and *Journal* in Aberdeen, for which Jon Connell was then working, for giving him the necessary time off; to Ceci White for her secretarial work and Annette Sutherland for typing the original manuscript; and finally to Rivers Scott, our editor at Hodder and Stoughton, for his patience and his guidance throughout.

Illustrations

Acknowledgments

1 Topix
2 Syndication International Ltd.
3 Private Collection
4 Popperfoto

5 London Express Pictures
6 Topham
7 Keystone Press Agency Ltd.
8 The Press Association Ltd.

'Flamboyant, arrogant and the
possessor of a misguided genius,
his cataclysmic life was a series
of headline-hitting grandiose
business deals and clashes with
governments . . .'

Kenneth Clark, 'Daily Telegraph'.

'A bumptious braggart, swelling with
rage or pleasure, consumed with his
egotism, loftily expounding his
plans and achievement, flying in
desperate panics at the advent of
disaster, rolling distraught with
crocodile tears running down his
fat cheeks - yet within minutes having
a miraculous recovery as disaster
was averted, and ascending to fresh
heights of lyrical self-
extolment . . .'

Peter Earle, 'News of the World'.

CHAPTER ONE

The Golden Age of Fraud

As THE HEAVILY-BARRED Black Maria drew away from the back entrance of the Old Bailey at the start of its four-mile journey to London's grimmest prison, Wormwood Scrubs, hostile eyes swivelled towards one passenger in an outstandingly elegant and expensive suit. From somewhere in the van a sneering voice was heard to say: 'So we're all peasants, are we?'

The remark was clearly directed at self-styled 'Doctor' Emil Savundra, who had just heard himself sentenced in Number One Court to eight years' imprisonment for one of the most heartless frauds of a generation. It was obvious that he was not going to be allowed to forget his contemptuous statement on television: 'I do not cross swords with the peasants.'

The man in the next seat, who had a well-earned reputation as a hard man, made a mental note: 'This joker is due for a going-over when we get inside.'

The forecast was to prove unfounded. Con-man par excellence, flamboyant bon vivant, brilliant financier and compulsive crook with an international record, he so prevailed upon his fellow prisoners, so convinced them that he was a victim of circumstances, and so enlisted their sympathy that he became a favourite of inmates and prison authorities alike.

The persuasive charm which had been his strongest card throughout an incredible career of deception did not desert him in his worst hour.

When we set out to write the life of Emil Savundra we were, of

course, familiar with the spectacular crash of Savundra's Fire, Auto
and Marine Insurance Company, which left 400,000 British motorists without cover; with his dramatic confrontation with David Frost
on television, and with the theatrical atmosphere of trial at the Old
Bailey; but these, we found as our researches progressed, were only a
part of a much more complex picture.

Savundra, although unique in the scale and sheer effrontery of his
fraudulent operations, was in the mainstream of crime in Britain in
the late nineteen-fifties and the early sixties.

The pattern of crime in the two decades after the war was determined by the economic circumstances of the time. The first decade
was the period of rationing, shortages, the black market and under-
the-counter deals. It provided limitless opportunities for the street-
corner spiv and the small-time crook.

In the second decade, however, the picture changed radically.
Restrictions were being cast aside. The affluent, never-
had-it-so-good society was taking shape. The black-market spiv had
become a quaintly out-dated figure. The word spiv, in fact, had
largely passed out of the language. But a new and more sinister spiv-
vish character, one capable of inflicting far greater damage on society, began to emerge: the con man who operated at board-room and
international level; the trickster who understood the intricacies of
company law, and who was capable of deceiving not only gullible
investors, but even governments and their agencies.

Savundra headed that league. He was a roly-poly Ceylonese who
spoke English with only the faintest of accents, and who, after taking
out British citizenship, strove to become more British than the British. He used his dishonestly gained wealth to ingratiate himself with
those whom he regarded as the 'right people'—the rich and the titled;
he plunged into the fashionable rich man's sport of power-boat racing; he aspired to a knighthood. All this after he had swindled the
governments of Communist China, Goa, Ghana, Costa Rica, and was
in the act of applying the insurance premiums paid by 400,000 British
motorists to his own uses.

Yet this cynical fraudster was deeply religious. He had a genuine,
lifelong commitment to the Roman Catholic Church. He supported
the Church with lavish generosity, and liked to give the impression
that he was deeply involved in its affairs.

Savundra had an immense capacity for making people like him.
Those who had experienced his charm found it almost impossible to
believe that all the time he had been using them for his own purposes.
This was so in the case of nearly all his senior colleagues in the Fire,

Auto and Marine enterprise. It was true, also, at a lower level.

When F.A.M. crashed, and Savundra found himself jostled in a hostile crowd, the voice of a woman policy-holder rose protesting above the hubbub: 'I know Dr. Savundra. He is such a nice gentleman . . .'

CHAPTER TWO

In the Beginning

IT WAS A SUMMER'S evening in 1937 in downtown Colombo. The sports meeting was over. The teenage competitors and their parents were gathered round the table on which the trophies were displayed, waiting for the presentation ceremony and the speeches. By custom the prize-giving was undertaken by a local celebrity and this time it was to have been by a distinguished law lecturer from the University—but the audience were in for a surprise. The lecturer, unable at the last moment to attend himself, had sent his thirteen-year-old son in his place.

The boy was equal to the occasion. He wore a smart new suit of rich silk, and he had been driven to the sports ground in a rickshaw, ordering the driver to take him by way of Colombo's smart Plaza Lane so that he could show off his finery.

One of those who was present at the ceremony vividly remembers his speech to this day and particularly the final words: 'In sports it *does* matter if you win or lose. If you lose nobody cares a hang about you. If you win, then you become somebody!' Everyone clapped enthusiastically.

It was the first taste of the limelight for Michael Marion Emil Anacletus Savundranayagam.* Perhaps the sentiments were not in accord with the amateur-sport outlook of the times, but they truly reflected young Emil's personal philosophy. His preoccupation with winning stayed with him for life—even if winning meant frequently changing the rules of the game as he went along.

In those last pre-war years, Ceylon was still firmly under the British

*He did not adopt the name of Savundra until he permanently settled in Britain in 1960, but for convenience we have used this name throughout the book.

16

Raj. The island's economy, based on tea, was dependent on British finance and British administration. The reins of power were in the hands of the men who gathered nightly to drink their ration of whisky at the bar of the Europeans-only club in Colombo's most fashionable quarter.

But the Ceylonese had their own elitist society which was both rich and exclusive. Most exclusive of all were the traditional land-owning families, many of whom still owned vast tracts of land and whose dynasties reached back many centuries. Immediately below the land-owners came the professional classes and the rich businessmen. The Ceylonese held the professional classes, in particular, in high esteem. The lawyers, the medical men and the academics lived lives of well-ordered elegance in sharp contrast to the great majority of the population who existed in conditions of unrelieved squalor.

Emil Savundra was born on 6th July, 1923, into one of the most highly respected legal families in the province of Jaffna which formed the north part of Ceylon. He could trace his ancestry back in direct male line to a Philippu Tisseru who came to Ceylon from India during the time of the Portugese and Dutch occupation. Tisseru was originally a Hindu, but he and his family became some of the earliest Roman Catholic converts. His son, Gabriel, was appointed private tutor in Tamil to the Rev. Daniel Poor, an early American missionary who came to Ceylon in 1816. Mr. Poor was a Protestant, and, in consequence, Gabriel Tisseru became as fervent a Protestant as his father had been a Catholic, and his life was featured in a contemporary religious book: *They Lived their Faith*. But later generations of the male line reverted to the Roman Catholic faith—Savundra's grandfather was a scholar and author, who demonstrated his enthusiasm for his Church by composing Roman Catholic hymns in Tamil. Meanwhile, the family's position in the legal profession was being established. Emil's father, Anthony Peter Savundranayagam, whose uncle rose to be a High Court Judge in Travancore, won a scholarship to London University and returned to Ceylon to practise as an advocate. Quite soon he received promotion to the Bench. He did not stay there long. He was hyper-sensitive and suffered acutely whenever he had to sentence a man to prison. He found it difficult to reject even the most improbable stories, with the result that his decisions were frequently overturned by a higher court. Eventually he found a happier way of life as a lecturer at Colombo College and devoted much of his time to writing legal text books.

'He was an awful magistrate,' remembers one of his students. 'A fine man, a fine lecturer but too good for the Bench.'

And another of his students, James T. Rutnam, records of him that 'he was always soft-spoken, courteous and gentle . . . more concerned about the ethics of an act than its legality . . . in sum, A.P. Savundranayagam was one of God's great and good men.'

Anthony Savundranayagam was also deeply religious and instilled his Roman Catholic faith into his family. It was something which was to have a particularly profound influence on his youngest son, Emil.

Emil's mother came from a land-owning family. Thus, according to the strict protocol of Ceylon society, it could be said that she married beneath her. The wedding had been a grand one. They had driven to the church in a maharajah's golden coach. Her husband was a cultured and kindly man, but, just as he had proved incapable of making cogent decisions on the Bench, so he was to prove ineffective in the home. He was an indulgent father, happy to give his four children anything they wanted. In return all he asked for was peace and quiet to pursue his studious way of life.

All the Savundranayagam children turned out, in the tradition of the family, to be remarkably intelligent. The eldest son, Aloysius, took a Bachelor of Arts degree at London University when he was only nineteen and went on two years later to come top in the Civil Service entrance exam. Tragically he died, only months later, of hepatitis. It was something which deeply affected the eleven-year-old Emil, who paid his first visit to London with his mother for the funeral.

Both Emil's elder sisters chose academic careers. Lolitta was to become administrative head of the Mount Sinai Hospital in New York and Indreni took a doctorate in psychology at Cambridge University before emigrating to America where she became a lecturer and author of books on education.

Emil was educated at the Benedictine College of St. Peter in Colombo, where he is remembered as having been erratically brilliant. His forte was figures. He could calculate in his head far faster than his schoolmates who had to resort to pencil and paper. Working out complicated sums was one of his boyhood hobbies. He also had an acute interest in practical and technical matters.

Some of his happiest hours at school were spent in experimenting and inventing. Radio, hi-fi and the potentialities of television fascinated him. So did engines and the problems of making machines go faster.

Unlike his brothers and sisters, however, Emil was more interested in cutting a dash in front of his school fellows than coming top of the class. Typically, on one occasion he devoted much time and trouble

learning how to make nitro-glycerine which he presented in a test
tube to his physics master. The master, goaded by Emil's constant
habit of going off on his own tangent, gave him a beating and kept him
in after school to complete the lesson he had been set. Emil occupied
the time making more nitro-glycerine with the inevitable result of
further punishment.

It was only in his last year at St. Peter's that Emil's desire to 'be
someone' brought about a change in his attitude to authority. Previously it had been enough for him to act big in front of his school fellows. Now when his contemporaries were competing to be made pre-
fects, Emil decided that he too would enter the lists. He eventually
became head of the school and captain of the shooting and squash
teams.

There was one other side to his make-up which may seem to be out
of character with his self-seeking ambition and desire for recognition.
This was his preoccupation with religion. Frequently when school had
broken up for the day and his classmates were hurrying out of the
school gates, Emil would quietly retire to the chapel where he would
spend a long time on his knees, deep in prayer. His was not the trans-
ient fervour of adolescence. It stayed with him all his life. Perhaps his
faith, in later life, was to provided the ultimate solace for a troubled
conscience; perhaps, too, there is a clue to his innermost self in his
observation: 'One does not cheat God.'

The master at school who knew Emil best, Father Gregory
Gunewardena, recognising his talents, urged him to be a scientist. But
for once Emil's father put his foot down. He insisted that his son
should follow the family tradition and study law. To soften the blow
he presented Emil, on his sixteenth birthday, with something on
which the boy had set his heart. This was a powerful Black Arrow
Norton motorcycle.

It was not a wise choice for someone of Emil's temperament. He
had scarcely learned how to master the controls before he was practising racing skid turns. He came off and broke his left knee. Riding
again within a few weeks he came off again and this time broke his
right one.

A few months later, roaring through the streets of Colombo late at
night very drunk and with two friends clinging on to the back, he once
more came unstuck. This time he broke his arm so badly that it had to
be reconstructed in plastic—but his two passengers were killed.

The family decided that the motorcycle was far too dangerous a
toy, and indulgently but illogically, they bought him a Tiger Moth aircraft instead. Within a year Emil had won the Royal Colombo Flying

Club aerobatics competition. It was his delight to take up passengers, the more nervous the better, and fly out to sea off Mount Lavinia. Then, turning for land, he would fly flat out for the steep side of the mountain, only pulling back the stick at the very last moment to swoop over the top.

It was now 1939. War had broken out, and Emil idled away the first two years of it waiting to be old enough to join the air force. At the time flying seemed to him to be the most important thing in the world—he was not to find such an all-consuming hobby until he took up power-boating in Britain twenty years later. But, when he reached eighteen, his father, with a rather belated concern for his safety, refused to let him take a commission in the air force and put him down for the Royal Engineers instead. Emil bitterly resented the decision. He later said he got drunk every day for three weeks in protest. But his father was not to have the opportunity of watching his son's career as an officer. He died on 17th September, 1941.

Emil soon became a captain, having drawn attention to himself by writing to the military authorities about various matters normally outside the scope of a junior officer (mainly the shortcomings of his superiors). The promotion was to be short-lived. With half-a-dozen other rich young officers, he formed a circle whose conduct was an odd mixture of strict protocol and riotous living. They would always dress in full mess kit for meals—but their conduct was often far from that to be expected from officers and gentlemen. There were 'incidents'.

Emil became a great womaniser, taking his affairs very seriously while they lasted. There was a W.R.N.S. Hostel, called Kent House, near the H.Q. of the Royal Engineers, and Emil frequently attempted late-night visits over the wall. He had a Cadillac car and to make his assaults upon the citadel easier to carry out he had an optional extra fitted to the vehicle—a ladder in the boot. When the boot was opened, the ladder would automatically extend.

His visits to that house led to one particularly serious episode. Emil's current lady friend—who came of course from Kent House— had broken off their romance. He returned to the mess and announced that he was going to drink a bottle of whisky, then shoot himself. Placing a loaded revolver on the bar, he ordered the whisky and settled down to drink it.

He was well down the bottle when a friend and fellow officer, Cecil Jonklass, came back from a night on the town.

'What are you doing?' he asked.

'I am just going to finish off this bottle and then I am going to shoot myself.'

'Good idea,' said Jonklass, putting his revolver on the bar beside Emil's. 'But why do we not drink another bottle first?'

In the end neither man could remember what exactly they had set out to do. Instead, they used the valuable mess china for target practice for their revolvers before collapsing unconscious.

Fortunately for Emil, Jonklass's father was a good friend of the Commanding Officer, Colonel Fernando. Both men were demoted for the escapade but there was no court martial. Later a report on Emil by Fernando described him as having 'inspired leadership powers' but adding that he was also 'lazy and fat'.

During the war Ceylon became a bastion of the Indian Ocean which the Japanese were never able to invade.

Emil saw no action. Instead he found that life as a member of the island's defence force offered plenty of scope for flamboyance and womanising. He was able to carry on making joy rides in his Tiger Moth. He was also at this stage a heavy drinker, although diabetes was eventually to force him to give up alcohol. One tale he was later to tell was of a wild party on a destroyer anchored off the coast, at the end of which one sailor died and many others were violently ill for several days. An officer who went below to find another barrel of gin unhappily brought up aviation fuel instead.

After the war Emil complied with his father's wishes and went to Colombo College to study law, but he took little interest in his course. As he had told his contemporaries when he was thirteen, he wanted 'to be someone'—and he felt the best outlet for his energies would be in the business world.

Without waiting to qualify he left his law studies in 1947 and joined a Ceylon-based English general trading company, called Taylor Mackay. Ceylon, like every other country which had been involved in the war, was suffering shortages and many goods were rationed for the civilian population. Emil Savundra met an American who was running the company and signed on as a broker. In this capacity he obtained large quantities of NAAFI stores which were hidden away until their price on the black market rose to a level where the firm could make a financial killing.

At that time corruption was widespread among Ceylonese officials. Savundra's apparent genius for obtaining desirable goods at ridiculously low prices resulted from the contacts he had made and from the use of bribery. His success soon earned him a directorship with Taylor Mackay.

He had only been working for the company for six months when, at a party given by a mutual friend, he met his future wife, Pushpam

Aloysius. Pushpam was beautiful, aristocratic and rich. The Aloysius family were the largest land-owners in North Ceylon and were directly descended from the old kings of Jaffna.

Emil at once decided that this was the woman he would make his wife whatever difficulties might be put in his way; and he was under no doubt that difficulties there would be. The Aloysius family were proud and steeped in tradition. In a country where arranged marriages were still the custom, it was unlikely that the head of Pushpam's family would look kindly on the son of a University academic as a suitable candidate for the hand of his daughter.

However, the attraction which Emil felt for Pushpam at that first meeting seems to have been reciprocated. Like many other girls who met Emil she found him a witty and amusing companion. But she detected in him something more.

Talking of him towards the end of his life she was to say: 'What a real man he was in those days—a man one could be proud to know and love, a man with the world at his feet and the imagination to take it in his hands. When I first met Emil he had the energy of twenty men. He had ability, imagination and drive and dominated any social company he was in. In his way he was a genius. Other men walked in his shadow and talked in tens while Emil talked in thousands.'

Within a week Pushpam's father had made it clear to her that he was violently opposed to the match. He forbade her to see the young man. The parental veto did not deter Emil. When he sent a van loaded with flowers for Pushpam to the Aloysius mansion, she, for fear of angering her father, refused them. For the next two days, every hour on the hour, Colombo's leading florist returned bearing ever more impressive floral offerings. Finally Pushpam accepted them and sent them to the nearest hospital.

Now the suitor used his Tiger Moth in the campaign. To keep her away from Emil's attention, Aloysius had sent his daughter to stay with her immensely wealthy maternal uncle, Chittampalam Gardiner. Gardiner was a senator in the Ceylon Parliament and a leading businessman who controlled a complex of cinemas and industrial enterprises worth over £3,000,000. He lived in a mansion on the outskirts of Colombo, but after Pushpam's arrival it ceased to be the peaceful retreat to which Chittampalam Gardiner like to return after a tiring day in the city. Its calm was shattered by the roar of the Tiger Moth's engine as Emil stunted crazily overhead. There were two tall coconut palms in the garden only a few feet further apart than the wingspan of the Moth. Emil's favourite trick was to hurtle between them and then swoop up over the swimming-pool where he hoped to catch a glimpse of Pushpam sunbathing, and throw out a bouquet of flowers. Then, with a wave of his hand, he would climb up once more into the sky.

For almost eighteen months Pushpam's father held out. Pushpam realised the anguish the affair was causing her family but she was becoming as determined as Emil that the marriage should go through.

In the end one of her aunts managed to bring round the stubborn Aloysius. In finally giving his consent, however, he made it a condition that Emil should abandon his career in business and return to his law studies.

The wedding, on 8th June, 1949, was one of the society events of the year in Ceylon. Aloysius, having decided to accept Emil into the family, did things in style and 3,000 guests toasted the bride and groom in champagne.

Such a bizarre courtship might not have seemed the best foundation for a lasting marriage, yet Pushpam remained devoted to Emil for the rest of her life, and he (in his way) remained devoted to her.

For a short time Emil kept his word to his father-in-law and went back to his law studies. He did this because it was convenient rather than because he felt it to be his duty. His self-esteem did not allow him to be overawed or to genuflect to his newly acquired relations, however important. But as it happened he had decided anyway to sever his links with Taylor Mackay. He had discovered that among his bosses was one whose idea of sport was to shoot elephants with a machine-gun. In Emil's view such caddish behaviour made him someone with whom he could no longer be associated. Having thus put himself out of a job, he felt he might just as well re-enrol at the law school. But the law did not offer sufficient challenge, or come anywhere near to satisfying his ambition to make money and be powerful.

In addition to her dowry, Pushpam had made a wedding present to her husband of a portfolio of shares which he promptly sold. Thus he had available a working capital of some £15,000. In 1949 it was a very substantial sum indeed.

Thanks to the money from Pushpam's dowry the young married couple were able to indulge their tastes for high living. They had six servants to wait on them in their luxurious home in Colombo, they had two cars, an expensive Riley and a Buick in the garage, and they entertained lavishly.

Emil had a near-professional talent as a jazz pianist and his ability to relieve the tedium of the dullest party, coupled with Pushpam's beauty, charm and high social standing, made them one of the most popular couples on the free-spending party roundabout. But it was an expensive way of life, and within weeks Emil left the law school for the last time and plunged once more into business. His initial ventures were diverse and dubious. One of his early deals was to arrange the insurance of a ship carrying a load of tea through the Straits of Malacca. Unaccountably the boat sank and Emil collected a generous proportion of the claim money. But rumours circulated as to how the ship came to be holed and there was even a suggestion that some of the tea had, in fact, been cement.

Then there was a flirtation with gun-running to Burma. Emil acquired some British ex-War Department weapons but they proved to be so out-of-date that the Burmese Government refused delivery. Savundra lost on this deal. There were other transactions conducted with varying degree of success but it must soon have become obvious to him that none of them offered the short cut to riches which he so eagerly sought. Then, still in search of the big prizes, Emil met a certain Mr. Renfro.

CHAPTER THREE

Prayers Answered

IN OCTOBER, 1949, JUST four months after his wedding, Savundra formed the first of the many companies he was to create in his lifetime. With a typical lack of modesty, it was called Trans-World Enterprises Ltd. Its capital was less grandiose—100 Reis, or approximately £7.

The shares were divided into four parts, one each to Savundra and Cyril Gardiner (Pushpam's brother) and two parts to Pushpam. The three shareholders were also directors and a Mr. S. Sellamuttu, who was a prominent lawyer and businessman as well as a member of the Colombo Municipal Committee, was elected as the non-shareholding chairman.

The Articles of Association described the company as being in the export-import business. All the slick, get-rich-quick operators of the time liked to describe themselves vaguely as being in the export-import business.

Shortly after the formation of Trans-World Enterprises, Savundra set out on a tour of Burma to promote the company's interests and it was while he was there that he met Mr. Renfro.

H.E. Renfro was an American businessman. In the post-war years men of his sort were to be found scattered all over the globe. They stayed in the best hotels and appeared to have access to extensive funds, but their long suit was in the people in high places whom they appeared to know and the important business contacts they claimed. Most were Americans and they tended to drop hints that in their operations there was some deeper political significance than they would care to admit openly. At all costs they wanted to avoid being recognised for what they were—opportunist entrepreneurs anxious to grab at any chance to make a fast buck.

Savundra and Renfro did not meet by introduction; they met by chance in one of those smart hotel bars which are the natural hunting grounds of their kind, but they at once recognised each other as kindred spirits. By the time Savundra was due to return to Colombo from Burma the skeleton of a deal had been set up. Renfro had explained to Savundra that Red China was in desperate need of certain strategic materials, particularly oil, but that supplying them presented difficulties. The Korean war was imminent. China, in opposition to the Western powers, would naturally support the Communist North. Because the West were justifiably convinced that any sinews of war sent to China would be used in support of the North Koreans, they had imposed a strict embargo which included oil and petroleum.

Now it so happened, Renfro told Savundra, that he had strong business connections inside Red China and at the same time had information that there were several petroleum companies in the West who might be willing to supply oil to China if it could be done discreetly. He felt that his new friend, Emil Savundranayagam, the principal director of a distinguished export-import business fortuitously registered in Ceylon where there were elastic trading regulations, might be able to be of considerable help to him.

Suddenly Savundra was presented with the opportunity of escaping from the round of local humdrum deals and becoming involved in the big international scene. The political element added spice to the whole affair and the fact that over a million dollars was to be involved excited his commercial instincts. Any percentage of a million dollars was worthwhile.

When the two men parted it was agreed that Renfro would occupy himself with securing a firm order for oil from the Chinese while Savundra would set up the necessary organisation in Colombo to see that the deal was carried through.

On his return to Colombo he at once got down to earnest discussion with his co-director, Cyril Gardiner. Cyril Gardiner enjoyed a unique position in the hierarchy of Pushpam's powerful family. He had been born Cyril Aloysius and was one of Pushpam's elder brothers. The Aloysius family was a large one; so when Uncle Chittampalam had taken a fancy to the boy and suggested that he undertake his education and bring him up with a view to training him eventually to take over his empire, the Aloysius family enthusiastically agreed. Thus it was that young Cyril came to change his name to Gardiner and set out on a career that seemed assured of success.

Between them, Savundra and Cyril Gardiner decided that they

would set up a second company, and it was thus that the firm of Eastern Traders Ltd. came into being.

Eastern Traders was, in fact, interlocked with Trans-World Enterprises, who controlled ninety-five per cent of the shares. At the same time it was agreed that because of the important business it would handle it must be suitably 'dressed up'. The issued capital was to be 1,000 Reis in units of 10 Reis each and a board of directors was appointed of such prominence that nobody could doubt the company's stability. Seven directors were named, each holding one 10-Reis share. The chairman was to be Cyril Gardiner's benefactor Chittampalam Gardiner himself; Savundra, Cyril Gardiner and Pushpam were also to be on the board. The remaining three seats were then offered to and accepted by Mr. Sellamuttu, the lawyer who was chairman of Trans-World Enterprises, a Mr. Mahendra who was described as a company director, and Mr. R.P. Senanayake, son of D.S. Senanayake, the Prime Minister of Ceylon.

The stage was set. All that was now needed was for Savundra's friend, Mr. Renfro, to turn up with the Chinese oil contract.

Eastern Traders was formed in May 1950 and in August Renfro arrived in Colombo as the accredited representative of the Chinese Company of Hwa Shih Co. of Tientsin with a mandate to negotiate the supply of oil.

On 23rd October Savundra was in a position as a director of Trans-World Enterprises to write to the Hwa Shih Co., c/o Mr. H.E. Renfro, Colombo, in the following terms:

Dear Sirs,
    We confirm our conversations of these last weeks and confirm our acceptance of your order for 45,000 drums of lubricants of various specifications to be shipped direct to Tsingtao, China, at a c.i.f. price of 1,230,000 dollars. It is agreed that you will open Letters of Credit in our favour with a Bank or Banks nominated by us in Ceylon and/or India and/or Switzerland to cover the cost of this shipment and that this credit will be in favour of our subsidiary firm, Messrs. Eastern Enterprises Co.
        Yours faithfully,
                    Trans-World Enterprises Ltd.

It was typical of Savundra's methods then and later in his career that he should introduce yet another subsidiary company into an already confusing situation. On the date this letter was written Eastern Enterprises had not yet even been formed. The omission was rectified on 8th November when the Eastern Enterprises Co. was registered as a company which was wholly owned as equal partners by Trans-World Enterprises Ltd. and Eastern Traders Ltd.

In the meantime agreement had been reached as to the exact specifications of the shipment and a letter of credit for 1,230,000 dollars for Eastern Enterprises had been opened at the Eastern Bank two days before the company officially existed.

Now matters started to move fast. In order to finance the operation of the deal, Savundra and Gardiner junior arranged for Eastern Enterprises to borrow 20,000 Reis from Chittampalam A. Gardiner Ltd. At the same time Hwa Shih Co. were persuaded to arrange for the transfer of the credit from the Eastern Bank to the Union Bank of Switzerland in Zürich, the Eastern Bank having refused to grant Eastern Enterprises an outgoing credit. At the same time the exact specification of how the shipment was to be made up was passed to the Union Bank with the condition that the money could only be released on receipt of the relevant documents showing that the oil had been bought and dispatched. The 20,000 Reis supplied by Uncle Chittampalam was to cover the initial expenses until the main sum could be touched. In consideration of this, Eastern Enterprises undertook to repay C.A. Gardiner Ltd. the sum of 200,000 Reis as their share of the expected profits.

These preliminaries having been satisfactorily completed Emil Savundra, armed with full powers of attorney to act for his company in the matter of the purchase of the oil, left for Europe on 28th November. He also carried with him a letter of authority, signed by Renfro as the representative of the purchasing company confirming the contract. The letter included a paragraph which read:

> We suggest that you approach in a very discreet manner one of the undernoted organisations who we have reason to believe will not be averse to helping you obtain supplies for shipment to China.
> Société Mediterranéen [sic] de Produits Pétroliers.
> Marseilles Petrole France, Paris.
> Association of Independent Oil Cos., Teheran.
> Anglo-Iranian Oil Co., London.
> You shall have the right to select any of the Companies mentioned in the above paragraph or any other at your sole discretion.
> Very truly yours,
> HWA Shih Co., Tientsin
> Sgd. by Accredited Agent and Foreign Representative.

Thus armed, Savundra, accompanied by Pushpam, flew to London and set up his headquarters at the prestigious Mayfair Hotel. Three months previously their first child had been born, and the baby, a boy named Peter, went with them.

Savundra arrived in London on the evening of 29th November. On the morning of 30th November he wrote to the Société Mediterranéen de Produits Pétroliers, 6, Rue de la Darse, Marseilles, as follows:

Dear Sirs,

We have been given your name as a firm of petroleum dealers who are out of the 'ring'.

There is a large order for approximately 1 million U.S. dollars worth of Petroleum products for the Far East which we are in a position to obtain for you. Should you be interested please contact the undersigned immediately at the Mayfair Hotel, Berkeley Square, London, before Sunday, the 3rd Dec., whereafter I am flying to Zürich and can be contacted at the Hotel St. Gotthard, Zürich.

The S.M.P.P. replied in a letter dated 1st December expressing keen interest. It was signed: Pierre Duval, Directeur.

Savundra's trip to Zürich was, of course, to tie up the arrangements with the Union Bank. He sent a letter to the managing director explaining that he would later be presenting the necessary documents in person to authorise the release of the credit in favour of Eastern Enterprises. Then he added:

We feel you will be interested in knowing something about our firm whose partners are the well-known Companies, Eastern Traders Ltd. and Trans-World Enterprises Ltd.

Our Chairman is Senator Gardiner, the well-known business-man and financier, Chairman of the 'Gardiner Group' of Companies, the largest group of Companies in Ceylon with a capital of nearly six crores.

Mr. R.P. Senanayake is the son of the Rt. Hon. D.S. Senanayake, the Prime Minister of the Dominion of Ceylon.

Mr. S. Sellamuttu is a member of the Colombo Municipal Council, a well-known solicitor and leading businessman.

Our other Directors are also on the board of various other companies in Ceylon.

The two partners in our firm (Eastern Traders Ltd. and Trans-World Enterprises Ltd.) are at present holding major contracts for services and supply to the governments of our own country and foreign governments in our part of the world.

Yours very truly,

[Signature illegible]

It now becomes immediately obvious why it had been decided to set up Eastern Enterprises Ltd. as the operating company for the oil deal. Apart from the imposing list of directors it enabled Savundra to disguise the fact the shareholders were two 'straw' companies, and to present them instead as important organisations with international ramifications without there being much risk of his having to substantiate the claim. The subterfuge was also designed, when the time came, to help hoodwink the taxman whom Savundra regarded as his natural enemy.

Savundra did not now, or ever, go to Marseilles to see Pierre Duval of the proposed supplying company, S.M.P.P. Instead Duval first flew to Zürich to meet Savundra and later conversations took place in London and Paris.

Meantime, back in Colombo, there was some unease. This was partly because Savundra kept his partners short of information as to the progress he was making. But there was another and more pressing consideration so far as the chairman of the board, Chittampalam Gardiner, was concerned. It was that he had been informed that he was to be granted a knighthood. If he had originally had any doubts of the wisdom of lending his name as chairman of Eastern Enterprises, they were now redoubled.

Should it come out that he was involved in a deal to sell oil to Communist China the consequences for him would be very serious indeed. Not only would it damage the close relationship which he enjoyed with the Prime Minister of Ceylon who had been quite explicit in his views about Ceylonese nationals who sought ways of getting round the embargo by the Western powers; it would also undoubtedly cause a change of heart in Downing Street.

In London Savundra was prevaricating and even trying to interest Eastern Enterprises in new business deals. Eventually, even his friend Cyril Gardiner was showing signs of losing patience. On Boxing Day, 26th December, he cabled:

BROWNS BUSINESS ['Brown' was the code name for Renfro.]

WHATS ACTUAL POSITION UNCLE MORE ANXIOUS THIS THAN NEW BUSINESS HAVE ASSURED HIM EVERYTHING IS ALRIGHT.

Savundra cabled that progress was being made and asked for more spending money. Cyril Gardiner snapped back:

PHONING TWELVE MIDDAY MONDAY IF YOU NEED FURTHER FINANCES
YOU MUST BE ONE HUNDRED PERCENT SURE BROWNS BUSINESS.

It would seem that the telephone call at least temporarily served to
take the heat out of the situation. Next day Cyril Gardiner cabled:

VERY GLAD EVERYTHING FINE STOP PLEASE PURCHASE FOR UNCLE
BOTTLE OF PERFUME DANDY DORSAY GOD BLESS.

Meantime desperate moves were taking place in Colombo to alter
the constitution of the board so that Chittampalam could be extri-
cated. Unfortunately it was his company, Chittampalam A. Gardiner
Ltd., which had loaned the money to finance the deal. Desperately he
even considered handing over his whole empire and backdating the
handover to before the loan had been approved.

Savundra's contribution was a typical, if rather garbled, cable:

ANTEDATE PROCEED ACTION STOP MY IDEA AVOID MAXIMUM RESPON-
SIBILITY POSSIBLE ALSO THOROUGHLY COMPLICATE ISSUE GENERALLY
RED HERRING ANY POSSIBLE SHOWDOWN WHICH HIGHLY IMPROBABLE
ANYWAY.

There must have been sighs of relief in the Gardiner mansion when
Chittampalam Gardiner's name duly appeared on the list of those
being granted knighthoods in the New Year's Honours List on 1st
January, 1951.

Now Savundra's anxiety was to receive the necessary documents
from S.M.P.P. to enable him to have the money released from the
bank in Zürich. The documents required were:

1) Affidavit signed by the Agents; 2) Certificate of Lloyds' Survey;
3) Bill of Lading (a guarantee that the correct cargo has been
loaded and signed by a representative of the shipping company
involved); 4) Export Licence; 5) Certificate of Sailing; 6) Analysis
Report (on the cargo).

By 10th January Savundra had everything cut and dried. It had
taken scarcely six weeks since he had first arrived in London but it
had been a time of considerable tension for him. It was his first
experience of operating in an atmosphere which must have made the
business world of Colombo seem parochial. And he must have
revelled in the thought that he was showing Pushpam's family the
mettle of the man she had married. It is not surprising to find that as
soon as he knew that the deal was near completion he did not bother
to pass on the good news to his business associates. Instead he cabled
his mother-in-law:

LEAVING LONDON TODAY HOMEBOUND VIA PARIS SWITZERLAND ROME
DUE COLOMBO IN ABOUT A FORTNIGHT ALL WELL LOVE EMIL.

The purpose of his stop in Paris was to pick up all the necessary documents from Duval. His next cable was from Zürich this time to his father-in-law:

> ARRIVED GOTTHARD HOTEL SAFE ALL WELL STOP TELL CYRIL SHIP
> SAILED FRIDAY NEGOTIATING CREDIT TOMORROW WILL CABLE
> DEVELOPMENTS PUSHEMPET.

(The last word of the cable was the abbreviation he used for Pushpam, himself, and son Peter.)

It is obvious that the whole of the family had been tensely following every report of the progress of the deal and it gave him the utmost satisfaction to ensure that it should be his stiff-necked father-in-law who had been put in the position of having to report the news of his triumph to the Gardiners. He was not left long in any doubt as to the success of the gamesmanship. Two hours later the cable in reply arrived for him at his hotel. It read:

> PARTNERSHIP VERY PLEASED SHIP SAILED OFFERING PRAYERS FOR
> SUCCESS NEGOTIATION GOD BLESS CYRIL.

One can sense the mixture of relief and jubilation behind the restrained message, and there can be no doubt that the Aloysius and Gardiner families, with their deep religious convictions, had indeed been offering frequent and fervent prayers for the success of the enterprise—nor that Savundra himself had been seeking divine intervention to hasten things along. He sincerely believed in the power of prayer, and resorted to it in every crisis in his affairs.

The date when he was due to present the shipping documents to the bank and draw the money was fixed for Tuesday, 16th January. Unfortunately the bank manager with whom he had his appointment was confined to bed with a cold and the meeting was put off until the following day. This caused Savundra to send an urgent cable:

> MOTHER SUPERIOR CARMELITE CONVENT MADAWELA ROAD KATUGAS-
> TOTA. UNEXPECTED DELAY AGAIN NOW WEDNESDAY PLEASE REMEMBER
> EXTRA SPECIALLY EMIL.

The prayers of the nuns were not in vain. At 2.30 the following day he issued a banker's draft for 825,552.50 dollars to Pierre Duval, the oil company's representative, in payment for the oil, and a further draft of 169,447.50 to the credit of Trans-World Enterprises at the Bank of Ceylon. He then drew the balance in cash and stepped out into the afternoon sunshine with a briefcase under his arm in which was 255,000 dollars in crisp new 50 and 100 denomination bills.

The business having thus been brought to a successful conclusion, Savundra did a complete about-turn in his attitude. Suddenly the compulsion to impress his family with his business acumen disappeared. Instead he became secretive and devious.

The day after drawing the money he sent a cable to Cyril Gardiner giving the most explicit instructions as to how the money was to be dealt with. It is too long to quote here in full but the opening sentence set the tone for the whole message.

KEEP FOLLOWING INFORMATION HIGHLY CONFIDENTIAL ESPECIALLY ISMAIL CAREEN AND NAZIM.

These were friends who had helped with loans of money at various stages of the negotiations.

The cable went on to insist that all members of the family should also be kept in the dark, and particularly Uncle Chittampalam.

Thereafter Cyril Gardiner was given minute instructions as to how the 169,000 dollars was to be dealt with. Firstly, when filling in necessary forms, the money must be described as commission on a deal outside Ceylon and not as profit. He laid down how much was to be transferred to his own account, how much to Cyril's and how much to Chittampalam's. All transactions were to be in cash. 'Don't ask questions,' he instructed, 'just do as I say with the utmost speed.' The cable ended:

ALSO BUY ME HUMBER HAWK FROM ROWLANDS AND RUN IN YOURSELF AS I RETURNING THE MIDDLE OF NEXT WEEK STOP EXPEDITE EVERYTHING ELSE GOD BLESS.

There was no doubt now who was in the driving seat. A year later he was to explain the need for secrecy to the Commissioner of Income Tax as follows:

'The information of how much money has been made was to be kept strictly confidential to prevent too many wolves trying to grab when the money came in. I did not want Uncle to know we were getting 7½ lakhs. He would have come for a loan of 5 lakhs probably. In any case I wanted everything kept extremely quiet for the same reason. If we started talking that we were making money all our poor relations would have pestered us.'

Savundra did not immediately return to Ceylon but first flew to London with Pushpam and the by now rather travel-sick child and booked in at Grosvenor House in Park Lane. It was at Grosvenor House that he first started to puff the bellows to create a smoke screen, an art at which he was to become increasingly adept as his career progressed. It will soon become apparent that in this instance a smoke screen was to be very necessary.

At Grosvenor House, he claimed he was interviewed by a man who said he was an American secret agent. This agent apparently told Savundra that the Americans were on to his scheme to beat the embargo on oil to China and that under no circumstances would the oil be allowed to get through. There was much talk of torpedoes and assassinations. Renfro, Savundra claimed he had been told, was to be arrested and tried under Federal law.

This was the story that Savundra telephoned to Colombo—not on this occasion, it appears, to Cyril Gardiner but to another member of the Gardiner hierarchy, Mr. Anandappa.

As it happened, on the same day a cable had been received from Renfro in Hong Kong, offering enthusiastic congratulations on the success of the deal and offering a further contract for a bigger shipment of oil at an improved price. A thoroughly shaken Anandappa at once cabled back:

> HAVE EXTREMELY CONFIDENTIAL INFORMATION REGARDING JUTE BAGS [Jute Bags was code name for oil] FOR YOUR REPEAT YOUR EYES ONLY STOP CABLE IMMEDIATELY SUITABLE TELEGRAPH ADDRESS TO CABLE YOU CONFIDENTIALLY.

The next day Savundra himself arrived in Colombo and lost no time in putting Renfro in the picture.

He urged Renfro not to cable him back unless absolutely necessary and particularly not to mention the question of further shipments which, he said cryptically, 'think they still unsuspect'. The text of the cable read:

> AMERICAN SECRET SERVICE DOING FANTASTIC UNBELIEVABLE THINGS CANNOT COMMUNICATE YOU WILL THINK ME COMPLETELY CRAZY STOP SHIP WILL NEVER REACH DESTINATION STOP INSURANCE WILL NEVER PAY THIS ABSOLUTELY CERTAIN STOP AMERICANS FIXED THIS ALREADY NOW TRYING TO PLUG MYSELF LITERALLY AND METAPHORICALLY STOP SUPPLIES ACTIVE PARTNER SERIOUSLY HURT GUN INJURY OFFICIALLY ACCIDENT EXPECT NOT TO RECOVER STOP I RETURNED HERE UNDER DIPLOMATIC IMMUNITY STOP AMERICA FULLY AWARE TIENTSIN AGENT BUT APPEAR UNAWARE YOUR CONNECTION STOP ACT QUICK OR YOU MIGHT ALSO GET HURT ACCIDENT STOP FLY COLOMBO IF YOU LIKE I CAN ARRANGE PROTECT YOU HERE STOP COLLECT YOUR SHARE NOW BEFORE EXPLOSION OCCURS MONDAY.

It will be noted that Savundra himself was so carried away with the melodrama he had created that he had forgotten that he had previously told Anandappa that the avenging Americans were already on to Renfro but in the general excitement such details were easily overlooked.

It appears, however, that the panic did not affect worldly-wise Mr. Renfro in Hong Kong. His reply arrived the following day. It read:

> UNCONCERNED YOUR INFORMATION STOP MY INTEREST PROFIT ONLY

AND I AM PERFECTLY HAPPY IF SHIP NEVER ARRIVES OR INSURANCE NEVER PAY ONLY CONCERN IF REAL DANGER EXISTS STOP DID YOU ALL PULL A FAST DEAL AND NEVER INTEND ARRIVAL STOP THIS OK WITH ME BUT WOULD LIKE SOME INFORMATION STOP DID SHIP ACTUALLY SAIL OR WERE DOCUMENTS FORGED STOP IS SHIP ALREADY INTERCEPTED OR IS THIS PLANNED STOP WHAT WILL HAPPEN ON MONDAY STOP IS SHIP CARGO FOR FORMOSA STOP FREELY OR UNDER COMPULSION STOP HAVE NO INTEREST IN SHIP BUT PERSONAL WELFARE WILL KEEP CONFIDENTIAL BUT MUST HAVE MORE INFORMATION TO DECIDE NEXT MOVE PLEASE OBLIGE.

In fact, the whole oil deal was bogus. There was no oil, no ship, and no Société Méditerranéen de Produits Pétroliers. That particular company did not exist. Pierre Duval—if that was his name—was a conspirator whom Savundra had brought into the game without Renfro's knowledge.

All the documents produced for inspection by the Union Bank were forgeries. They must have been skilful, convincing forgeries and whoever produced them must have received expert advice—presumably from Savundra—on the appearance and technicalities of the various documents.

There was no ship of the name given in the documents. And the Société Méditerranéen was incapable of supplying oil to Red China or anywhere else because it was just a name which had been invented by Savundra.

It is clear from Renfro's cable that although he was considerably bewildered by Savundra's activities, he was not in the least surprised that Savundra had pulled a huge confidence trick, the details of which were not yet clear to him. The non-existent Société Méditerranéen was, of course, one of the companies that he authorised Savundra to deal with. But the probable explanation is that when he and Savundra discussed the project in Colombo, Savundra had provided him with a list of petrol companies—three genuine ones, and one 'ghost' company. Savundra, of course, would have had no problems over writing to and receiving replies from this 'ghost' company.

Safely back in Colombo, Savundra's main problem was not how to explain matters when the would-be purchasers of the Hwa Shih Company inevitably discovered that there was to be no oil. Indeed, that was one of the least of his worries. From the very outset he had realised that as the shipment was illegal, the Chinese had little hope of redress if no oil arrived. His concern was to ensure that he could hang on to the major part of the loot. It was no longer the Chinese whom he was most anxious to hoodwink but his friends. One of Savundra's unwritten rules was only to allow his fellow plotters to hold certain pieces of the jigsaw. He alone held the key as to how they fitted.

He arrived back with the 255,000 dollars he had drawn in cash still in his briefcase. To a friend who had enquired anxiously whether carrying around such a large sum of money was not a dangerous proceeding, Savundra had replied airily: 'That is not my problem. It is a problem for my insurance company.' However, when he came to pass through the Customs at Colombo Airport he was in for a shock. He declared the money quite openly, explaining that it represented commissions on a business deal which he had to pay out to third parties. Asked by the Deputy Governor of the Colombo Branch of the Bank of Ceylon where the money had come from, Savundra replied, not altogether untruthfully: 'I got it gambling.' The worldly-wise Deputy Governor appreciated the joke and laughed. But in spite of Savundra's violent protest, the dollars were impounded and their equivalent in Reis credited to Savundra's bank account.

Savundra had known what he was talking about when he had declared that the vultures would be waiting to divide the spoils when he got home. Even the immensely wealthy Sir Chittampalam who had tried so hard to back out of his involvement did not now hesitate to accept 200,000 Reis as his reward for an investment of 20,000 Reis and there is evidence that one of Savundra's accomplices managed to extract 50,000 Reis in repayment of a personal loan to Savundra of 5,000 Reis.

To combat the cupidity of his friends and family there had to be some reason why the 255,000 dollars, which he had wanted to leave in bond at the airport but which had now been so unfortunately converted into local currency, should not be available to be divided up.

Savundra was equal to the occasion. It was money, he claimed, which he held in trust to be paid to Mr. Duval for his services. Duval had instructed him that he was to go to New York and personally hand over 50,000 dollars to a Mr. Tembros and then to proceed to Singapore where Mr. Duval would be waiting to receive his just reward of 185,000 dollars.

To bolster up his rather fragile story Savundra instituted an imaginative correspondence with the non-existent S.M.P.P. On 26th January he wrote that he was unable to comply with the arrangements for the payment of the dollars because they had been confiscated. He could now only pay them in Reis.

The reply signed this time not by Duval but by a Jean Duvat, was a masterpiece of simulated outrage. It read:

Sir,

We have just received your letter of 26th January. We regret that we are not disposed to accept the excuses you offer.

You full well know the conditions of our contract and know that you are responsible for paying us the amount mentioned.

As to your relations and negotiations with your Government, they are not of the least interest to us. It was at our own peril that we and our friends persuaded the officials to authorise the deal and in consequence we do not intend to allow you to escape your obligations.

We are daily awaiting the arrival of your telegram assuring us that the matter is now in order. Should this telegram not arrive before the end of the month we will be obliged to take steps, the nature of which you will be able to judge, to remedy the injury you have done us.

Finally, it will not be necessary for us to point out that if you break your word and do not honour your contract, it will be impossible for you to do any further business with this country; you will already know of our position and the influence we have.

We would therefore beg you to abandon your excuses and honour your contract . . .

Meanwhile the day of reckoning with the Chinese company when it would be discovered that there was no oil was drawing ever closer.

Renfro, still apparently unaware of the true position, was desperately trying to pull a stroke of his own. Believing that there was indeed a ship on its way he cabled with an offer of 100,000 dollars to be divided between Savundra and the captain of the vessel if it could be diverted to a 'safe island'.

A few days later he cabled an amendment, stating it was essential that the ship should proceed as arranged to the mouth of the Canton River.

Savundra, now signing himself A.W. Perera, sent a spate of cables to Renfro about American intervention. 'Five Russian ships disappeared this week en route here to collect rubber.' 'Wait for conflagration.'

It was a game of cat and mouse which could not go on forever. By the beginning of March Renfro himself was getting impatient.

On the 7th he cabled:

BUYER INSTRUCTS YOU TELEGRAPH IMMEDIATELY TO ASK SHIP OWNER IN SWEDEN TO INFORM THEIR TIENTSIN AGENT WHEN DO THEY EXPECT SHIP TO ARRIVE NEW DESTINATION.

This time Savundra remained broodily silent. Four days later Renfro, now thoroughly under pressure, cabled again:

BUYER MAY TAKE STIFF ACTION AGAINST US IF YOU KEEP SILENT CABLE REPLY.

Finally, no reply being forthcoming, Renfro himself had to take action. On 12th March he cabled:

SWEDISH COMPANY AND THEIR AGENT HERE GILMAN COMPANY HAVE NO KNOWLEDGE OF SHIP STOP PLEASE CABLE OPERATORS NAME.

To this Savundra replied simply:

MY NEW POSTAL ADDRESS 30 HORTON PLACE COLOMBO.

At this stage Savundra cabled Renfro about a completely different matter. So far as he was concerned the oil deal was now dead. It was also a convenient time to start new hares. It was typical of Savundra that during the China affair he had found time to offer to supply coal cheaply to the Ceylon Government, to fire off letters to a firm about developing and widening Colombo harbour, and to try to persuade an Indian telephone company to re-organise Ceylon's telephone system. (Savundra, the entrepreneur, would handle the 'inducements' necessary, he assured the company, as he knew the people who counted in high places and how to deal with them.) Now he cabled Renfro, asking him to supply the plant to manufacture neon signs, together with skilled operators.

Obligingly Renfro replied:

NEON PLANT AND THREE SKILLED WORKERS READY STOP CABLE WHETHER YOU ARE DEAD SERIOUS IF SO WILL WRITE FULLY STOP OWN MATTER BUYERS IN A FRANTIC STEW STOP I RATHER AMUSED BUT PLEASE DONT INVOLVE ME IN ANYTHING.

However, the problem of the angry Chinese would not go away. Renfro was now cut out of the picture and the Hwa Shih Co. started an acrimonius correspondence direct with Savundra.

They openly accused him of being a crook. Savundra countered by claiming that all the 'irregularity' was at their end and demanding an apology.

Savundra seemed to be mainly worrying about whether Renfro had collected his commission, in which Savundra undoubtedly had a share. Renfro replied:

WE COLLECT 40 PERCENT ON SHIPS DOCUMENTS SIXTY PERCENT WHEN ARRIVE STOP HAVE NOW COLLECTED FULLY FORTY PERCENT NEVER DID EXPECT TO COLLECT OTHER SIXTY PERCENT STOP I SATISFIED WITH PROFIT ALREADY IN HAND AND MAIN INTEREST NOW IS TO LET WHOLE MATTER DIE AS QUIETLY AS IT WILL.

It was not a view held by Hwa Shih. 'It is clear that you have swindled us,' they wrote on learning that the shipping documents had been forged. 'Nobody can get away with a crooked deal of this size.'

Savundra calmly pointed out that it was their representative, Mr. Renfro, who had suggested his approaching S.M.P.P. (Apparently the Chinese had not yet realised there was no such company.) It was not his fault if they turned out to be crooks. Claiming that he had had very little money out of the whole thing, he replied to their demand for the return of the money: 'It is not possible to squeeze blood out of a stone. We suggest you treat this as a gamble which you took and lost, or alternatively, that you take it out of the hide of the bankers whose negligence has caused you this great loss and us so much unnecessary worry.'

The frustrated Chinese now resorted to threats. Stating that they were taking legal action for the return of the full amount of their investment, they added, 'Also we will take against you the personal action which we have already taken against your friend and accomplice, our former foreign representative, who begs to inform you that the sooner you pay the better it will be for him. Will you not realise who you are playing with. Please we beg you, do not force us to take harmful steps which you can only avoid by paying us back what you cheated us.'

Shortly afterwards, however, they were to modify their brave words. On 18th June Mr. C.Y. Fang, General Director of the company wrote:

Gentlemen, without altering our rights to our claims for 1,250,000 dollars we beg to request you to inform us how much you will be prepared to pay and how soon you will pay. A rice grain to a starving man is better than the rice bowl next day. We are, Gentlemen
       Very truly yours.

There was to be a great deal of further correspondence but from that moment on Savundra must have known that he had won the battle.

As for Mr. Renfro, there is no evidence that Savundra ever heard from him again.

What, it must be asked, happened to the 825,552.50 dollars which were supposed to have been paid to the mysterious Pierre Duval, the representative of a phoney oil company? It is certain that Savundra would have considered this far too high a remuneration for Duval's help in setting up the fraud. It would seem that the money was split between Savundra and Duval, with the greater share, perhaps in the region of 500,000 dollars, going to Savundra.

Strangely, just about that sum was given to the Roman Catholic Church through a friend of Savundra, Monsignor Asta. This munificent gift was to found a Carmelite convent in Kandy. In future, Savundra was going to have his own establishment to intercede on his behalf with the Almighty.

CHAPTER FOUR

La Salle
des Pas Perdus

THE BUSINESS COMMUNITY IN Ceylon was an exclusive one. Its members all knew each other and not to be accepted by them was, for the aspiring businessman, a considerable handicap.

Emil Savundra, before his involvement in the bogus Chinese oil deal, had already done much to erode the goodwill to which his own family's social standing and particularly that of his wife would normally have entitled him. His post-war dealings in the black market and other dubious activities had been noted. Now, as some of the details of the Chinese affair became known, the chilliness of the Establishment became more pronounced. The banks were reluctant to handle Savundra's business.

Pushpam's distinguished family, however, stood by him loyally, especially Sir Chittampalam Gardiner, who was satisfied at the outcome of the China oil deal so far as he himself was concerned. It was Chittampalam who now suggested that Emil might do better to employ his talents in the wider scene of Europe.

Savundra seized on the idea with enthusiasm. His brief visits to England and the Continent had born in him a very real admiration for the Western world, and particularly for all things British. He was convinced that Europe was indeed the land of opportunity where he could spread his wings and soar like an eagle, untrammelled by the petty bourgeois outlook of Colombo, a place which he once described as being 'a town with the mentality of a village'.

Pushpam accepted without question the Eastern convention that a wife's duty is to obey her husband in all things. She now had two sons, Peter and Emil junior; and if it should be her husband's wish that she and they should be uprooted from her homeland to launch into an entirely new way of life, so be it.

It must have been some compensation for Pushpam that Uncle Gardiner did not believe that a young man should necessarily start at the bottom and work his way up. He believed that the higher up the ladder you started the quicker you would reach the top.

Thus it came about that early in 1953 the whole Savundra family found themselves established in a suite in the Georges V, one of the most expensive hotels in Paris. Savundra's richly engraved business cards proclaimed that he was the head of a Colombo-based firm, rather grandly called Modern Industries Ltd. His style of living indicated that the firm was a prosperous one.

It was, in fact, a company in name only. This was even more of a façade than Eastern Enterprises had been. Savundra put it about that the firm was owned by a Mr. A.W. Perera which, it will be recollected, was the nom de guerre he himself had adopted in the later stages of the Chinese oil affair. If there were other paper directors, there is no record of them. Emil Savundra had full power of attorney for European operations.

The mantle of the well-to-do businessman was one which fitted Savundra perfectly. With uncle paying the bills and possibly providing suitably influential contacts, he set about establishing himself in his new surroundings. With his charm and open-handed generosity it was not long before he had gathered round a circle of acquaintances anxious to be of mutual benefit to one another.

To project his image as a budding tycoon, he appointed a personal assistant to deal with any matters considered not to be of sufficient importance to merit his personal attention. This aide was an impeccably dressed, well-spoken young English engineer, called Charles Dade, whom Savundra had first met in Colombo. It was the very Englishness of Dade which impressed Savundra. Dade was never allowed to know the intricate details of the schemes which were passing through his new master's fertile brain, but he added just the right touch of urbanity and respectability.

As well as Dade, Savundra was often seen at this time accompanied by a six-foot-six Irishman known as Packie whom he liked to tell people was his bodyguard-cum-chauffeur. One of his duties was apparently to open all mail because of the danger of letter bombs.

Savundra now talked quite freely about the Chinese oil episode. It was, he would explain to anyone who wanted to listen, something he had undertaken at the request of the Vatican. The Red Chinese had abolished the Catholic Church in China and seized all their very considerable property. He had been given the task of obtaining some redress. As a result of his success in this direction the Chinese were trying to kill him. That was why he had to have a bodyguard.

It seems likely that while he was establishing himself in Paris, Savundra, through Modern Industries Ltd., conducted one or two perfectly legitimate business deals. He was quick to see money-making opportunities and, in spite of his innate laziness, he had an active brain and was only happy when it was being put to some pro-ductive use. On the other hand, it is certain that very soon after his arrival in Paris he was already engaged in hand-picking the team for his next major fraud and planning it down to the last detail. It is a measure of his misguided genius that the operation he was then engaged in setting up is still remembered by Interpol as one of the most baffling cases they have ever been called upon to investigate.

The Chinese affair had left Savundra convinced on one thing—that the vulnerability of the European world of high finance lay in the par-ticipants' implicit trust in pieces of paper. Provided things looked right, the most preposterous fraud could long go undetected. There-fore, the first moves in what became known as 'The Case of the Phan-tom Shipment' were precisely those which merchant banks encoun-tered in their normal, honest everyday transactions.

On 16th April, 1954, just over a year after Savundra had set up his headquarters in Paris, the Kreditbank in Antwerp, Belgium, received a request from the Banco Nacional Ultramarino of Lisbon to open a credit for 865,000 dollars on behalf of the Government of Portuguese Goa. The money was to be for the credit of the well-known Belgian shipping firm of Hantra.

The purpose of this conventional banking transaction was to finance the purchase and shipping of 8,000 tons of Italian and Bur-mese rice to the Goan port of Mormugao where it was urgently required for the relief of local famine conditions.

The essential documents against which payment could be made, such as bills of lading, insurance policies and consular invoices, would in due course be forthcoming from a Colombo company called Mod-ern Industries Ltd., who were handling the whole deal on behalf of the Goan Government. When all the required documents had been received, the available money was to be apportioned as:

8,290 dollars to Messrs. Outschoorn and Landau, Antwerp underwriters.

6,850 dollars to be retained by the Kreditbank for Messrs. Hantra.

669,860 dollars to be transferred to the Banca Report of Lugano, Switzerland to the account of a Mr. George Kaufman.

The payment of the bulk of the money into a Swiss bank was not in the least out of the ordinary. It was common practice for firms involved in international deals to channel them through Switzerland in order to earn their commissions in Swiss francs, the hardest currency in the world at that time.

At the start of the project Savundra had received from the Goan Government a sample of the rice they required so that he could make sure that the rice he was to buy on their behalf was of the right standard. Savundra put the package firmly in the bottom drawer of his desk in his Paris office. Far from worrying about such trivialities as the quality of the rice his sole concern was how to ensure that the Kreditbank duly made the payment of 669,860 dollars to Lugano so that he could convert it to his personal use. So far he had gone through all the formalities of setting up a perfectly legitimate deal. But from now on every move was to be fraudulent.

On 21st May, 1954, a Swiss forwarding agent presented himself at the Kreditbank and asked to see Mijnheer Verbruggen, the Managing Director. He was a Herr von Hornung, the head of Hantra's shipping firm's branch in Basle. He explained to Verbruggen that he had been instructed by Modern Industries to handle personally the Goan rice deal rather than the Hantra head office. Mijnheer Verbruggen would understand the reason for his clients wanting the deal to be transacted through a Swiss bank. Mijnheer Verbruggen did. He handed over copies of the correspondence with Modern Industries from Ceylon, which confirmed Hornung's claim and, most important of all, presented an invoice showing that the rice had indeed been bought and shipped.

The fuse was lit. Now it was a matter of Savundra's syndicate each playing their part to an exact time schedule so that they could get their hands on the money before, as was inevitable, the bomb exploded.

Within hours of von Hornung leaving the Kreditbank a messenger arrived and handed over a consular invoice purporting to be signed by the Portuguese Consul in Antwerp certifying that the rice had left port. Duly endorsed with official-looking stamps and ribbons, the invoice stated that the ship in question was the Norwegian freighter, the *Trianon*, owned by the well-known shipping company of Wilhelmsen in Oslo.

In the meantime, a man named Mayers who ran the Antwerp office of another shipping firm, Marinex, had done his part. In his official capacity as the shipping agent for Modern Industries he had obtained from the highly respectable firm of Outschoorn and Landau, insurance brokers, a completely genuine insurance policy paid for by the 8,290 dollars thoughfully put in their name at the Kreditbank. Now he handed the policy to Verbruggen, who then had all the necessary documents. Verbruggen immediately airmailed them to the Goan Government and, believing his part in the transaction to be successfully completed, at once transferred the 669,860 dollars to the Banca Report in Lugano for the account of a Mr. Kaufman.

The Banca Report, of course, were not interested in the details of the rice deal; so that when Herr Kaufman presented himself at the bank counter within hours of the credit being received and demanded payment of 366,860 dollars, in Swiss francs, they had no grounds for demur. At the same time Kaufman ordered that the balance of 303,000 dollars be immediately transferred to the Hofman Bank in Zürich to the account of a Herr André Klotz. Again the bank, used to the wheelings and dealings of their customers, complied.

The money was not allowed to remain in its new resting place for long. Immediately it had been received, Herr Klotz identified himself to the manager of the Hofman Bank and instructed them to contact a large bullion dealer in Zürich and purchase four cases of fine gold for almost the whole amount of the deposit. The gold, Klotz commanded, was to be handed over by the bullion dealers to anyone presenting an Italian 1,000-lire note, Serial Number 6/85/18364. Within an hour of this James Bond type arrangement having been agreed, an unknown caller presented the note, collected the gold, and disappeared.

While these frenzied arrangements for the disposal of the money were being executed in Switzerland, the fuse in Antwerp was burning dangerously short.

Four days after the Kreditbank had transferred the money to Lugano, Verbruggen received a cable from the Banco Nacional Ultramarino in Lisbon asking on which ship the rice had been loaded and when it was expected to arrive in Mormugao. Verbruggen lifted the telephone receiver and called the offices of the Wilhelmsen Line's local agents. He was in for a severe shock. The agents reported that not only was Mormugao not one of the *Trianon*'s ports of call, but that the ship was not carrying rice.

Incredulously Verbruggen insisted in calling Hantra's head office and Wilhelmsen in Oslo before he would accept the truth. Then he called Antwerp's police headquarters and within hours Interpol had been alerted. A cable was sent to Lugano with an order to freeze the money. It came twenty-four hours too late. Herr Kaufman had been and gone.

Armed with the information which Verbruggen was able to give them, Interpol were faced with what appeared to be a simple, if bold, case of fraud. Their first step was to interview Mr. Mayers of

Marinex. Mayers protested his innocence with the utmost vigour. He agreed that not only had he obtained the insurance certificate from Outschoorn and Landau and had been in touch with the Kreditbank about financing the rice shipment to Goa but he had received his instructions from the highly respected firm of Hantra through their Basle office. He had no reason to believe that there was anything sinister about it. Apart from that he had put his offices at the disposal of Herr von Hornung of Hantra's Basle office. Von Hornung had arrived on 21st May with three other men, two of whom spoke French and the other English. They had held a series of meetings and made a number of overseas telephone calls. Otherwise he knew nothing. Interpol were unimpressed and placed Mayers under arrest before going after von Hornung.

Von Hornung was more frank about his part in the affair. He knew that his services were being used to facilitate an illegal currency transaction but in his line of business he regarded that as a venial rather than a cardinal sin. He was as violent as Mayers had been in his protestations that he had no idea that the whole deal was a fraud and that the rice did not exist. He underwent a rigorous and protracted grilling by the Swiss police before being finally allowed to return to his home under strict surveillance.

When the police returned to resume their questioning the following morning, von Hornung was dead. He had shot himself through the head.

At this stage the trail might have gone cold but for one thing. Von Hornung left behind him a signed confession. In it he claimed that he had been drawn into an affair he did not fully understand. It was started with an innocent enough letter from a firm called Modern Industries in Ceylon asking for his co-operation in a deal which would earn for them much-needed Swiss francs which were required to finance other European operations in which Modern Industries were involved. As a result he had gone to Paris where he had met the top man in Modern Industries Ltd.—a Mr. Emil Savundranayagam. It was he who had spelled out the exact course von Hornung was to follow and it was he who had provided him with the shipping invoices, which only now he had learned were forged.

Savundranayagam had ordered his personal assistant, a Mr. Charles Dade, to accompany him back to Basle with instructions to see that he caught the next train to Antwerp to deliver the invoices to the Kreditbank. It was true that he was prepared to be a party to bending the currency regulations and, on Savundra's insistence, neglected to inform his head office in Antwerp of the details of the transaction, but when he realised the full extent of the fraud into which he had been drawn he knew that his career was in ruins and a bullet in the head was the only way out.

Von Hornung's confession and suicide, was something Savundra had not anticipated. The signed statement that it was Savundra himself who had provided the forged invoices was a body blow.

Savundra's instinct for self-preservation, however, had not allowed him to rely completely on the loyalty or elusiveness of his fellow plotters. Shortly before the balloon was due to go up he had sent Pushpam to London. There she acquired a flat in St. James' Court. Within hours of the police picking up von Hornung's confession, Savundra and Charles Dade were on a plane to London. They arrived on 30th May.

There is little doubt that Savundra had hoped that the elaborate smoke screen he had left behind him would have been sufficient to make it impossible for the police to make a case against him. But von Hornung had changed the picture. Within days of Savundra's arrival in England the Belgian police had applied to the courts for the extradition of himself and Charles Dade to stand trial in Brussels. Both men were taken into custody and a week later they appeared at Bow Street Court to answer the allegations made against them.

Savundra's hope that he had effectively covered his tracks had not been realised. But he was still buoyant. He had convinced himself that British justice would somehow protect him from these troublesome Belgians.

An eminent counsel, Mr. Gerald Gardiner, who appeared for Savundra, put his client's case with quiet confidence. Savundra had fallen, he claimed, into the hands of unscrupulous continental financiers who had used his name to perpetrate a vast fraud. He had no need to become involved in affairs of this sort. He was, it was explained, a member of one of the wealthiest families in Ceylon and he had come to London with his family purely to conduct a business deal. There were two prominent bankers in court who were ready to stand bail for him.

Mr. Bertram Reece, the presiding magistrate, was unimpressed. He remanded both men in custody.

The case for extradition brought on behalf of the Belgian Government suffered a minor set-back when it came up in court again a fortnight later. Charles Dade's own innocence of any fraudulent activity was accepted. He was adjudged to have no case to answer and discharged with an order against the Belgians to pay him £200 costs.

Savundra was not so fortunate. The case against him dragged on to the end of July, with bail finally fixed at his own recognisance of £5,000 and two other sureties of £2,000 each. The British authorities were taking the matter rather more seriously than Savundra had expected, and on 27th July Mr. Reece declared:

'I have found that in this case there is a case to answer on charges of forgery, uttering documents which were forged and obtaining money by false pretences, either as a principal or an accessory.'

Savundra was asked if he wished to give evidence or call witnesses. He replied that he wished to do both. The case was further adjourned for two months.

Now he resorted to a tactic which he was to use again many times when in a tight corner. He had a heart attack. It would perhaps be doing the team of distinguished doctors who were called in less than justice to say that his condition was entirely simulated, but there is no doubt that their efforts to arrive at a correct diagnosis were considerably hampered by their patient's histrionic ability.

There were to be many occasions in the future when he was to use the excuse of a weak heart as part of his defensive armour; so it is relevant to consider to what degree he simulated the condition.

Savundra took his health very seriously, almost to the point of hypochondria, and he would certainly have equipped himself with an exact knowledge of the symptoms from which any doctor would diagnose a coronary thrombosis. Even in the absence of confirmatory symptoms which could be easily recognised, it would only be necessary for him to claim that he had excruciating chest pains, adding that they were extended down his left arm, for any doctor to consider the case seriously.

Once the results of X-rays, cardiograph readings and blood tests were available, it would be difficult to sustain the fiction even with the most sympathetic of doctors. But Savundra did undoubtedly have medical problems and quite possibly a genuine heart condition. He was certainly a diabetic and probably also suffered from angina. And of course he could constantly claim to be under severe mental stress which can cause a coronary.

In this instance, when faced with the possibility of his being extradited to stand trial in Belgium, he was able to convince the court over many months, with the aid of medical certificates, that his condition made it impossible for him to face proceedings. He had himself moved into the expensive London Clinic at No. 20 Devonshire Place. If he was going to be ill, he was going to be ill in the greatest comfort and in the best company.

'The Clinic', as it is generally called, is the common ground where

A man of property—Savundra
outside White Walls, his Hampstead
residence.

His wife Pushpam, with one of their sons.

**The Savundra family after Morning Service at
The Church of Our Lady of the Assumption, Englefield Green.**

the richest patients and the most distinguished members of the medical profession meet to their mutual advantage. It has an exceptionally fine wine cellar and the catering arrangements are of such a high standard that the Duke of Windsor once remarked that he wished the food was half as good in London's West End hotels. It has 180 beds and a staff of 350, with more trained nurses than there are patients. It has a secret exit through which the famous can come and go, unobserved by Press and public, but inside the atmosphere is stately, calm and reassuring, rather like that of a very good club. Even in that exalted company Savundra made sure that he was regarded as a special case. He insisted that his room should be on the second floor, which had something of the cachet of the Royal Enclosure at Ascot. At one stage there were no fewer than fourteen of the country's leading heart specialists, headed by Dr. Wilfred Oakley and Sir Philip Hanson-Barr, advising on his case.

There is a story, no doubt aprocryphal, about an occasion when he had temporarily been moved to another room just down the corridor. One of his doctors, paying a courtesy call, put his head round the door of his usual room and, seeing the bed empty, jumped to the conclusion that his munificent patient had passed away and promptly collapsed from shock.

If nothing else, Savundra's retreat to the Clinic bought him time. When his case was called again on 27th September, his counsel, now Mr. James Burge, announced that he was not fit to attend court. A doctor had said that he was a dying man. The case was adjourned for a further month and then for a further three months, the court no doubt being persuaded by the very numbers of his medical advisers that he must indeed be a in a critical condition. Meanwhile Pushpam, who had given birth to a third son whilst in Paris and a fourth within weeks of arriving in London, had also been admitted to the Clinic suffering from nervous exhaustion.

Savundra's delaying tactics could not, however, continue for ever. When the period of the final adjournment had expired, the long-suffering Mr. Bertram Reece decided that if Savundra could not attend the court, the court would have to attend on him.

The Clinic is not normally averse to publicity but it must have been less than delighted when, one grey morning early in February 1956, a cavalcade of cars drew up at its front entrance. From them emerged Mr. Bertram Reece, closely followed by defence counsel, and Mr. Gilbert Paull Q.C., (counsel for the Belgian Government), the Clerk of the Court, shorthand writers and other officials and behind them a bevy of solicitors and Press reporters.

It was impossible to crowd enough chairs into Savundra's sick room. Many of those attending had to crush in standing while clerks balanced files and documents on their knees and cupboards were pressed into duty as desks.

Savundra had now changed his mind about calling witnesses and giving evidence himself. Instead, his counsel declared that if an order for committal to prison were made, he would apply for a writ of *habeas corpus*. Mr. Reece contented himself with granting the extradition order and left it to the police to decide whether to move Savundra to Brixton Prison or leave him in comfort in the Clinic.

He remained in the Clinic.

The final stages of the protracted legal battle were fought out in the Queen's Bench Division of the High Court of Justice before the formidable Lord Chief Justice, Lord Goddard, Mr. Justice Ormerod and Mr. Justice Gorman. Savundra was represented by a team of four counsel. Mr. Geoffrey Lawrence, Q.C., led for the Belgian Government.

Savundra must have been gratified at the plethora of legal talent which was being employed in his affairs but he cannot have been at all gratified by the result. In spite of a plea by Savundra's counsel, that his client did not have long to live, his application for *habeas corpus* was turned down.

One month later Savundra was put on board an aircraft at Heathrow Airport on a stretcher and flown to Melsbroeck, where an ambulance awaited him on the tarmac to take him to Antwerp Prison. Shortly afterwards he managed to have himself moved from prison to the luxurious Catholic St. Elizabeth Hospital, after representations had been made about the state of his health. There the loyal Pushpam could visit him every day. And until the case was heard at least he would be living in comfort.

In fact, although the Belgian police, on the posthumous evidence of von Hornung, had not delayed in bringing charges against Savundra and Interpol had pressed vigorously for his extradition, the case for the prosecution was far from complete. The long months while he had successfully delayed his extradition had been busy ones for Interpol. Under their direction intensive police enquiries had been conducted in Belgium, Switzerland, England and France and followed a number of baffling trails which criss-crossed all over Europe.

Interpol had been quick to identify Klotz, already a well-known gold smuggler. He was picked up easily enough but there was nothing for which he could be held. He admitted being an intermediary in buying the gold but in Switzerland that was not illegal. He had not been the man who collected it. He did not know where it was.

The tracing of the mysterious George Kaufman, into whose account in the Banca Report the missing money had been paid, was a more difficult matter. Finally he was identified as a Swiss citizen who had been resident in Paris, where he was known as Fernand Geissman. He eventually surrendered to a warrant issued for his arrest and he, in turn, implicated a Dr. Bera, who was an 'adviser' to the Report Bank. At the same time Geissman involved two Yugoslavs, also resident in Paris, called Miljusz and Sorz. Sorz had hired Geissman to draw the money from the bank and deliver it to a Mr. Horn in Olten. On being questioned Horn denied ever having met Geissman. It eventually emerged that Horn had been paid a sum of money to allow a Pole named Mniszek to represent himself as Horn to Geissman and meet him in Horn's house. Geissman had handed over the money to Mniszek. Mniszek was the manager of a firm called Tewes, based in Paris, which had close business connections with Hantra . . . and so on and on.

Apart from the phonetic strain the names of the conspirators put on the Interpol investigators, they were faced with the difficulty of assessing who were the principals in the plot and who the catspaws.

It eventually became obvious that apart from the ill-fated von Hornung and Dr. Bera of the Lugano Bank who had only been enlisted because they were Swiss and in a position to take advantage of their country's flexible currency regulations, all the others were based in Paris which had been Savundra's own seat of operations. In the end Mniszek was arrested as he tried to board a plane in Bordeaux, Sorz was picked up in an apartment in Montparnasse and Dr. Bera, who had disappeared from Lugano, was finally found by the Sureté at Le Bourget airport. It was these three who were eventually to stand trial in the dock with Savundra.

At the same time there were one or two notable absentees. A warrant issued for the arrest of a certain Edward Johnson, suspected of being responsible, with Savundra, of planning the whole deal in Goa, had not been served. All trace of him had been lost in Bombay. As in the case of the Chinese oil, whoever carried out the excellent forgeries on which the whole scheme depended had also never been traced. Was the same man responsible for both? On the face of it, it seems likely. Yet another absentee, perhaps as much to the regret of the accused as of the accusers, was the Yugoslav, Miljusz, who was the last in the chain to receive 410,000 of the missing Swiss francs. Like the four cases of fine gold, he and the money had completely disappeared.

On the interesting subject of the final destination of the money, it is difficult to imagine that someone with Savundra's planning ability would not make foolproof arrangements to ensure that it did not end up in the wrong pocket. The elaborate arrangements to draw the hounds off Miljusz may indicate that his role was to do precisely what he, in fact, did do—disappear with the money and lie low until the hue and cry had died down. Otherwise, why should he have been introduced into the picture at all? Although the gold's final destination is not known, it may be conjectured that arrangements had also been made for its reappearance when wanted.

These were questions which Interpol, with all their resources, were never able to solve but the court which the four accused were now to face was not concerned with assessing by how much they had profited from their actions—only in proving that their actions had been with fraudulent intent.

It was six months after Savundra had been extradited before the prosecution finally completed their case and the trial opened on the afternoon of 25th January, 1956, in the Tenth Chamber of the Palais de Justice in Brussels under the Presidency of Mr. Wildiers. Pushpam elected to remain outside the court, unable to bring herself to watch her husband in the dock. A lonely figure, she sat by herself, wrapped in a mink coat which seemed too big for her, in the entrance hall, picturesquely known as the 'salle des pas perdus'—the room of the lost footsteps.

Savundra the death's door patient now became Savundra the showman. From the moment he filed into the dock with the co-accused he proceeded to dominate the entire proceedings. He exuded good health and confidence, whilst his immaculate appearance made everyone about him look shoddy by comparison.

Asked by the President whether he spoke French, he replied that he did not but that he understood it.

'In that case,' said Mr. Wildiers, 'do you mind if the initial submissions are made in French?'

'It is a matter of complete indifference to me, providing they are kept short,' Savundra replied languidly.

The trial had been expected to last for perhaps ten days but every piece of evidence brought forward by the prosecution was so strenuously challenged, largely by Savundra, that the case dragged on into weeks and then months.

Early in the proceedings Savundra had asked Pushpam if she would change her mind and sit in the court. It would, he told her, give him added confidence and comfort.

Now, each time he considered he had scored a point or when he felt things were going well for him, he would turn to where she sat and, raising his thumb and forefinger in a gesture of triumph, give her a grin and a broad wink. It was as if he considered there could be one outcome to the whole dreary business—his complete acquittal.

Predictably he claimed that he was merely a go-between in the whole matter. The company he represented in Europe, Modern Industries Ltd., was wholly owned by a Mr. Perera in Ceylon. It was Mr. Perera who had instructed him to discover the most profitable way to ship the rice. 'With the exception,' he could not resist adding, 'of the most profitable way of all which would have been to ship no rice at all.' There was an outburst of laughter. Even the President gave a wry smile.

Day after day, while Pushpam sat near him, her enormous dark eyes constantly fixed on him, Savundra fought every point. One moment he was lecturing his co-defendants in the dock, the next gesticulating wildly in protest at some statement made by a witness. Even the prosecution had to acknowledge his brilliant advocacy and grasp of detail, but it was all to no purpose.

After nearly three months, the calling of hundreds of witnesses, and the sifting through of a mountain of documents, Savundra, Sorz and Mniszek were found guilty. Savundra, as the ringleader, was sentenced to five years in prison and fined 40,000 Belgian francs. Sorz and Mniszek were also fined in addition to a four-year sentence. Only the Swiss, Dr. Bera, was acquitted, but he died soon after, it was said from the strain of his ordeal.

Savundra had lost the battle in court. But there was to be a truly astonishing sequel. He returned to St. Elizabeth Hospital pending the hearing of an appeal, where one of his most constant visitors was the ubiquitous Monsignor Asta, who had been so opportunely at hand at the prize-giving after the China oil affair.

The appeal was heard on 11th July, where the fine was cut to 2,000 francs but the five-year sentence was confirmed.

But two months later, on 6th September, Savundra was on an aeroplane to Milan a free man. The purpose of his trip was to pay his respects to Cardinal Montini, later to become Pope Paul VI. Then he returned to his family in England.

Just how had this reversal of fortune been achieved? And what part was played by his clerical visitor? While this book was being prepared, we wrote to Cardinal Asta, now Apostolic Pro-Nuncio in Turkey.

His reply from Ankara read as follows:

Dear Sir,

In reply to your latest kind letter of the 13th of this month, I am very sorry to inform you that I am not able to meet your wishes.

The case you are interested in is already so far-off that it would be very difficult for me to give you useful information: it has been one of those many circumstances in which Christian charity recommends to take care of people in need of help.

With best regards,

Yours sincerely,

[signed] Salvatore Asta.

In fact, immediately after the appeal had been dismissed, Savundra suddenly became ill again. The energy he had displayed in court had mysteriously vanished. He called in an eminent specialist who certified that his condition was critical.

Above all, it seems that Savundra prevailed on his friend, Monsignor Asta, to intercede with the Belgian Minister of Justice. Asta's high position in the Church would have assured him of access to the minister of a country which has a substantial Roman Catholic population. Whether Asta did see the minister, and if so, what passed between them, is a matter for conjecture. But Asta may well have believed Savundra's claim that he had been used by others. He may well have pleaded that Savundra was basically a good man, and a generous benefactor to the Church. Now he was dying, and wished to spend the last months which remained to him in peace with his family.

Such a plea could have been put forward on the grounds of Christian charity.

Whatever the reason, whatever pleas and advice he received, the fact is that the minister agreed to Savundra's release.

Back in England, after his astonishing deliverance, Savundra took steps to ensure that the case should not be re-opened.

His first action was to have his obituary published in the Belgian Press. Later he was to explain that he did this to avoid the wrath of the Portuguese and Goan Governments who might have been incensed by the clemency shown by the Belgian authorities. It had, however, the more immediate and practical effect of causing the Belgian police to remove all documents and records relating to the case from files under active consideration. The ruse served its purpose. Subsequent enquiries from interested parties failed to unearth details of Savundra's part in the affair.

Savundra himself put around a typically grandiose explanation of his involvement in the rice affair. All his actions were not for personal gain but sprang from deep and unselfish political motives. He had acted after being approached by the Prime Minister of India, his friend Pandit Nehru.

At the time of the phantom shipment the Goan population was in a state of near revolt against Indian domination and invasion by Indian troops.

'Whether the Goans rebelled against the Indian troops or greeted them with open arms, depended on one factor—how much food there was in Goa,' he said. 'No food could come in from India, the Indians saw to that. The only other way in which the food could come into Goa was through the port of Mormugao. But the food ships did not enter port. One man was given the job of ensuring that they did not.' With an expressive shrug of his shoulders, Savundra let his enquirers in no doubt as to who that man was.

CHAPTER FIVE

The Original
Black Englishman

HAVING PAID HIS RESPECTS to Cardinal Montini, Savundra flew back to London, where Pushpam had acquired on his behalf a pleasant family house at 80 Hendon Lane in Finchley. It was perhaps not quite as grand as Savundra himself would have wished but it made a comfortable enough home for him and his family, which by now consisted of four boys.

In spite of the fact that Savundra, at the age of twenty-eight, had pulled off two of the biggest international frauds of the decade, he was short of money. Most of the cash from the Chinese oil deal had passed into the hands of the Ceylonese authorities and the Catholic Church, and much of the profit from the phantom rice shipment to Goa had been spent on lawyers and a battery of doctors.

Savundra's father had instilled in him at an early age the importance of giving a proportion of his earnings to the Church, and Monsignor Asta is known to have been a guest at family gatherings of the Savundras in fashionable West End restaurants. He. was the one exception to Savundra's practice of placing his guests, however important, at the bottom of the table. Savundra, like a Godfather in the Mafia, insisted on sitting with his whole family grouped closely around him. Only Asta was allowed a place of honour at his right hand.

This was the life that Savundra really enjoyed. Nothing gratified him more than to be seen dining in distinguished company, and surrounded by his family. At the same time it was something that he could not afford, even with the financial support that Pushpam and Uncle Gardiner could give him. But his sensitive nose told him that the climate was right in London to make the big killing he dreamed of—a killing which would catapult him into high society. Pushpam often expressed a desire to return to Ceylon where their position would be recognised, but her husband was obsessed with proving that he was 'the original black Englishman'. Now, like a tiger, he started to prowl around in search of fresh prey, and there was no one more qualified to show him the jungle paths than the genial, giant Irishman, James Drury Dickinson Pyper.

London in the immediate post-war years could be not unfairly described as the crime capital of Europe. There were gangs like the appalling Messina brothers, who nightly drove round Mayfair's square mile in their enormous black limousine ready to leap out and slash the face of any prostitute who dared to poach on their territory. Gambling, which had not yet been made legal, was, with a few exceptions, in the hands of ruthless operators, and there were men like Billy Hill, self-styled 'King of the Underworld', and Jack Spot, forerunners of the Krays and Richardsons.

By the nineteen-fifties, however, a new type of criminal was beginning to emerge and James Pyper was of this breed. Men like Spot and Hill, although sometime drinking companions, he held in contempt. 'They will use a club on a deal,' he used to say, 'when the stroke of a pen would achieve the same effect.' His was a world of dubious private banks, obscure holding companies and shady continental connections.

Pyper had a talent for exploiting other people's weaknesses and he was quick to recognise that Savundra's Achilles heel was women. Not that Savundra made any secret about it. His first question to the most casual of acquaintances was likely to be: 'Do you know of any pretty little things for me?'

This appetite for extra-marital diversion does not alter the fact that he remained all his life devoted to his wife and family. Nor would it ever have crossed his mind to chase after a friend's wife. That he would have regarded as highly immoral. Like the Victorians, his solution was to pay for extra-marital sex. Paying, in his eyes, made it all right. Jimmy Pyper not only provided him with a list of telephone numbers of suitable call-girls but also allowed him to use a flat he owned near Marble Arch as a love-nest. Friends remember that the girls he preferred were red-haired or blonde with long legs and very white skin.

His love-making provided him with a splendid opportunity to indulge his vanity. He liked to strut around the bedroom preening himself like a peacock. He would then stand in front of a full-length mirror stroking his stomach and declare: 'There is no dobut, Emil, that you are a genius. There is nobody in the world who can hold a candle to your wit, charm, brilliance and ingenuity. All others are *pygmies.*' And then, in almost child-like delight, he would cap his performance with a little dance around the room.

It was little peccadilloes like this which led Savundra to be labelled by underworld acquaintances as 'the clown prince of high finance'.

When Savundra settled in London, there was a circle of fraudsters, whose contacts were wide-ranging and who freely exchanged ideas. It was to this company that Pyper was able to introduce him. In the early 1950s, the favourite haunt of this criminal 'think tank' was a remarkable public house tucked away in a mews on the west side of Belgrave Square, the Star Tavern. Although Savundra was always disdainful of pubs and is not remembered as a frequent visitor, a brief glance at The Star is the best way of suggesting the atmosphere Savundra found in London—and the outlook of the men with whom he was to rub shoulders.

Run by Paddy Kennedy, an ebullient Irishman known for his caustic wit and lavish style of living, and patronised by the famous as well as the fraudulent, The Star was a jokey sort of place. When the Maharanee of Cooch Behar, in a fit of pique at some real or imagined slight, had a load of horse manure from her country estate piled against the door of the bar so that the customers could not get in at opening time, it was all taken in good part. Paddy Kennedy turned the tables on her by having the manure packed in plastic bags which he sold to local residents for their window boxes and asked her if he could have another load.

One of the most popular of the regulars at The Star was Charles de Silva. Like Savundra he was keen to keep on good terms with God and never failed to turn up for Mass at Farm Street Church in Mayfair every Sunday. Apart from that the two men had little in common. Savundra took the business of making money with great seriousness. If he could beat the law, he did not regard it as criminal but rather as a tribute to his own genius. For de Silva, however, the whole thing was a game and if he got caught he paid the penalty—a spell in one of Her Majesty's prisons—philosophically.

A typical de Silva exploit was the conning of an ageing American multi-millionaire. This elderly playboy had a well-known weakness for schoolgirls and de Silva managed to extract a large sum of money from him in exchange for an address where his needs could be supplied. When it turned out to be a convent the American was understandably angry but there was little he could do.

De Silva, however, was a born loser. He committed suicide when forty-seven, in 1973, and although it is estimated that by his swindles something like three million pounds had passed through his hands, he had managed to keep none of it. 'There's no future in the rackets,' he told a friend sadly. 'The mugs are not mugs any more.' In the end even the police had a kind word for him. A Scotland Yard detective said: 'He was one of our best clients, a perfect gentleman. We'll miss Charlie.'

But the type of comparatively small-time fraud in which de Silva indulged was not for his friend and compatriot Savundra. He took as his heroes men who thought big, like the pre-war Swedish match king Kruger and the genius manqué Horatio Bottomley, with the reservation that where they had finally failed to beat fate or the law, he would succeed.

Meanwhile, in Ceylon Pushpam's loyal uncle, Sir Chittampalam Gardiner, had not deserted him. Far from being deterred by the outcome of the Chinese business and the brush with the Belgian police, Sir Chittampalam considered Savundra capable of great things which might rebound to the advantage of them all.

Thus it was that Savundra's next involvement was not as a result of anything which was dreamed up by his new, assiduously cultivated friends in London, but came through an introduction by Sir Chittampalam to one of the most colourful of the new type of business tycoon now beginning to emerge.

CHAPTER SIX

Prayers Unanswered

JOHN DALGLEISH, A BURLY forty-five-year-old Tynesider, born of Scottish parents, was a man whom the City watched warily. He was certainly a remarkable fellow. Before the war he had been a fifteen-shillings-a-week shipyard apprentice, then a newspaper reporter, before enlisting in the army and rising from the rank of private to lieutenant-colonel on the General Staff. On his discharge he turned out two best-sellers about his wartime experiences, which gave him a small amount of capital. It was enough to launch him into big business.

His big coup was to acquire control of the ailing complex of companies known as Camp Bird. Camp Bird had originally been a mining company in the romantic tradition. A lone American miner in the wilds of Colorado struck a rich seam of gold. For months he had toiled in one of the most desolate regions in the world, with only the vultures wheeling overhead and the friendly, cheeky little camp birds which hopped around his bivouac for companionship. So he named his company Camp Bird and it made him a vast fortune.

By the beginning of the nineteen-fifties, however, with the original founder long dead, the assets of the company had become diversified into many not-very-profitable activities unconnected with mining. John Dalgleish took a long look at it, bought some shares and then, at the next annual general meeting, persuaded his fellow-shareholders to sack the board of directors and appoint himself and his nominees instead.

His appointment was to herald a startling change in the company's fortunes. By cutting out the dead wood and investing in growth industries, like hi-fi and television, he brought a welcome new look to the annual balance sheet of his diverse empire.

In 1957, three years after he had taken over the reins of office, he had made a considerable fortune while at the same time paying ever bigger dividends to the gratified shareholders. The City had to acknowledge the indisputable evidence of success, but in the more staid circles his activities still caused a certain amount of unease. He was a flamboyant character who did not fit into the conventional City pattern. There were mutterings in the clubs of Pall Mall that he was over-reaching himself.

This was the man whose Rolls-Royce drew up one morning in July 1958 outside 80 Hendon Lane. The company secretary of Camp Bird was later to recollect that Savundra had paid several visits to the Dover Street offices of the company earlier in the year but nobody knew what it was he discussed at such length with the chairman. The two men had in fact been drawing up plans for an ambitious operation. And the spearhead was to be Emil Savundra.

The plan was nothing less than the acquisition of the whole of the mineral rights in Ghana in West Africa, which had only recently been granted its independence under President Nkrumah.

In the days when Ghana was the British Colony of the Gold Coast, the mining concessions had been tightly controlled by a handful of powerful companies. Savundra with his ability to turn political situations to his own advantage had been quick to appreciate that with Ghana in the first fine throes of anti-colonialism, the atmosphere was ripe for persuading the new rulers that the existing mining concessionaires were reactionaries, who put their own profit before the national interest. If this point could be pressed home, it should not, Savundra's thinking went, be difficult to get them to cancel all concessions granted prior to independence and hand them over to someone who would operate them in the best interest of the nation.

Sir Chittampalam, with whom Savundra first discussed the matter, was quick to see the possibilities and to realise it might appeal to his old friend, the adventurous John Dalgleish. He was not mistaken. Dalgleish took up the idea with enthusiasm. Now all that required to be settled was the delicate matter of coming to a suitable financial agreement with Savundra and this was something he preferred to discuss outside the office. Hence the journey by Rolls-Royce to Hendon Lane.

In the privacy of his study Savundra explained what he wanted. He stressed that political persuasion would be of no avail in a newly independent country like Ghana, where officials might lack both the experience and the integrity of the old regime, unless the arguments were backed up in a practical way. Bribery of top government officials was an expensive business. The only way he could agree to co-operate was if he was granted an open-ended credit and should not be required to account for his expenditure to anyone.

Dalgleish agreed.

A few days later Savundra flew to Ghana with Dalgleish and introduced him to President Nkrumah, with whom he seemed to be on terms of friendship. (In fact, some time earlier, hearing that Nkrumah was celebrating his birthday in London's then most fashionable restaurant, the Mirabelle, Savundra had booked the next-door table and had managed to introduce himself.) As a result of the meeting in Ghana Dalgleish was convinced that Savundra's plan had every chance of success and returned to London to set things in motion.

At the beginning of December Camp Bird announced the formation of a new subsidiary company, called Ghana Minerals Corporation, and intimated that they had put down a capital sum of £50,000 to cover initial costs. If their expectations for the new company proved justified, they would subscribe a further £1 million to cover the cost of detailed geological surveys. In return, the parent company would control two and a half million £1 shares in Ghana Minerals.

Camp Bird was a company of world-wide repute. They had an authorised capital of £5 million so their ability to fulfil their promises was not in doubt. The Ghanaian Government, with a creaking economy, could not afford to ignore the scheme.

There was only the question of Savundra's own qualifications. Obviously the man who was already declaring himself to be the saviour of Ghana could not just be taken at face value, but Savundra had anticipated this and had laid his plans well.

On his visit to the country in August he had taken great care to leave a good account of himself, not only with Nkrumah but with as many of the high officials as he could talk to.

He was, he told them, an investor and financier, who believed that to make a profit in Africa was only compatible with Christianity if it was on an anti-colonial basis. He was himself a Christian who took his religion very seriously (witness the convent which he had founded and maintained in Ceylon). He was also fervently against colonialism as being anti-Christian. This was all music to the ears of the new Ghanaian regime but it was only his introduction.

He was, he said, one of the first businessmen to deal with the People's Republic of China. Further, he was so strongly against colonialism that he had been actually imprisoned for his views by the

Belgians, the oppressors of the Congo. He had been freed by the intercession of the Apostolic Delegate in Brussels.

It must have looked, even to the uncorrupt members of the Ghana Government, as if a saviour might indeed be at hand. It was known that many of the existing companies owning mineral rights in the country were in a sad financial state. What more desirable than that someone should appear who was willing to invest vast capital sums?

And it seemed the Ghana Minerals Corporation really meant business. Savundra registered it with an authorised capital of £50 million which he went on record as saying 'should be sufficient for this company's immediate needs'. Nor were the dazzled Ghanaians left in any doubt that this immense capital investment was regarded by Savundra as petty cash. Shortly afterwards he registered three other Camp Bird-backed companies, each with an authorised capital of £100 million—one of them to carry on business as a bank.

What was not made clear to those who did not have a knowledge of Ghanaian law was that, unlike other countries where the authorised capital of a company was in direct relation to the fees for registering it, this was not so in Ghana. To register a company with £100 capital in England at that time would have cost in the region of £30. To register a company with an authorised capital of £100 million would have required an astronomical sum. In Ghana, however, anyone could register any company of any size for a flat fee of precisely £7!

When the details of the scheme were announced in London by Dalgleish at the end of 1958, there was immediate uproar. The fence-sitters in the City were quick to forecast disaster but their reaction was nothing to the rage which the announcement engendered amongst those companies which already had mineral rights in Ghana. There was the British-owned Consolidated African Selection Trust, who owned diamond concessions, there was the British Aluminium Company, who were already in the middle of a row about bauxite rights, and above all there the £5 million Ashanti Goldfields Corporation, whose chairman was the formidable Sir Edward Spears, K.B.E., M.C., Commander of the Legion of Honour, Croix de Guerre with three palms, Etoile Noir, Grand Cross of the White Eagle of Serbia, Czecho-Slovak Croix de Guerre. Spears had many friends in high places. He had been Churchill's personal representative with General de Gaulle, a Member of Parliament, and the head of the famous Spears Mission to Syria and the Lebanon.

Spears was altogether a larger-than-life character. From his office in St. Stephen's Buildings on the Embankment close to the Houses of

Parliament he wielded considerable influence. His forthright esp-
ousal of the Arab cause had made him a prime target for Jewish ter-
rorists. Spears took the precaution of having a steel plate fixed to the
front of his huge desk and keeping a loaded revolver in his drawer lest
any visitor should be so unwise as to try to assassinate thim. Now he
watched events in Ghana closely and prepared to take his own measures.

This was the man whom Dalgleish now had to face. By an odd coincidence immediately after Dalgleish had announced his plans for
Ghana, there was a burglary at his offices. The thieves risked a sixty-
foot drop to seize certain papers relating to Savundra's scheme,
including a million pounds of debenture stock raised for the
venture—valueless to an ordinary thief but invaluable to a business
rival. The raiders did not get everything they came for but it made
the Camp Bird Directors realise that they had caught a tiger by the
tail.

The Ghana Chamber of Mines in London wrote a strong letter to
Camp Bird, telling them of the unfavourable reaction of the existing
mining concessionaires, but Dalgleish ignored them.

There was, however, at least one person in high authority in Ghana
who was quite unimpressed by the big money talk. This was ex-
Labour M.P., Geoffrey Bing, Q.C., who had been appointed by
Nkrumah as his Attorney General. Bing thought it strange to say the
least that just one of Savundra's new companies should require an
authorised capital very much larger than that required by any of the
Big Five Banks and that only £7 in cash, as the registration fee, had
been subscribed for £100 million. There was, however, nothing
illegal about it. True, it was not permissible to operate a bank without
a government licence but, as Savundra smoothly pointed out, the
Camp Bird Bank was not operating—only in existence—and so long
as he was not doing any business there was no offence.

Savundra arrived at Accra with all his family in October 1959 in a
blaze of publicity. He took a whole floor at the plush Ambassador
Hotel and must have been gratified when the following morning
Nkrumah's morning newspaper, the *Ghana Times*, hailed him as a
saviour and as the man with £350 million who had come to develop
Ghana and abolish poverty.

The family, suddenly transplanted from their relatively modest
existence in Hendon Lane, found themselves in a world of fantastic
opulence. 'I lived like a king at this time,' Savundra said later. 'Company directors in Africa were expected to.' By now, in addition to the
four boys, there was the latest arrival, the apple of Savundra's eye, a

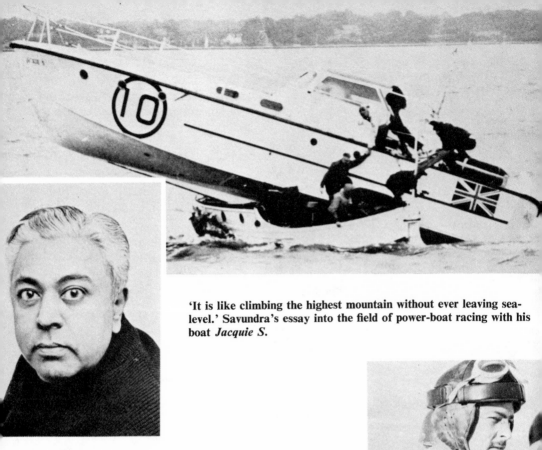

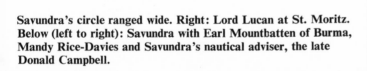

'It is like climbing the highest mountain without ever leaving sea-level.' Savundra's essay into the field of power-boat racing with his boat *Jacquie S*.

Savundra's circle ranged wide. Right: Lord Lucan at St. Moritz. Below (left to right): Savundra with Earl Mountbatten of Burma, Mandy Rice-Davies and Savundra's nautical adviser, the late Donald Campbell.

Savundra's reaction to the Board of Trade's investigation into his business affairs.

Below left: Stuart de Quincey Walker, Savundra's closest colleague in FAM.

Below right: Back from Rome in 1967—'I am like General MacArthur. He said "I shall return" when the Japs drove him out of the Pacific. And I, the great Savundra, am returning in likewise fashion.'

girl, Jacqueline. Servants waited on the family's slightest need and Pushpam found herself in the role of hostess to a constant succession of guests whom her husband would from time to time abduct to his study for long private conferences.

The publicity Savundra received in Ghana newspapers was the prelude to a massive advertising campaign to win support for his project. What he wanted was a guarantee of exclusive rights in new mining operations in Ghana for the next fifty years. All existing companies there would have to give ten per cent of their proceeds to his mining corporation. In return for this he promised his companies would pay huge sums of money to the Government. The advertisements assured people that he would pay far higher wages than any existing company and announced his intention of providing water, electricity and hospitals in all the villages adjoining the six areas where the companies planned to operate. Just the kind of approach to appeal to a struggling, emergent nation.

Nobody (except Geoffrey Bing) seemed to worry that only £14 had been subscribed, as the registration fees, for two £100 million companies. Champagne flowed. Politicians were entertained on a lavish scale. Ghana's citizens were regaled with expansive announcements made from a suite in their country's best hotel.

Mr. Bing remained unaffected by the general euphoria. He realised that he could not simply chuck out an individual who was promising to bring riches to the country simply because he personally had doubts. To do so might have deterred future genuine investors. But Bing discovered that only £50,000 of the £1 shares had been issued for cash. The balance of the shares were in form of 'suspense' shares converted into what were called bearer warrants. It was a stroke of luck for Bing that where the laws of Ghana were old-fashioned enough to allow Savundra to operate without proper public safeguards they were also old-fashioned enough not to provide for bearer warrants. Indeed, the issue of such shares was contrary to the Ghana exchange control law. All the same it was doubtful how far the law, drawn up in the old colonial days, would apply to the new Ghanaian pound, which was never mentioned in the regulations.

Bing sent officials to Savundra's three business addresses to inspect the books, which they were entitled to do for the payment of a fee of one shilling. They could have saved themselves the money. There were no books to examine.

The only effect of the inspector's visit was to alert Savundra that Bing was suspicious. The failure to produce books, Savundra realised, could be sufficient grounds on which to apply for a search warrant with a view to subsequent prosecution, if only for technical offences.

The warrant was duly granted and the inspectors moved in. It is not clear exactly what they expected to find but what they did find was certainly not what they expected.

There were, for example, copies of cables sent to the Mother Superior of Savundra's convent in Kandy, Ceylon, asking her and her nuns to pray for him. They were pinned to items of business correspondence which referred to crucial meetings. Also in the file was a cabled reply from the Mother Superior which read simply: ALL DOCU-MENTS DESTROYED—PRAYING, and a mysterious letter confirming that she had burned the 'black bag' unopened as he had requested. What was in this mysterious black bag? Did it contain details of religious or financial transactions?

The officials stumbled upon one other revealing document in their search of Savundra's papers—a copy of a letter to a British M.P., explaining how easy it was to fool the Africans . . .

All this was interesting material—but hardly damning evidence. What was certain in Bing's mind was that Savundra was not relying on prayers alone for his success. There was nothing directly incriminating among the papers, but there was one find which it was thought might be significant. Tied together in a bundle were the receipts for four packages of stated weight and measurement deposited in a Ghanaian bank. On the back of these receipts were pencilled notes which led Bing to believe the packages contained the missing share warrants.

After various formalities the packages were surrendered by the bank and delivered to Bing's office by senior bank officials. He had gone to a great deal of trouble to ensure that the packages should be opened before witnesses of undoubted integrity. There were police officers and prominent public figures, as well as the bank officials, to witness the disclosure of what Bing hoped would be damning evidence.

But, in the intervening days since the abortive search, however, while an order for the production of the packages was being applied for, Savundra had been to the bank to inspect his packages. Whatever they had previously contained, when they were opened in Bing's office they were found to be full of torn-up magazines, toilet paper and obscene poems about Bing's wife written on the same writing paper as an unposted letter to the convent.

There was, of course, nothing illegal in this. Savundra could not even be prosecuted for publishing obscene poetry. Indeed he had done just the opposite. He had locked the material away under such circumstances that it could normally be read by nobody but himself!

The collapse of the whole pack of cards, when it did occur, was brought about by a miscalculation for which Savundra was not primarily to blame. Shortly after his arrival in Ghana, he had persuaded a junior Ghanaian Minister, Mr. I.S. Iddrisu, M.P., who incidentally was in no way connected with the mining industry, to write him a letter which said that the Ghana Government had approved in principle Savundra's proposals. Savundra knew that it would not stand up as a binding document because the minister had no authority to write it. Nonetheless Savundra sent the letter to Dalgleish as evidence of the progress he was making.

Most of Savundra's communication with headquarters, as was usual with him, was by means of cables (on this venture to Camp Bird's bizzare telegraphic address, 'Yours Charmingly'), so whether he put Dalgleish wholly in the picture as to the background of the minister's letter is not known. But the result was disastrous. Dalgleish, annoyed by official denials in Ghana that any agreement had been reached with Camp Bird, impulsively published the letter.

Bing at once seized upon this to declare that Savundra's presence in Ghana was 'not conducive to the public good'. On 3rd December summonses alleging infringement of the Ghanaian Companies Ordinance were served on Camp Bird, Ghana Minerals Corporation and Savundra himself. Bing then contacted Interpol, but when the police raided Savundra's suite in the Ambassador Hotel, they found him ill in bed. A doctor with him said he could not be moved as he was suffering recurrent bouts of angina. It was impossible to take him into custody.

The balloon was now well and truly up and the rumpus spread rapidly from Ghana to Britain and the Commonwealth Office.

The first reactions in Britain were contradictory. The Press, and particularly the *Daily Telegraph*, criticised Nkrumah for instigating a purge against foreign investors in his country but the City and the shareholders of Camp Bird were not so naive. The Stock Exchange immediately suspended dealing in Camp Bird shares, pending clarification of the position in regard to Ghana Enterprises in spite of a hurried statement by Camp Bird that it had withdrawn its proposals regarding mineral rights. The statement went on to say: 'Camp Bird will thus have no capital commitment in connection with Ghana Minerals Corporation, other than the £50,000 originally subscribed. Similarly the options granted to Mr. Emil Savundra and his Far Eastern colleagues (principally Pushpam's ubiquitous uncle, Sir Chittampalam Abraham Gardiner), now automatically lapse as does Camp Bird's provisional commitment to provide services over the next few years to the extent of £2,450,000, had the concessions been granted.'

Meanwhile the Ghana Government issued a statement explaining why they were acting against Savundra. This not only accused him of the technical offence of failing to keep a record of his companies at their registered offices. It also claimed he had set up the Camp Bird Bank without being issued a licence and that he had lied about Ghana Minerals Corporation when he stated it had £5 million fully paid up share capital.

The statement indicated that the 2,450,000 shares said to be issued to 'suspense'—in other words for a consideration other than cash—must be illusory because neither Savundra nor Camp Bird in London could show an agreement substantiating the issues.

Despite this Savundra had put half-a-million pounds' worth of these shares on the market by converting them into bearer warrants.

These warrants were for sums of £5,000, £1,000 and £100. The seal of the company was affixed to them, and they were signed by Mr. Dalgleish, the chairman of Camp Bird Limited, and apparently of the Ghana Minerals Corporation, and by Mr. Savundra, and were dated 21st October, 1958.

'Taking all these matters into account,' said the statement, 'the Government of Ghana considers that the Ghana Minerals Corporation has not the financial stability which would justify any Government Department entering into any contract of any sort with it and the company is being so informed.'

The statement vehemently rejected the idea that Savundra was about to be given exclusive mineral rights. The Ministry of Trade had never accepted the proposal, and as for the letter which had been sent . . .

'The Parliamentary Secretary of the Ministry of Information and Broadcasting, Mr. Iddrisu, is in no way concerned with the granting of mineral rights in Ghana and it is difficult for the Government of Ghana to accept that Mr. Savundra could have believed that any such letter constituted any authority.' The fate of the Parliamentary Secretary to the Minister of Information and Broadcasting was predictable. After the police had called at the Ambassador Hotel, they made a late-night raid on the home of the thirty-nine-year-old Mr.

Iddrisu and seized various documents. Shortly afterwards, he was sacked.

Savundra had gambled on the proposition that if you are going to tell a lie make it a big one. It had not come off. His plans lay in ruins. The would-be 'Saviour of Ghana' lay in bed in his luxurious suite, waiting for the knock on the door which would herald his arrest on charges of fraud.

The knock never came. Taking into account Bing's lack of concrete evidence and Savundra's physical condition, it was decided to expel him instead. Deportation proceedings were instituted on 14th December and twenty-four hours later, two weeks after the fatal letter had been published in London, Savundra and his family were on an aircraft bound for Ceylon, leaving behind not only crates of empty champagne bottles but a business tangle of such complexity that it was never to be finally sorted out.

It is to Dalgleish's credit, however, that he did not now desert Savundra. Instead he sprang to his defence. John Gordon in the *Sunday Express* had described Savundra as 'the convicted criminal'. But at the company's annual general meeting after the Ghanaian debacle, in February 1959, Dalgleish stated: 'He [Savundra] has a high family position in Ceylon where his uncle is chairman of five or six of the largest public companies and, in fact, the introduction to Camp Bird was made by the uncle.' A further recommendation, Dalgleish told the meeting, came from 'a leading premier in the Far East', who referred to Savundra as 'this brilliant man'. The Indian Press Office in London thought this statement sufficiently pointed to merit a heated disclaimer that the premier referred to was Pandit Nehru.

'I have been to Scotland Yard,' Dalgleish went on, 'where I saw an assistant commissioner whose words were: "Nothing to the detriment of Mr. Savundra is known in this country." That is my personal feeling and I stand by it.'

The shareholders were unimpressed. Their leading spokeswoman was Miss Nancy Maurice, personal secretary to Sir Edward Spears of Ashanti. She held a single share in Camp Bird. Her single share not only gave her the entrée to shareholders' meetings but also the right to express her views which of course were the views of her employer. She was a general's daughter, a forceful woman and prided herself on the possession of a sharp brain and a strong will. (When she was seventy, and Sir Edward seventy-five, they married.)

During Savundra's adventures Ashanti had sent a team of investigators out to Ghana, who discovered that Nkrumah and other members of the Government, besides Mr. Iddrisu, had been bribed.

And in January, a month after Savundra's deportation, Spears himself and Nancy Maurice flew to Accra. When interviewed on arrival at the airport, Spears congratulated Nkrumah on having 'seen Savundra off'. On his return he commented: 'I consider that Savundra's behaviour in Ghana was extremely undesirable and I'm not at all surprised at the subsequent developments.'

Savundra threatened to sue for libel but never in fact did so.

The Camp Bird coup had come unstuck but Spears was not taking any chances on Dalgleish's making a second attempt.

Dalgleish found himself faced with the most hostile shareholders' meeting of his career as the determined Miss Maurice angrily tried to discredit him. While Dalgleish tried to stop her turning proceedings into a 'bear garden', she interrupted him time after time.

She asked how much, if any, of the £50,000 had been spent. Dalgleish replied that £25,000 had been 'repatriated' and a further £3,500 was expected shortly. The balance had been spent on offices, a motor car and 'other expenses'. At the news that almost £22,000 had sunk without a trace the meeting was in uproar.

'Let's not be petty,' shouted Dalgleish, spreading his arms. 'This company is earning £3,000 a day.'

It was six weeks before the Stock Exchange allowed a resumption in the dealing in Camp Bird shares and the row with the shareholders rumbled on for almost three months before they agreed to stop pressing for a Board of Trade enquiry.

The Ghana incident, however, marked the beginning of a downturn in the fortunes of Camp Bird and its chairman. Within two years the annual profit of about £1 million had turned into a loss of the same amount. Like many companies which have once tarnished their image, it became fair game for the sharks of big business, never slow to scent a wounded reputation. One of the City's most mysterious financiers, Dr. William Wallersteiner, who had fled to Britain from Hitler's Germany as a young scientist, intervened in its fortunes and accelerated its decline.*

Camp Bird was eventually wound up and the Official Receiver called in. He arrived too late. Most of the capital had already disappeared. For months the Receiver tried to make some sense of its affairs, in particular the Ghana episode.

In a statement issued in 1963 he confessed himself beaten. It read:

---

*Attempts are currently being made to get Wallersteiner, now in Frankfurt, to settle debts in Britain estimated at some £3,000,000. A former Lloyd's underwriter, he also faces claims from Nigeria, East Germany and Czechoslovakia.

'This company was formed sixty-three years ago, but its affairs have become complicated and involved. It seems it had some hundred-and-forty subsidiaries and sub-subsidiaries. £2,400,000 has disappeared and we cannot find the books.'

By the time this statement came to be made, Savundra had put his ignominious exit from Ghana out of his mind and was deeply involved in new ventures. But a friend remembers his reaction to the Official Receiver's report. 'The poor dim British', he gasped, before dissolving into fits of helpless laughter.

CHAPTER SEVEN

The Rise and Fall of a Mystic Financier

AFTER BEING KICKED OUT of Ghana, Savundra spent almost two months in Ceylon, no doubt explaining to Uncle Chittampalam, who had taken such a close interest in the affair, what had gone wrong. Then, in February 1959, he flew back to London.

In fact, he had not come out of the whole business too badly. John Dalgleish's spirited defence of his reputation had been highly gratifying. And newspapers, some of whom were hostile to the new regime in Ghana, had not treated him too unkindly.

There was just one immediate problem. Though Savundra drove round Mayfair in his Rolls, he was short of cash. Nothing remained of the £22,000 Camp Bird had invested in him. It was a man named Frank Prater who pointed out a simple way of overcoming his difficulty.

Prater eventually became a respected and successful businessman, but he had been involved in a massive air ticket swindle which defrauded airlines of something like £300,000. He was one of the most exuberant and fast-talking of the new breed of fringe operators who flourished in the late fifties—men who preferred to use brains rather than brawn to relieve others of their money, an occupation which he regarded as a kind of game.

Prater was not in the least surprised that the elegantly dressed Savundra with his Rolls-Royce parked beside them on the kerb should be pleading poverty. In fact, the Rolls gave him an idea. Why not, he asked Savundra, put the car on hire purchase? Surprised that worldly-wise Prater should have thought otherwise, Savundra explained that the car was already pledged for as much as he could lay his hands on.

'Well, you do it again, don't you?' said Prater.

He had spotted Savundra's personalised number plate, ES 6262, and had rightly surmised that the plate had been acquired separately from the car. Now he explained the significance of this to Savundra as if he were outlining something of elementary simplicity to a child.

At that time hire purchase companies, when considering an application for finance, relied entirely on checking with the central hire purchase index, where the registration numbers of all cars under hire purchase were recorded. The weakness of this system, which has since been tightened up, was that there was no guarantee that the number plate quoted actually belonged to the car.

All that Savundra had to do now was to apply for a hire purchase agreement quoting the 'clean' number plate. It helped, of course, to have an agent who was *persona grata* with the various hire purchase companies and again Prater was able to help—by suggesting a contact.

Savundra and the contact pulled off this trick two or three times, using different number plates, and raked in several thousand pounds. Fraud on this petty scale was not really Savundra's handwriting but it served to keep him in what was known as 'marching money'—the ready cash to enable one to put up the prosperous front so necessary to the fraudster—until the opportunity for the next stroke should present itself.

When that opportunity came, however, it was not his own idea but that of James Pyper. Pyper had a life-long habit of reading the small items in the City columns. It was a habit which had proved profitable in the past and now he was about to strike lucky again.

The paragraph which caught his attention simply stated that the Costa Rican Government were in the economically embarrassing situation of over-production of the coffee on which the prosperity of the country largely depended, and were about to launch a strenuous sales drive abroad to try and increase exports.

There are a number of conflicting accounts of how matters developed from there but undoubtedly the possibilities arising from that simple paragraph were floated around the 'think tank', with Savundra participating eagerly.

One morning soon after the paragraph had appeared, he presented himself at the Costa Rican consulate and asked to see the consul, Franz Hacke-Prestinary, on a matter of the utmost importance.

To Prestinary he introduced himself as an international financier of the highest repute. There followed exactly the same routine as he had adopted in Ghana. He had close connections with the Vatican and he had a philanthropic interest in helping under-developed countries.

He now wanted to put forward a plan which would enable Costa Rica to live up to the English translation of its name—the 'Rich Coast'.

Prestinary listened. He could hardly do otherwise to the man who almost casually offered his country economic salvation. In turn, he introduced Savundra to his sister, Virginia Prestinary, who had recently arrived in Britain to head her country's export drive of coffee.

Savundra explained that he had made a careful study of the problems facing Costa Rica and felt he could be of practical help. Senora Prestinary was impressed. She arranged for Charles Vincent, close friend of the President of Costa Rica and, more important, chairman of the Costa Rican Coffee Brokers' Association, to fly to London accompanied by a team of bankers.

To Vincent, Savundra claimed that he had a buyer for a considerable amount of Costa Rican coffee for distribution throughout Europe through his wide contacts. The proposed broker, he added, was an extremely rich man, who would finance the whole deal. His name was Shiv Kapoor.

The son of a passingly wealthy tea-planter in Assam, Shiv Kumar Kapoor had had some success in his home country in the import-export business. Then, in 1949, he had come to England, and to begin with had flourished. His first venture after arriving had been to buy up old railway lines and sell them rerolled as steel. There were other ventures in the same field and he seemed to be the man with the golden touch. Soon he was controlling several thriving companies.

Then the scrap metal market collapsed and soon the high-living Kapoor, who let many people believe he was an Indian prince, found himself heavily in debt. However, the cracks were not yet beginning to show in his life style.

At the time the Costa Rican deal was being thought up, Kapoor was living at Buckhurst Park, near Ascot, which was of such magnificence that he could ask for a rental of a thousand guineas during Ascot week. It was even to be considered as a home for the newly-wed Princess Margaret and Lord Snowdon. It stood in twelve acres of parkland. There was a miniature golf course, a 600-foot lake teeming with fish, and a floodlit swimming pool shaded by high cypress trees. The house itself was lavishly equipped. There were three kitchens, six bathrooms with gold-plated taps, and even the door knobs and keys were gold.

It could hardly be doubted that anyone who lived surrounded by such evidence of wealth must indeed be a millionaire and quite capable of financing a coffee deal on the scale envisaged by Savundra.

Savundra and Kapoor had met socially, and Savundra's role was, ostensibly at least, that of 'contact' man. He knew Kapoor's image as a 'prince' was perfect for the project about to be launched and he performed the necessary introductions. Underworld associates of the two men who remember the deal being set up are in no doubt that Savundra provided the impetus and that Kapoor, when the affair was publicised three years later, suffered more harshly than he deserved. As one of Savundra's former Ceylonese friends put it: 'It was obvious it was Emil's deal, even though his name was not mentioned. It had his blueprint all over it'.

At the time the bargain was struck Kapoor was certainly vulnerable. He was desperate for money. In addition to Buckhurst Park, he had another fabulous glass and wood house to maintain in Virginia Water. It had a carpeted pit sunk in the drawing-room floor, a goldfish pond and a fountain in the sitting room. A bemused gossip columnist once described it as 'a futuristic cricket pavilion gone mad'. Kapoor called it 'Gurjveer', which may be translated as 'lovemaking', but the neighbours, recalling the wild parties held there, nicknamed it 'Gertcher'. The thought that he might shortly have to give all this up must have weighed heavily on Shiv Kapoor. The coffee deal seemed to offer a way out.

When Charles Vincent flew over on a second trip to London to finalise the deal with Kapoor, he was immediately swept into a world of fantasy. A Silver Cloud Rolls-Royce was waiting at the airport to waft him to Buckhurst Park. As he was driven up the long driveway, he gazed in astonishment at the private yew forest and the formal gardens ablaze with colour.

Later he was to say: 'My eyes were popping out with the splendour of it all.' He found 'Prince' Shiv Kapoor charming, and most of all, he found the deal which was being suggested overwhelming.

Kapoor, who said he had already found a willing buyer on the Continent, offered to buy 6,000 tons of coffee for the at-that-time extremely generous price of £359 a ton. To the one and a quarter million people of Costa Rica it was their biggest-ever export order. It amounted to one tenth of their entire coffee crop. The bill was £2,153,571.

Vincent knew it was a tremendously important deal for his country. Sitting in the lavish surroundings of Buckhurst Park, he signed the contract and flew back to his country a happy man. That was October 1959.

To handle the coffee deal Kapoor used one of his companies, Reevaham Commerce Ltd. It had two 'sleeping' directors, but

Kapoor made all the decisions. Like Savundra, he was very super-
stitious, calling his companies after Oriental gods (Reevaham in
reverse means 'great power') and using as file references on his contracts the numbers 7, 11 and 151, regarded as lucky in Indian
numerology.

A month after the meeting with Vincent, Kapoor secretly 'contracted' to resell the coffee. The Continental merchant on the receiving end was to be a French-born count called Maxim de Cassan Floyrac.

Small and dapper, with a penchant for what might be described as
unconventional business deals and a life-style to match, Floyrac lived
in the exclusive Rue Mignard in Paris but was a frequent visitor to
London. With his expensive tastes and his liking for making money
fast, he was well-known to many in London's more dubious business
circles. He was described to us by Prater as having 'that little bit of
society that nobody else had'.

Kapoor's private contract with Floyrac was signed unbeknown to
Reevaham's stooge directors. And in it was a condition by which
Reevaham had to pay Floyrac the massive penalty of £271 a ton for
any shipment which did not arrive on time.

The coffee was to be shipped in twelve monthly instalments of 500
tons each, to be delivered at three European ports, Hamburg, Rot-
terdam and Antwerp, and early in January 1960 the first consignment
started out on its journey to Europe from the Caribbean port of
Limon.

But of course all was not as it seemed to be. In the first place, there
was no intention of reselling the coffee to Floyrac. Coffee was the last
thing he needed. It was to be resold cheaply in East Germany. In the
second place, there was to be no payment for most of it. This was to be
a phantom shipment in reverse; instead of there being money and no
goods there were to be goods but no (or virtually no) money.

Kapoor had continental associates to handle the spoils. There was
the American and Foreign Bank in Tangier, run by a sixty-year-old
American, Tom Stangbye, into which the penalty money due to Floyrac was religiously paid out of the money obtained from the genuine
sale to East Germany, only to be paid out again to others in the proportions ordered by Kapoor; and there was the Privat und Kommerz
Bank in Zürich of which the President was an associate of Kapoor's,
Dr. Joachim Teitler. Teitler's bank was Kapoor's nominee, which
held all the shares, but two, in Reevaham Commerce Ltd. So the
machinery was set up for the smooth disposal of the revenue, well out
of reach of the British tax authorities.

After some delay and after the second shipment of coffee had arrived, the sum of £137,000 was paid for the first shipment. If Vincent had had any passing moments of unease in his mind about the delay, they were immediately set at rest. When the contract was being signed, it had been explained that international currency regulations sometimes made payment slower than could have been wished. Incredibly the Costa Rican financial advisers had been taken in to the extent of agreeing to a 180-day settlement. Such a clause can only be understood against the background of the measure of their desperation to conclude any sort of deal.

In the meantime, the aura of limitless opulence was kept up on the home front. Among Kapoor's acquaintances \ ere industrialists, MPs, socialites—even a Chief Constable (but if his visitors were bastions of the English Establishment, a slight smell of incense generally pervaded Gurjveer, reminding them that there was a touch of the Oriental mystic about their host). Franz Hacke-Prestinary remembers a visit in which he talked to both Kapoor and Savundra at the house, and at New Year, 1960, Vincent was flown over to a lavish party where, he was later to say at Kapoor's trial, he 'met a crowd of distinguished people who fitted into the picture Kapoor had created around himself'. Kapoor's wife, Lilamani, formerly a noted classical dancer in the East, was then rated one of London's most beautiful hostesses.

While the shipments took place with conscientious regularity to the designated ports in Europe, Kapoor continued to live in style.

It was not until late July, when no further payments had been received, that a reluctant and dismayed Vincent ordered the shipments to stop, by which time the sum of £1,169,000 had been received from the East Germans and had been paid, under the Floyrac penalty clause, into the Tangier bank.

There had been one or two casualties on the way. Tom Stangbye, who had been negotiating to buy Buckhurst Park from Kapoor, had mysteriously vanished, taking his bank with him. It later reappeared in Panama, but Stangbye himself was caught in Germany and thrown into prison in Morocco. It was estimated that depositors had lost one and a half million pounds, but Floyrac was not amongst them.

As for Dr. Joachim Teitler, the deal had hardly got under way before he shot himself. Kapoor was deeply shocked by his friend's death. He collapsed and had to be treated in London by Dr. Susarta Sen, who had been Pandit Nehru's personal physician. Perhaps it was at this point that he fully realised for the first time how deeply he was in the deal, but he was in a position of no return.

Apart from the initial £137,000 which had been used to pay for the first shipment, £490,000 was paid to Reevaham and £563,00 went into the Floyrac account. It is known that Kapoor was able to pay off a £49,000 mortgage on Buckhurst Park and £46,000 in personal debts.

And what of Savundra? There is no direct evidence that he made anything out of the deal—indeed, he later vehemently denied that he had—but James Pyper at least believed otherwise. In 1970, dying on his bed in a one-room flat in Artillery Mansions, Victoria, surrounded by empty whisky bottles and a battery of pills, he cursed bitterly about him to a friend:

'To think that I set that stinker Savundra on the road to riches. He was a nondescript, down-at-heel little man when I took him in on a fiddle I thought up against the Costa Ricans. My idea was to make a few thousand pounds on a coffee deal—but what does he do? He takes the entire bloody crop!'

Yet the only man to stand trial for the fraud was Shiv Kapoor, and it was three years before he was brought to justice. After the fraud he had vanished to Switzerland but he came back, he claimed, to clear his name. He did not succeed. His beautiful wife, Lilamani, who daily brought in delicacies for him to eat in his cell with a flask of tea—but never coffee—wept openly in court as her husband was sentenced to six years. Even the judge seemed to have a certain amount of sympathy for him. Stating that it was obvious he had had associates who had not been brought before the court, he described Kapoor as a man of 'genteel background, ability and opportunity'.

'It is sad,' he said, 'when a man of your education allows himself to fall into dishonesty.'

The Costa Rican Ambassador in London was less charitable. As Kapoor went to prison, Senora Mimi Chittenden went on record as saying: 'The President of my country will be glad to hear this news. So, too, will our state-nationalised banks. We have still not recovered from the paralysing blow Kapoor dealt to our economy.

'Even at a million pounds the trade would have been three times the country's annual exports to Great Britain.

'All the top people employed by the Anglo-Costa Rican Bank—which carries the burden of the fraud—have lost their jobs. My brother, the Assistant Manager, was one.'

It was not the bank officials, however, who were the hardest hit on a personal basis. That role was reserved for Charles Vincent. 'Even if I save my name,' he said after the crash, 'I have lost my fortune. I was rich. I had a successful business. Now I face a £250,000 debt because of guarantees I gave our State-run bank. All my property and resources have been destrained. I have got to start again.'

Although Floyrac's part in the conspiracy came in for severe criticism during the trial, the name of Emil Savundra was never even mentioned. Yet typically, even while the coffee deal was being carried through, he had been trying to interest the Costa Ricans in another scheme, which involved the purchase by their government of the country's British-owned Northern Railway.

Nothing came of it. And now, four years later, with Kapoor still in gaol, he embarked on a new scheme which was to shake the roots, not of a small country like Costa Rica, but of Great Britain itself.

CHAPTER EIGHT

The Smuggler in the Old School Tie

WHILE SAVUNDRA WAS BUSY with the Costa Ricans, things were not going so well for the man who was to become closer to him than anyone, except his family, and with whom he was to be associated in his most spectacular fraud. That man was Stuart de Quincey Walker, ex-public schoolboy, bar-owner and smuggler, operating from the mecca of smugglers, the 'free port' of Tangier. Because Stuart Walker was to play such a prominent and controversial role in subsequent events, it is fitting that we should devote some space here to describing his background.

He was born on 11th January, 1924, of reasonably well-to-do parents. He was sent to prep school near Bath, then to Wellington, where he is remembered as a quiet, middle-of-the-road boy with no outstanding abilities. From an early age his main interest was the sea and when war came he tried to join the Navy, but failed to pass the entrance examination. Bitterly disappointed, he had to find work on cargo boats. But at least he had one opportunity to show that, whatever his shortcomings, he didn't lack the courage of an officer. In 1941 he received a commendation for bravery for rescuing two comrades, at great personal risk, from a gas-filled hold.

After the war he settled in Penzance and married the daughter of a Norfolk clergyman. They had a daughter, Julia, but the marriage proved disastrous. After only three years they were divorced and Walker was left, restless and without roots. His one thought was to get out of England and seek some of the excitement of which he felt somehow he had been cheated. Tangier, with its raffish reputation, seemed to be the place.

Of all the odd characters who established themselves in the Tangier of the nineteen-fifties, Walker was one of the oddest. It was his very *lack* of flamboyance which made him remarkable in that polyglot community. The late Vincent Mulchrone of the *Daily Mail* once wrote: 'There is a gentle air about him, the young Englishman sipping his beer in the corner of the bar. The dark suit, the Wellingtonian tie, the spectacles and the receding hairline add up to a picture of a City gent waiting for the 5.27 to Surbiton.'

In fact, Walker was one of the most diligent, if one of the most unlucky, of the band of smugglers plying their trade around the Mediterranean and his boat, the *Vanadia*, was a familiar sight in the harbour.

He had, however, other interests. With the profits from his contra-banding he bought one of the many seedy bars in Tangier which were always coming on the market and, with a stroke of genius, installed one of the town's most outlandish figures to run it. Paul Lund was quite the opposite of Stuart Walker. The story that he was a self-confessed thief who had jumped bail in Birmingham—although too good to check—was no doubt apocryphal, but he delighted in pub-licity and soon the Bar Nevara in Musa Ben Nusair became known simply as Paul Lund's.

There were bars to suit every taste in Tangier. There were queers' bars for men and bars like Nora Lumb's smart Carousel, where the lesbians used to gather, and less exotic bars like Dean's in the Petit Soco, where a copy of *The Times* was supplied with your drink, and social bars like the Minza and the Riff.

Walker's bar, as run by Paul Lund, attracted a complete cross-section and it certainly lived up to its reputation of being the most colourful of them all. It was far from luxurious or even sanitary. One of Lund's habits was terrifying the uninitiated by shooting the cock-roaches as they crawled up the wall, with a revolver which he kept behind the bar.

There was always something happening in Lund's bar to keep the gossip-hungry tongues of Tangier wagging as, for example, the time when an elegantly dressed socialite was rash enough to use the primi-tive apparatus under the stair which served as a lavatory. One moment all was comparatively quiet. The enormous house cat sat sleepily at the bottom of the stairs, watched balefully from three steps up by Lund's boxer dog. There was soft music and a handful of cus-tomers were sipping their drinks peacefully.

Suddenly, the door of the lavatory burst open and the elegant cus-tomer rushed out, yelling at the top of his voice, with his trousers round his ankles, closely followed by a gigantic rat which had sprung at him out of the lavatory bowl. The cat caught sight of the rat and set off in hot pursuit, and the boxer, not to be outdone, set out after the cat. In an instant, all was chaos as the cavalcade crashed round the tiny bar, knocking customers off their stools and spilling drinks in all directions. It gave the locals the best laugh they had had for weeks.

It was typical of the quiet, self-effacing Walker that he should have been involved in an enterprise such as the Bar Nevara. Everything he touched had a habit of turning out unexpectedly, if seldom to his advantage.

Eventually Walker decided that he would do better to try his luck elsewhere and let it be known that his boat was on the market. It was then that he met William Lindsay Pearson, who introduced himself as a prospective buyer. Walker found Pearson witty and charming. His life seemed to revolve around water ski-ing and pretty girls. Most important of all, he appeared to be rich and he wanted the *Vanadia*. When Walker explained that negotiations with other would-be purchasers were nearly complete, Pearson immediately offered £1,000 more than they had done. He produced impressive letters of credit and when Walker hesitated, counted out £2,000 in cash as an advance. The deal did not end there. Pearson wanted the boat in Aden and suggested Walker deliver her. Dazed by this sudden turn of luck and delighted at the prospect of a long voyage on completely innocent business, Walker accepted.

The next morning he sailed out of Tangier, bound for Gibraltar, where the boat was to be fitted out to Pearson's specifications and take aboard fuel and Pearson's own crew. A week later and he was on his way to Aden.

The trip, however, did not live up to his expectations. Barely two days out of port, the *Vanadia* was arrested by the French Navy and Walker was ordered to sail her to Bizerta on the North African coast. One of the crew hired by Pearson, it seemed, was a deserter from the French Foreign Legion. And, in addition, both Pearson and Walker himself were suspected of arms-smuggling. Only after days of intensive questioning were they finally allowed to set off for the next leg of their voyage—the 1,500 mile stretch to Port Said. Here, precipitously, Pearson left the *Vanadia*, pleading urgent business in London and instructing Walker to go to the British Bank of the Middle East in Aden, where he would be paid in full for the trip and the boat.

It was at Aden, after travelling through the crisis-torn Suez Canal, that the trusting Walker first began to have misgivings. There was money for him at the Bank but only a very small proportion of the sum due. There were also instructions to proceed to Zanzibar, calling at Mombasa on the way where more money would be waiting with the Standard Bank of South Africa. When Walker called there was no money at all. Worse, the Standard Bank had never even heard of Pearson.

By now almost penniless, Walker struggled on to Zanzibar in the belief that Pearson would be bound to get in touch with him sooner or later. Walker may have been naive and gullible but he was a great survivor. With no sign of Pearson he began to make a living for himself, trading ivory and explosives round the Zanzibar coast.

Then, suddenly, he was arrested by the British Navy on a charge of piracy. But the charge, it soon appeared, was a blind. Interrogating Walker the Senior Naval Officer made an extraordinary statement. 'Archbishop Makarios,' he declared, 'is the responsibility of the British Navy. Any attempt to abduct him from the Seychelle Islands will be forcibly prevented.'

Eventually Walker was able to convince the S.N.O. that he had no idea what he was talking about. It was then revealed to him just how he had been duped. Pearson, it appeared, was an Australian confidence trickster and was believed to have been the mastermind behind the recent huge Oppenheimer diamond robbery in South Africa. Now the authorities had been alerted to the possibility that he had been hired by the Mafia chief, Lucky Luciano, to kidnap Archbishop Makarios, who was in exile in the Seychelles from Cyprus. That was what Pearson had wanted the *Vanadia* for. The British Navy had kept a close eye on her progress but it seemed that Pearson had realised that they were on to him. It was now less likely than ever that he would show up in Mombasa or Zanzibar.

The one compensation for Walker was that at least he still had his boat. After a few more months trading he sold it to an Arab syndicate, bought a Land-Rover and with two acquaintances, an engineer and a Special Branch policeman, he set off to return to England.

An element of farce was never very far away from anything Walker did and the journey home proved no exception. On the way back they stopped off for some time at Dr. Schweitzer's famous hospital at Lambarene where they made an elaborate film which they hoped to be able to sell when they got home. Unfortunately it was only when the reels of film came to be developed that it was discovered that they had neglected to take the lens cap off the camera.

Later, Walker's two companions fell out and in the ensuing fight the engineer lost an eye.

Finally, back in London, he discovered that Pearson had, since deserting him, been involved in an arms deal in Tangier. There had been a quarrel with his associates which had resulted in a gun battle. The police had arrived and Pearson had been arrested, tried and sentenced to eighteen months in a Moroccan jail.

Walker had a feeling that if he could get Pearson out of prison, there was a chance that he would get the rest of his money. He flew out to Tangier and met Pearson's blonde girl friend, who had already made a romantic but unsuccessful attempt to help her lover by smuggling a grenade to him in prison inside a cake. From her, Walker learned that Pearson's plot had been to supply guns to the Moroccan Independence Movement, the Istaquel party. An official of the party, Achmed Zirie, now told Walker that if he could find another arms supplier, he could have Pearson released from prison.

At once Walker returned to England and started to make enquiries. Arms dealing was not really his scene but he had contacts who knew their way around. Eventually he got the name of a man who, he was told, could help him. He was taken to an office in Warren Street; and to what was to be the most fateful meeting of his life.

Seated behind the desk was Emil Savundra.

'I am the original black Englishman,' he greeted Walker. 'Tell me what I can do for you.'

Walker outlined the deal and Savundra immediately showed interest. He gave the impression that he had handled many similar deals before. As a result it was arranged that Achmed Zirie should be brought to London to meet Savundra when all would be arranged and Walker, believing he had achieved what he had set out to do, left the matter there.

In fact, all that Savundra did was to contact an arms dealer who drew up convincing proposals for the Moroccans. These Savundra showed to Zirie who agreed that they were satisfactory.

But Savundra was not content to sit back and to take his commission. Instead of going ahead and arranging the shipment, he contacted the French authorities and asked them how much they would pay him to block the delivery. This time, however, the double cross did not come off. The French did not want to know and Zirie was far too cagey a customer to pay money in advance. Thus the whole scheme foundered. Pearson remained in jail and Walker returned to Tangier to take up smuggling again—the only trade he knew.

Soon, under Emil Savundra's persuasion, he was to enter another one; with calamitous results.

While the consequences of the Costa Rica fraud were still in the future, Savundra, who in any event knew he would not be involved in the proceedings, set about revarnishing his image. On 10th February, 1960, he became a naturalised British citizen under Section 61 of the 1948 British Nationality Act. Shortly afterwards he began to put it about that he had been granted two doctorates. Plain Mr. Savundranayagam now became Dr. Emil Savundra, Ph.D, D.C.L.

When he came to be questioned about the origins of his new academic honours, he was to claim that they had been granted to him by Avatar University, in consideration of two theses he had written. Avatar University was a tiny concern run in a Kensington cul-de-sac by the Greek Apostolic Church. It no longer exists, and the Greek Apostolic Church does not give degrees.

Savundra at least looked the part. His prematurely iron-grey hair and his heavy-rimmed glasses gave him an air of dignity and learning calculated to impress the most sceptical.

There was another more significant prop to the image which was created at about this time. The ever loyal and industrious Sir Chittampalam Gardiner now set up a series of companies which he put under Savundra's control. Sentimentally they were all called after Savundra's three-year-old daughter, Jacqueline. They were, variously: Jacqueline Holdings, Jacqueline Finance, Jacqueline Nominees, Jacqueline Securities and Jacqueline Enterprises.

They were all small companies with an authorised capital of only £100 each but they were to provide the foothold in the British business world which Savundra needed. Sir Chittampalam's reason for setting them up was, according to Savundra, that 'he wanted to provide a degree of stability for his niece who was married to what he called the spendthrift of the family—me'. That the companies were eventually to be used as vehicles for a massive fraud was something Gardiner was never to know. He died only a few months after they were established.

For Savundra most of 1960 was spent in rearranging the scenery, while the seeds of a really gigantic fraud were germinating in his brain.

The end of the fifties and the beginning of the sixties ushered in the age of the big business fraud both in America and in Britain. One field of finance particularly vulnerable to the high-level fraudster was insurance.

The attraction of insurance in this context was obvious. It was a business where the customer paid cash in advance and most of them never wanted anything back except a piece of paper. Those who were tiresome enough to submit claims could be stalled, haggled with, and given false promises. At its most simple, all that had to be done was to borrow money, usually on the strength of forged securities, buy a company and pay one's self a huge salary and generous expenses whilst engaged in stripping the company of all its premium income, capital reserves and other assets.

But when the day of reckoning came, the man seen to be in charge of the operation might have some explaining to do. Therefore the fraudulent insurance operator had to prepare carefully his 'front'. And it was while Savundra was making his preparations that, for the second time, he met Stuart de Quincey Walker.

Walker, after his meeting with Savundra over the abortive arms deal, had for a time tried his luck in England but was unable to settle into the conventional life. Eventually he managed to raise the money to buy another boat, the *Ace of Clubs,* and returned to Tangier.

However, his reputation for being 'a bit of a Jonah so far as ships were concerned', as one friend put it, remained with him. Returning from successfully delivering a cargo of cigarettes to Italy, the *Ace of Clubs*, an ex-German E-boat with three powerful 1200 h.p. motors, broke down off Corsica. She wallowed helplessly in rough winter seas for days on end before the British aircraft carrier, *Victorious*, appeared. Unfortunately their offer of a tow to Carthaginia had to be rejected as to land there would have meant certain imprisonment for the Spanish members of his crew. Much later a Norwegian super-tanker came on the scene and suggested a tow to Tangier. Again fortune was not on Walker's side. The lowest speed of which the super-tanker was capable was fifiteen knots and, after the tow rope was fixed, Walker and his crew watched helplessly as the foredeck of the *Ace of Clubs* was pulled off and went bounding over the waves into the distance. Next an elderly Russian freighter arrived but, in trying to get close enough to fix a rope, she got too close and her counter knocked the wheelhouse into the sea.

At this final ignominy the dispirited *Ace of Clubs* sank. The Russian freighter landed Walker and crew in Malta. They found their way back to Tangier where Walker received the final blow. The news of his misfortune had preceded him and the fellow members of his syndicate had appropriated all the money from the cigarette cargo, transferred it to their bank from Italy, and made off.

Walker did not give up. Somehow he managed to acquire a launch, the *Dunbar*, but scarcely had he taken possession than a storm blew up and she sank in the harbour.

Once again, almost penniless, Walker returned to London. Life for him had reached its nadir. It was at this point, however, that he met an old friend from Tangier, Bobby McKew, who told him he thought he could find him an interesting, well-paid job.

McKew was, in fact, acting as a contact man for Savundra, whom he had known for some time. The son of a wealthy Irish film distributor, he went to Dublin University where, although he is supposed to have had a reputation in society as a tearaway, he is today remembered for nothing more outrageous than sending a large crab scurrying across the floor at a tennis club dinner. Later, however, he was involved in a robbery from film producer Jack Warner's home in the South of France and had served a three-year sentence in France. Back in London, his name was frequently linked with those of debutantes, and he eventually married the daughter of 'Lucky' Jack Gerber, the South African millionaire.

There is no doubt that McKew was deeply involved in the initial stages of setting up what was to be Emil Savundra's most notorious memorial: the giant motor insurance company, Fire, Auto and Marine.

For one thing, he was to help with the hard cash which would be needed to acquire offices and buy such mundane essentials as tables, chairs and typewriters. His police record made it inadvisable for him to be openly involved, but he was able to supply someone who would project the right image; his choice was his old friend Stuart Walker. The three men met towards the end of 1962 in a modest coffee bar in Conduit Street.

Walker was at first uneasy. Tentatively he asked what had happened over the arms deal. Savundra brushed the question aside with an impatient shrug of his shoulders. 'That was something I didn't make any money out of,' he said brusquely, making Walker feel that it had been his fault. Then he smiled benignly, as if to intimate that he readily forgave Walker, and, his mesmeric eyes taking on an almost soulful expression, he pressed the palms of his hands together as if in prayer, and said: 'Now, let us talk about making real money.'

Savundra and McKew sketched out for Walker the plans they had for the founding of a business which would offer the public car insurance at irresistibly low rates and thus corner the market. They did not find it difficult to carry Stuart Walker along with them in their enthusiasm. It was a field in which he had no knowledge or experience but these were not considerations. A week before he had been sitting glumly in Tangier with no money and no future. Now, suddenly, he had the chance of taking part in what promised to be an exciting and challenging adventure. More important, it smelt of money. When Savundra offered him a job as his aide in the new company, he accepted eagerly.

At that moment an out-of-work smuggler died and an industrial tycoon was born. Only someone who trusted in the strange ways of fate as completely as Stuart Walker could have accepted the metamorphosis with such equanimity.

CHAPTER NINE

Benefit through Care

WHEN EMIL SAVUNDRA TOOK his first long, cool look at British insurance, he must have rubbed his hands with joy.

He saw an industry which worked to a set of rules more appropriate to a gentleman's club than to a highly competitive business. The quaint idea seemed to persist that insurance was a public service rather than a commercial enterprise.

It was this aura of respectability and the fact that the members of the industry, with remarkably few exceptions, lived up to their reputations which made London the insurance capital of the world, with seventy per cent of all business transacted coming from abroad and providing the country with one of our biggest invisible exports. However, it was not an industry geared to cope with someone of Savundra's shark-like propensities.

Basically the conditions under which it operated had remained unchanged since the turn of the century. Anyone who could show a capital of £50,000 could set up a company dealing with motor insurance. No professional qualification or previous experience was required. A man could be digging ditches one day and sitting behind a big desk selling insurance the next.

To open the door even wider to the unscrupulous operator, once the £50,000 had been 'shown' it did not have to be deposited or invested in gilt-edged securities. All that was necessary was to produce a piece of paper indicating that the sum of money was available. The money could have been borrowed for the purpose and returned the following day or invested in other enterprises, however dubious.

It is true that all insurance companies were required to show in their annual accounts that they had a liquid capital of £50,000 or ten per cent of the premium income, whichever was the greater. This eminently sensible provision, however, was effectively invalidated by a clause excusing newly set-up companies from showing this solvency margin for the first two years of trading—surely the most perilous period for any industry.

Furthermore the industry as a whole was protected by special legislation from over-zealous investigation by the Board of Trade. If the Board considered a *prima facie* case existed for examining the activities of a company, the management concerned had the right of appeal in court in the hope of blocking the investigation. Even if the court supported the Board, there would probably be a delay of several months during which time all manner of irregularities could be perpetrated.

Certainly there existed a sort of Jockey Club of insurance in the shape of the British Insurance Association, but membership was not obligatory and there was no compulsion to abide by its principles.

It is almost as if the legislators were deliberately playing into the hands of men like Savundra. But the traditions of the industry had been forged in an atmosphere of mutual trust and were not geared to cope with the fraudulently-inclined. Certain members of the B.I.A. agreed among themselves to abide by a rough tariff system, charging similar prices for policies. But this was purely a gentleman's agreement, in the same way as it was customary to offer ten per cent commission to insurance brokers. There was nothing to stop a new operation offering cut-price premiums and higher commissions.

In fact, behind the image of solid respectability the industry in Britain had become complacent and over-expansive. The laws of the market place—production at the cheapest possible cost and selling at a competitive price—did not apply and Savundra frequently declared, during his years in the business, that insurance should and could be sold in exactly the same way as baked beans.

To put the cherry on the cake from Savundra's point of view there was no restriction on the movement of an insurance company's money. The contribution to Britain's balance of payments from the insurance industry was a vital one. It was desirable that firms should be able to invest funds overseas.

For a man who liked to boast 'When you English see a loop-hole in the law, you drive a Mini Minor through it; I, Savundra, drive a Rolls-Royce', the temptation to set up as an insurer was irresistible.

His immediate problem was to convince the Board of Trade that he had £50,000. He would never have dreamt of using his own money, even had he been able to, and the man to whom he turned for help was his old friend, Count Maxim de Cassan Floyrac.

During his frequent visits to London the Count stayed in a small flat in Mayfair, and it was here that Savundra outlined his plans and asked Floyrac to help him with the problem of instant capital. When asked later how Floyrac reacted to the proposition, Savundra was to say: 'He dived in like a seal.'

The proposition was a simple one and would have the effect, at first, of making Floyrac the largest shareholder and the nominal controller of the proposed company.

Yet it was important that both Savundra and Walker should be shareholders from the beginning. Walker put up £1,000—money he had received from a marine insurance company after the sinking of his last boat, the *Dunbar*, in Tangier. Savundra magnanimously matched this, or rather Jacqueline Securities (one of the companies set up for him by the late Sir Chittampalam Gardiner) did. This meant Floyrac had to guarantee £48,000. Of course he did not have to produce this amount in cash but merely provide a banker's certificate to show he was good for the amount. The way he did this was ingenious and was to set the pattern for future manipulations.

He visited a Zürich lawyer, Dr. Paul Hagenbach, who was one of the leading experts when it came to setting up investment trusts in Liechtenstein, a tiny country, but one of great significance to international financiers because its so-called 'banks' are about the most easily manipulated and obliging in the Western world. Hagenbach set up for Floyrac a company called Western Bankers Trust, and one of their first acts was to provide their proprietor with the note of credit for £48,000 required by the Board of Trade. This was, of course, just another example of the way impressive-looking pieces of paper figured in Savundra's life.

The formalities having been thus completed, the new insurance company under the important and comprehensive title of Fire, Auto and Marine was registered on 14th February, 1963.

At this stage Savundra did not appear as a director of the company. Until he had tested the temperature of the water he was anxious not to become too deeply immersed, lest somebody with an inconveniently long memory might start asking questions.

Instead, in all his negotiations on the company's behalf, he described himself as the company's attorney, representing the interest of the backers whom he claimed were an important group of foreign investors.

The man in at the sharp end was Stuart Walker, who was appointed managing director (and the only director with executive power). Until the company started trading, he was to be paid expenses only.

After that he was to draw a salary of £1,500 a year, plus the use of a company car.

Bobby McKew, who like Savundra preferred to remain in the background, put up £6,000 in cash for the company's immediate needs and at the same time secured the company's printing contract for a printing works which he owned at Herne Hill on the outskirts of London.

The Floyrac money was not, or course, available for use, so the limited working capital made it urgent to start the inflow of money from premiums.

It is at this point that another advantage peculiar to the newly-formed insurance company becomes apparent. Launching a product for a new company in almost any other line of business, is a long, expensive and painstaking process, involving the building up of a sales force and a money-consuming advertising campaign.

An insurance company, however, starts with the inestimable advantage of having immediate access to a nationwide grid of brokers and agents, who either sell insurance to the public or perish. Their income comes from the commission earned from the insurance companies whose policies they sell.

Savundra was quick to realise that, amongst the less scrupulous agents, enthusiasm for selling policies was likely to be kindled by offering them a higher commission than other companies. And the fact that the policies, however sound, were at cut-rate prices made selling them easy. They appealed to the type of customer who liked to pride himself that he had a sharp eye for a bargain. And who was the agent to counsel caution when his own generous commission was at stake?

Not that F.A.M. policies were available to everyone. Insurance companies generally worked on the basis of making the good risk customers subsidise the bad ones. This did not appeal to Savundra. The only business he wanted to encourage was what was considered to be the jam of motor insurance—the responsible family motorist. Under no circumstances would he underwrite fleet schemes, young drivers and motor cyclists, while at the same time he made the novel stipulation in his policies that he would accept no liability if a car involved in an accident had been driven 'in an unsafe or unroadworthy condition or manner'. One Lloyd's broker was to remark acidly that this ruled out 'everything but an act of God'.

Lest such disturbing thoughts were to cross the mind of a potential customer, the company's letter headings were designed to set his mind at rest. The motif which appeared on all the company stationery and documents was a lion rampant on a scroll bearing the comforting words: *Benefit through Care.*

Fire, Auto and Marine opened its doors for business in untypically modest premises—an office suite consisting of three small rooms in Baker Street. The advertisements placed in trade magazines and some national newspapers were less diffident. Readers were left in no doubt that a new Messiah had appeared to rescue the long-suffering motorist from the high premiums which had been extracted from him in the past. At the same time, and much more important, insurance brokers throughout the country were discreetly circularised, and offered as inducement a commission of up to twenty per cent, as opposed to the traditional ten per cent, on any business put in the way of F.A.M. Savundra had shrewdly put his finger on the insurance world's Achilles' heel. By appealing to greed he had penentrated the entrenched position of an industry which had hitherto relied for protection on its own reputation for honour and integrity. If Savundra had made a mistake, it was to underestimate the accuracy of his diagnosis.

Within forty-eight hours of the launching of the sales campaign for F.A.M. the proposal forms started dropping throught the letter-box in Baker Street—singly at first, but soon in battalions.

So great was the avalanche that within weeks neither the existing staff nor the premises could hope to cope with the volume of business.

Frantically, Stuart Walker committed himself to taking over a spacious office block in Orchard Street, just off Oxford Street, and moved in overnight. The staff requirements were not solved so simply. Qualified men were not easy to obtain. Savundra met the problem by waiving the need for qualifications. In consequence, the situation began to acquire an Alice in Wonderland air of unreality.

Normally, before engaging assistants, Savundra made enquiries which had nothing to do with the applicant's professional qualifications. He placed great reliance on astrology. He regularly consulted the stars as to whether an enterprise was propitious or not, and would never think of involving himself closely with another person until he had discovered the time and date of that person's birth and had a horoscope cast to establish his or her suitability. The smaller fry among his associates only warranted a token clearance from his astrologer, but somebody appointed to fulfil a senior role, like Stuart Walker, called for the closest investigation. In this case Savundra only approved the appointment after the close study of a detailed thirty-page astral report (which, Walker says, referred to a possible catastrophe in June, 1966).

Now, however, was not the time for such niceties. He just had to have staff, quickly. The urgent need for an office manager was satisfied by a man whose only qualification for the job was some experience as an assistant manager in a supermarket. The highly technical job of running the renewals department was given to a former clerk in the World Health Organisation. An Australian boy and girl, seeking to extend the duration of a European tour by taking gainful employment, were surprised to find themselves jointly running a department after submitting their names to their local Labour Exchange.

While Walker was forced into a situation where he had to grab at any willing pair of hands, however unsuitable, Savundra adopted a more choosey, if no less logical, attitude in making appointments. There may have been some justification in his appointment of the Earl of Suffolk's younger brother, the twenty-three-year-old Hon. Maurice Howard, to head the claims department because of a brief experience of the insurance world, but his other appointees betrayed Savundra's snobbish weakness for graduates from the older universities, or the possessors of double-barrelled names.

One appointment which made rather more sense than most came several months later when the chaos, caused by the inability of the unqualified staff to deal with the ever-rising tide of business, was at its peak.

Reg Stratton, who had been in insurance all his working life, was between jobs when a friend told him that in the currently depressed state of the insurance market F.A.M. were almost unique in advertising to take on new staff. Stratton applied and was immediately hired, only to find that at the age of thirty-seven he was very much the odd man out in a firm where the accent was on youth and inexperience. His first job was to understudy a twenty-year-old who was struggling to understand the complexities of his responsibilities, but it was not long before the youth came to rely on Stratton's expertise to keep his head above water.

It quickly became clear that Stratton was a valuable man. Within a month he was appointed to take over control of the endorsement and renewals department.

Stratton took over his new duties with an enthusiasm which was rapidly to become frustrated. He found that there was a traffic jam involving the processing of some 60,000 endorsements and the customers, tired of chasing their brokers, were telephoning direct to F.A.M. and making their views clear. Stratton's problem was that he did not have the staff to deal with the emergency. Or rather, he had the staff, but he could never find them when he wanted them. The reason for this was not far to seek.

To cope with the ever-increasing volume of business, Walker had had to acquire another office building about five minutes walk away, where space could be found for the additions to a staff which already numbered over 150. Many of them, however, found the definition of their duties so vague, and were so inadequately supervised, that they adopted the practice of clocking on in the morning and then slipping across the road, usually to Selfridges, where they spent the day working as counter assistants. In the unlikely event of anyone asking for them at F.A.M. their colleagues declared that they were in transit from one office to another.

Happily for them, too, the double wages thus collected could be further supplemented by overtime without any real risk of being found out. It was simply a case of clocking in again as soon as they had clocked off. Then they were free to return home for a meal or simply curl up in a quiet corner and go to sleep before clocking out again at 10 p.m.

It did not take Stratton long to discover what was happening and he immediately reported the matter to Savundra who, in spite of not appearing on the letter heading as a director, was known by most of the staff as the real power behind the company.

Savundra was outraged. He did not like to be taken advantage of. Immediately he put Stratton in charge of all night work with the power to sack anyone on the spot whom he found to be slacking. The first person Stratton caught was duly fired. Unfortunately he turned out to be the head of the department which had hired him. When the matter was duly reported to Savundra, he amended his instructions. 'You can fire anyone,' Stratton was told, 'except the heads of departments.'

In the end Stratton managed to select six reasonably efficient aides but it still took him three months to clear the backlog.

While pandemonium reigned amongst the lower echelons, Walker and Savundra were largely aloof from the general chaos. Occasionally Walker could be seen wandering like a ghost from one department to another, but Savundra was seldom on view. In line with his policy of maintaining a low profile he did not even have an office of his own but used Walker's when he visited the building to count the money or direct the next step.

Such an astonishing overnight success could scarcely have gone unnoticed in the closely-knit world of insurance. While high officials of the Board of Trade looked on nervously, unable to interfere because of the two-year free-from-inspection clause, there were many experienced insurance men who forecast disaster. No company, they claimed, could both cut premiums and increase commissions and remain solvent. There were many others, however, particularly among outside brokers, who dismissed such forebodings as sour grapes.

Savundra himself was very well aware of the suspicion with which his company was regarded by the more conservative elements of the industry and decided that he must do something about it. He had recently had the staff circularised with a memorandum entitled 'Chain of Command', which showed Stuart Walker as Chief Executive. But Walker's name carried no weight. The board, decided Savundra, needed 'dressing up'. To that end he started looking for a chairman whose social standing and integrity were beyond question. It was not long before he found one.

CHAPTER TEN

An Officer and a Gentleman

AT THE OUTSET OF 1963, life was placidly pleasant for Cecil H. Tross Youle, O.B.E. For close on twenty years, following a distinguished war-time career in the Navy, he had been general secretary of the RmN.V.R. Officers' Association, which he had founded with his friend, the Hon. W.W. Astorn later Lord Astor of Clivedenm

The club premises in Mayfair's Hill Street were a convivial meeting place for ex-Naval Reserve Officers and the genial, bon vivant Tross Youle steered the ship with just the right touch. It was, as they would have said in the Services, a 'cushy billet'. By tea-time he would be free to drive down to his luxurious country house, Bix Bottom Farm, near Henley-on-Thames in Oxfordshire, where, with his attractive wife, Elizabeth, he was a popular member of the county set. He knew all the right people, was seen in all the right places and there had never been a breath of scandal attached to his name.

Yet, Tross Youle was not entirely content. He had reached an age when he must try to do something positive with his life or resign himself to coasting unambitiously into old age. Then there was the financial aspect. His life style cost money. His son was at Cothill, arguably the most expensive preparatory school in England. His daughter, a talented and beautiful girl, suffered tragically from deafness and her special educational needs were also a big drain on the family excheq-uer. Although his wife was comfortably off, Tross Youle felt that he himself should do more to provide for their future.

The opportunity to do so arose indirectly from a decision taken a few years previously by the R.N.V.R. Club's committee.

When Tross Youle and 'Bill' Astor had founded the club in 1945, it had immediately attracted some 20,000 members, but over the years the numbers, through resignations and deaths, had started to fall away. To combat this, it had been decided to admit as members amateur yachtsmen who had had no previous connection with the Navy. It was under this new regulation that Emil Savundra, who had recently acquired a pleasure cruiser on the Thames, became a member.

For Savundra, with his high-flying social ambitions, it was a feather in his cap and he lost no time in making himself an agreeable and generous companion to his new circle of friends, who provided such a welcome contrast to his 'business' acquaintances. It was equally inevitable that he should come into frequent contact with Tross Youle, part of whose job was to make everybody feel at home.

It was out of this situation that a friendship started to grow. Savundra played his hand carefully. So much so that Tross Youle, who was very conscious of the social status of the people he met, was later to go on record as saying: 'I always found him a charming man, who invariably brought to the club very pleasant guests of good standing.'

Savundra's first approach to involve Tross Youle in the affairs of Fire, Auto and Marine was cautious. In April 1963, he wrote to him at the club:

Dear Tross Youle,

I have been hoping to run into you at the Club during the week, but we did not meet.

Certain foreign friends of mine have finally been permitted by the Board of Trade to set up a new Insurance Company in this country. As you know, the B.O.T. are quite fussy about Insurance Companies in general and are very loath to allow new ones to be formed.

These people have as their only Director in this country, so far, an Insurance expert [A reference to Stuart Walker]. He is more a technical man than anything else. They have asked me, as I am to be their legal adviser, to organise a powerful Board for them, composed of Englishmen of the highest repute and integrity, and also social standing.

The work is not going to be heavy, meetings will probably be held monthly and should be mere formalities during the first couple of years in any case, and my friends have mentioned fees of around £1,000 per year.

I know that money means very little to you, but perhaps you might be interested in such an appointment and if so, you might care to contact me.

I should be glad to meet you in town and tell you all about it.
Very sincerely yours

It was not a letter which was likely to arouse the suspicions of even a much more experienced businessman than Tross Youle, who wrote back immediately, inviting Savundra to lunch with him at the Connaught Hotel.

After that the letters came thick and fast and couched in progressively warmer terms. Savundra urged Tross Youle to ring him at any time 'at my ex-directory most heavily guarded telephone Finchley 0946'. If Tross Youle did not think he would fit the bill as chairman, would he approach some of his important friends?

Tross Youle would and did. He invited, amongst others, Sir William Slayter, a recently retired Admiral, and Conservative M.P. Sir John Langford-Holt. Both refused for personal reasons, although Langford-Holt was later to agree to serve on another board in the empire Savundra was beginning to create.

Savundra also sought candidates on his own. Among his acquaintances was Lord Bingham, a young man who spent most of his days and nights gambling at John Aspinall's Clermont Club in Berkeley Square. Very soon his father was to die and he became Lord Lucan. To Savundra, Lord Bingham seemed an ideal choice. He had a title, a little money and not too much brain. Thus while Tross Youle was still lobbying for candidates in his rather more select social circle, Savundra jumped in and offered Bingham the chairmanship of Fire, Auto and Marine.

Tross Youle was horrified and lost no time in making his views clear. Savundra was immediately contrite. Tross Youle was one of the few really respectable allies he had and he did not want to offend him. Hence this letter of 31st May, 1963:

Dear Tross,
I again want to assure you that the Insurance Company's status is of paramount importance to me and the interests I represent in this matter, and it is for this singular reason that I first invited you to join their Board.

I would not ever allow anything to happen which might even remotely or indirectly affect this venture and least of all would I embarrass someone whom I respect and whose friendship I value very much by making him look an ass by putting him anywhere alongside a complete chump!

It is cases like the one I am thinking about that makes me often think that the system of hereditary titles is completely outmoded and should be abolished. Additions like this to your nobility makes the entire Upper House system into a complete comedy and brings the nobility into disrepute!

I am so glad that the air is now completely cleared and I look forward with pleasant anticipation to your continued interest in our venture.

Incidentally, we topped £1,000 for 1 day's takings yesterday!
Very sincerely

The friendship between Savundra and Tross Youle flourished. There were invitations to each other's houses and Tross Youle did all that was expected of him in introducing Emil and Pushpam into his own circles. To quote from yet another letter:

Dear Tross,

For a start, it is I who must thank you for all you have done for F.A.M., Pushpam and me.

To start with F.A.M., as I said to you, there are strange catalytic processes in human affairs, as yet quite unknown to us; but you have yourself seen many examples of what I mean. There are associations which breed success and good fortune, and others which spell disaster and chaos . . . not because of any particular definable factor, but because of this strange catalytic ability of certain people in certain situations.

Now, Tross, I am fully convinced that our association is one of these which will spell complete success all round and I think events to date have proved this completely. [—and so on and on.]

All other candidates forgotten, Tross Youle now became chairman of Fire, Auto and Marine. He had also accepted the chairmanship of another Savundra company, Champion Assurance.

His association with Savundra, however, did not run as smoothly as they both would have liked.

He had devoted twenty years of his life to the R.N.V.R. Association and he was not anxious to surrender what had always been for him a very pleasant, not to say convivial, way of life, but others in the club had different views. Chief amongst these was the vice-chairman, Commander Colin Campbell, who had gathered round him a number of supporters who wanted a shake-up in the club's affairs. There had been an unsuccessful move to unseat Lord Astor as chairman of the council, and now the target was his right-hand man, Cecil Tross Youle.

Here they were on stronger ground, for Colin Campbell knew a lot about Savundra's past record. A study of Tross Youle's contract with the club uncovered the fact that he was not allowed to take on outside directorships without the express approval of the committee, and this had not been obtained. Campbell made clear his dislike for Savundra and did not hesitate to tell anyone who would listen about his past. He even arranged a meeting with Tross Youle and Savundra outside the club, when he made his allegations to Savundra direct. Tross Youle and Savundra reacted in different ways. Savundra, who so openly despised the law, now rushed to it for protection. On 17th March, 1964, he wrote furiously to Campbell:

Sir,
I have now got the definite evidence that you have repeatedly slandered me, and in particular at the Naval and Military Club, at the Cocktail Party of the Royal Yachting Association on the evening of the 26th February, 1964.

I have to advise you that unless a full apology is received by me *by noon tomorrow the 18th. instant*, I shall forward the matter to my Solicitors for further action without reference to you. Finally I have to warn you that if you ever make a further slanderous statement about me to any person, I shall not hesitate to take immediate and drastic action to put an end to the unnecessary nuisance you are making of yourself as far as I am concerned.

There are more than sufficient legal processes available to ensure that decrepit old has-beens with one foot in the grave are not allowed to go free having slandered people who have done them no harm and who leave them severely alone.

We move in different circles, Thank God, and there is no reason in the whole world why you should go out of your way to collide with me.

I would request and require you therefore to mind your own business in future and leave me entirely out of your conversations, as I have always been delighted to do in respect of you, in spite of the very distasteful and disgraceful matters about you which I have learned.

Threats of writs flew in all directions. Tross Youle, his loyalty to Savundra in no way diminished, came to his defence. In a long letter to Lord Astor, who had warned him that he had been told that Savundra had a conviction for fraud, he claimed that his friend was being slandered.

17th March, 1964.

Dear Bill,

With reference to Colin Campbell's proposed allegations in connection with Emil Savundra, I am going to give you as brief details as is possible but I would be quite willing to fill in the gaps if you require me to.

Emil has for many years been an agent of the Vatican and one of the cases which I imagine Campbell will bring up is in the matter of Emil acting for the Vatican to transpose Vatican funds which were in China and India and which amounted to many thousands of pounds. He, being an international banker, was able to transpose the funds and this was done through the Bank of Belgium. You can imagine the intricacies of such an arrangement were very great and that obviously devious methods had to be used. This included the lodging of a great deal of money in Goa, which was done with Nehru's knowledge and agreement, and in fact Nehru was considerably involved in this matter. Unfortunately the question of Goa's ownership was very much in the boiling pot at the time and Portugal, who naturally had no friendship with India and having a knowledge of the transferring of the various funds, looked for a scapegoat. They were able to persuade the Belgian Government, the two countries being largely of the same faith, that Emil had been acting contrary to the good of either Portugal or Belgium, and Emil was duly arraigned and had a trial in Belgium. He was given a sentence of five years imprisonment. Twenty-four hours later he was released from the hospital in which he spent the day after his judgement on a decree signed by King Badouin and he was then flown directly to the Vatican where he was entertained by Cardinal Montini, who is now the Pope, and then flown back to this country.

I would mention that Emil and his family are naturalised British subjects. As a result of the successful dealings in the question of transfers, Emil received a warm letter of appreciation from Cardinal Montini, who was then Vatican administrator. I have seen this letter myself and Montini purposely did not mention the inconvenience that Emil had suffered since it was obviously not politic to do so. To satisfy the Portuguese, who would have been outraged had they known of the action taken, Emil's obituary was printed in the Belgian papers shortly after his departure.

Emil still has the ear of the Vatican and he and his family were received by the Pope last year.

The other case which Emil describes himself as part of his more unfortunate experience was that of Camp Bird. You may remember that a year or two back negotiations were in train for Camp Bird to retain certain reservations and rights in Africa. Emil was dealing with this matter with Nkrumah but he had no connection at all with the chairman of that company's stock exchange dealings which were going on at the time of the negotiations and which I believe brought the company down. The chairman was Dalgleish and I cannot remember what the final outcome of this matter was but Richard Jackson (the head of Interpol), now Sir Richard, publicly announced in the English press that nothing was known or could be held against Emil Savundra in the whole affair. Richard would re-affirm this if called upon to do so.

For Emil himself and his family I can speak highly. I have known them for some time and he and his wife have visited our house and met a great many of our friends, as we have done his. Three of Emil's sons are at St. John's, Windsor, and the fourth has moved on to Beaumont. I have met the headmaster of St. John's only very recently and he has invited me to go over the school to see the boys of whom he is very fond.

Emil himself is a great motor-boating enthusiast, as you will no doubt see when he takes part in this year's *Daily Express* power boat race, in which he is entering *Jacquie S* which ran last year and also a new boat which is being built for him at the moment by Clark of Cowes. Closely working with him on this venture is Lord Lucan, who I believe has some connections with Bruce Campbell, Colin's son, who does not share his father's dislike of Emil.

So far as Colin Campbell's animosity is concerned, this arises from the fact that at a certain time he himself was endeavouring to raise some funds and he came into contact with Emil. Things did not work out satisfactorily and I imagine that he has ever since then had this hate. There is a firm of stockbrokers in London who work for Emil, who, when they first began to do so, were approached by Colin Campbell with his story, whatever it may be, and were asked and advised not to represent Emil, but who made their own enquiries and have acted for him ever since.

I can only think that Campbell's dislike of Emil, coupled with his recently acquired dislike of myself, is why he is acting to the extent that he is. I would ask you to appreciate the fact that his upheaval last year and again over the question of the resignation of members of the Council were both hampered by my personal intervention, which I made plain to him. He was not successful in his intentions and I think that he is now trying to take things out on me.

You may remember that before I was married there was a little clique of members of the Council who endeavoured to oust me from my position, but who gave up their efforts when they were directly challenged by myself as I was able to prove to them that they would be on very dangerous ground if they went ahead with their untrue allegations. In this clique there was, of course, Bill Cutts, who, although he has resigned from the Club for some time now, is still a close friend of Campbell's and they have meetings at one house or another from time to time, in which these policies are discussed. I have first-hand knowledge of these meetings because they have been attended by Ian Hunter, who is always very open to me.

It is perhaps unfortunate that this matter also involves Leslie Cocke [at that time chief accountant of F.A.M.], who is now firmly established in the Fire, Auto and Marine Company and has a great future in front of him. Leslie has spoken to me about Colin Campbell's utterances and I am quite sure that if anything arises Leslie will himself speak to Emil who would not hesitate to issue writs. So far as I am concerned I find it rather heartrending that Campbell should raise the matter, which has long since been forgotten, with a view to hurting me and, although I will naturally accept your advice as I have always done, I shall be placed in a very unfortunate position if I am asked to take any action, as I do not see that I can allow Campbell to go around giving me a bad name without doing something about it.

Your sincerely

This letter shows with great clarity just how Savundra was able to mesmerise his victims. A few deft passes and the criminal image disappears and in its place there appears the martyred hero. Tross Youle was so under the Savundra spell that even the publishing of Savundra's obituary in the Belgian newspapers seemed to him perfectly natural and understandable.

He was, however, in an impossible position. He was forced to choose between his directorships or his position as secretary of the R.N.V.R. Association. He elected to nail his colours to Savundra's mast. There were the usual farewell dinners and speeches and presentations and by the beginning of May 1964 he had left the job he had done so well for so long and had launched himself in the perilous world of big business, about which he knew little or nothing.

It was not long before he began to realise that in his job as chairman of the company he was only the most remote of figureheads.

While the premiums from trusting motorists took on avalanche proportions and the organisation over which he ostensibly presided mushroomed overnight his activities were restricted to little battles about his company car and whether he should have the services of a secretary. If he attempted to involve himself in matters of importance, Savundra was horrified. He wanted Tross Youle as a 'front man', but neither he nor Walker would tolerate any interference with the running of the company. Within a few months the iron fist was beginning to show.

Memo from Emil Savundra to Stuart de Quincey Walker, 30th November, 1964:

My dear Stuart,

I am far from happy about Tross.

Let me be very blunt and ask you to speak to him under the old pals act and try and find a solution to the problem.

. . . in my opinion he is clearly unsuited to anything like a full time job with Champion for reasons which are really very simple.

His way of life for years has been to come to town in the morning, arrive at the Club around 10 a.m., do a solid job of work till around 11.30 then retire to the Bar followed by a very elaborate lunch washed down with plenty of excellent wine, brandy and Port . . . then he returns to his office around 3.30 to sign letters, possibly polish off a few bits of work still remaining undone and then off home or to another social engagement.

. . . To cut a long story short can you see Tross doing a *9–12 and 1–4 routine?* and managing to live on the standard lunches of higher executives—highest executives for that matter even if not our own monastic luncheon arrangements.

The memo goes on to say that Tross Youle was to have a small office of his own at Jacqueline House and the use of a girl to take messages and deal with his personal affairs. He could conduct interviews but never in the afternoon after one of 'his expensive alcoholic lunches'.

The final paragraph spells out Tross Youle's true status at F.A.M.:

'This will allow him to have the "front" he needs, now that he is not at the Club, and occupy his time to some extent, to have a "home from home", but not get underfoot as far as we are concerned.'

So, while de Quincey Walker and Savundra presided over the growing F.A.M. empire, and the thousands of pounds poured into it, Tross Youle was restricted to writing little memos to the accounts department, asking them to pay his petrol and entertaining bills out of the petty cash.

It was perhaps just as well for, when the crash came, it was perfectly obvious to the Fraud Squad officers investigating the affair that Tross Youle had no knowledge of what had been going on and his name was cleared completely. His financial loss, however, was to be considerable and brought him close to bankruptcy.

CHAPTER ELEVEN

Gentlemen
Prefer Blondes

IT WAS IN THE initial stages of the F.A.M. adventure that Emil Savundra became involved in what was undoubtedly *the* scandal of the sixties. By the time it was over a respected Minister of the Crown had been disgraced and forced to resign, and a fashionable osteopath and portrait painter, Stephen Ward, had cheated sentence at the Old Bailey by committing suicide. Some famous names were to receive unwelcome publicity. Savundra's name, however, was mentioned only once and escaped notice. He was generally referred to as 'the Indian Doctor'. Few people knew the 'Indian Doctor's' identity.

It was Bobby McKew who introduced Savundra to Stephen Ward. Ward was later to treat Savundra for back injuries he had sustained in a power-boat accident, but meanwhile they had another common interest: beautiful girls. At different times, two such girls, Christine Keeler and Mandy Rice-Davies, shared a flat with Ward.

Christine Keeler formed an association with a member of the Government. She also had an affair with a Russian diplomat who was suspected by M.I.5 of spying. When, after cover-up attempts had failed, these facts emerged, the minister resigned.

It was while this scandal was in the making that Savundra, for a time, became a regular visitor to Ward's flat in Wimpole Mews and there he met Keeler. At the time Stephen Ward's cosy domestic arrangements were in a state of flux. Mandy Rice-Davies had moved out to have a stormy affair with the notorious property racketeer, Peter Rackman, and Keeler herself was about to move to a flat of her own in Dolphin Square.

If Keeler was nice to Dr. Savundra, the ever-helpful Ward suggested, Savundra might, in return, pay for Keeler's new flat. Savundra wanted to rent a room where he could take girl-friends and

Keeler's new place would be ideal. Before she could decide, however, Ward introduced Savundra to Mandy Rice-Davies in a coffee bar in Marylebone High Street and Savundra at once forgot all about Keeler.

He was later to say that Mandy Rice-Davies was the ideal mistress—beautiful, vivacious and undemanding. Ward now put to Mandy that she should provide a room where Savundra could take his girls. He showed her £25 in notes which Savundra had given him, presumably to try and fix the matter.

'Why let outsiders in?' Ward asked her. 'Why don't you go out with him instead?'

Mandy agreed and so her affair with Savundra started. Savundra paid her generously in gifts and money. The affair did not last long but when Ward was brought up for trial at the Old Bailey for living on immoral earnings, Mandy Rice-Davies' evidence was damning. 'The Indian Doctor', she claimed, always left between £15 and £20 on her dressing-table and she, in turn, gave Ward a share of it.

In retrospect what is extraordinary is that Savundra should have escaped almost untouched. The one time his name was mentioned in court it was subsequently spelt wrongly in the newspapers. He was the only one whose anonymity was preserved. Each time his part in the affair came up he was referred to as 'the Indian Doctor' and most people assumed the man involved was a doctor of medicine.

He would not, of course, have been able to testify on the vital matter of whether Rice-Davies gave any of his money to Ward, but had he not paid Ward £25 direct?

Even Savundra, it appeared, was uncertain whether his anonymity would be preserved. When the trial began, he took his family to Guernsey. From there he kept in regular touch with Stuart Walker to get the latest news of how the case was progressing. Walker was later to say that he had never known anything to worry Savundra so greatly.

It was a sordid affair which excited world-wide interest and brought shame to many.

Only 'the Indian Doctor', with the luck of a black cat, escaped.

But this affair was not the only one which might have threatened his image.

There was, for example, an enquiry into his Swiss bank accounts. This arose, oddly, from the genuine interest which he had had since childhood in amateur radio.

In his study at Hendon Lane was one of the most sophisticated transmitting and receiving systems on the market, which he used to call up fellow enthusiasts all over the world. One of them was Barry Goldwater, the unsuccessful Presidential candidate in America in 1964—Savundra called him on the eve of the election to wish him luck. Another fellow 'ham' was Herbert Hoover Junior, with whom Savundra had long discussions about the formation of a special society. This was to be one of his grand gestures aimed, he said, at helping the under-developed countries. The society was to organise the supply of government surplus radio equipment to people who could not otherwise afford it. His interest was purely charitable. When asked about this later, in the Old Bailey, Savundra was to say cryptically: 'It was to amend for the sins of omission and commission in my life.' But some of his calls at least were connected with his financial transactions. The G.P.O., to whom he paid £2 a year for his operator's licence, and the highly-respectable Radio Society of Great Britain, of which he was a member, knew nothing of this—but the police, who monitored many of his calls, did. For them, G3SDN—or –. ...– ... –.. –., the official licensed call sign of Dr. Emil Savundra, began to have dubious connections. The police knew that some of his calls were being made to colleagues in Switzerland and they eventually managed to persuade the Home Office to ask for a Commission Rogatoire (a commission of enquiry) to investigate Savundra's bank accounts there.

Just after dawn one morning in late 1963 Savundra called Stuart Walker and persuaded him to come immediately to No 80 Hendon Lane. Walker found him already up and showing signs of stress. Savundra explained the situation: he could not go to Switzerland himself, he said—that might be inadvisable. There had to be an intermediary.

Two hours later Walker was on an aircraft to Geneva, where he went to the Union Bank de Suisse and talked to its manager, Willy Suhner.

There the purpose of the Commission which had been set up was explained to him. Its task was to investigate the source of funds arriving into Savundra's numbered account. The only interest of the Commission was to be satisfied itself that the funds were not the proceeds of crime. If irregularities were found, details of them would be sent to the Home Office on the understanding that they could never be used as evidence—only as a source of information. Even this was something Savundra could not afford.

The same evening Walker was back at Hendon Lane explaining the situation to Savundra. Savundra, for his part, said he was in a difficult spot—the source of the funds was not easy to establish. The nearest he came to explaining them to Walker was to mention commission earned for the recovery of Vatican funds.

Walker, still very much in the dark, next day found himself bound for Tangier. He had contacts there, one of them a banker, whom he persuaded to co-operate. In the end the banker (for a sum of £3,000), signed an affidavit saying that Walker had paid the money into the Swiss account via the Tangier bank—and, for a gift of £3,000, the banker agreed to give evidence to this effect if required. Walker then flew back to Berne and presented the statement to the judge via the Union Bank, who accepted it at its face value.

The potentially awkward enquiry was blocked, but what the helpful Walker did not foresee was that his efforts were later to prove decidely embarrassing for him. Savundra was to claim that the affidavit (which on paper showed his managing director as having a spare £6,000) suggested Walker was the key financial figure in F.A.M.—not Savundra himself.

Amongst the staff of Fire, Auto and Marine at this time there were continuous rumours of other dubious involvements of their founder. Some were based on Savundra's own claims. He told his personal secretary—a headstrong Irish girl—that he had smuggled arms for the I.R.A. Apparently he thought she would be impressed. She was horrified and said so, and Savundra found it necessary to add, with a smile: 'Oh, it's all right, none of them worked.'

It was typical of his attempt to inspire in others the belief that he had always been a secret but powerful influence in world politics. One of his favourite conversation pieces at luncheon parties later in F.A.M.'s history was his claim to have helped to 'fix' an election in Ceylon. He had helped Mrs Bandaraniake to power, he maintained, by arranging for voters to be ferried from polling booth to polling booth in lorry-loads, so that they could register their votes several times each.

His relationship with the Vatican was another cause for speculation. Walker remembers him saying Cardinal Montini had helped 'smooth the way' for his children's schooling in England, and one particular morning when Savundra had greeted him with the words: 'My man at the Vatican is now Pope.' Savundra was later to scornfully dismiss this recollection. ('Unfortunately the man at the Vatican is a man of God and not a man of mine'.) But he did not deny that he had performed special duties for the Vatican, and he told some of his executives that he was the Pope's economic adviser.

On a less exalted level, there were even rumours that Savundra had been involved in the Great Train Robbery. One report had it that he had masterminded the whole thing, but the one which was more generally believed was that he had had a hand in getting rid of some of the money. A van, it was said, arrived at the Baker Street rooms one day—when F.A.M. was in its embryonic stage. In the back were two trunks containing £300,000 in notes. Savundra was asked by the van driver—a minor accomplice in the robbery who never came to trial— if he would transfer the money into his Swiss account and then bring it back into the country 'clean'. In return, he would receive a two and a half per cent commission. Some say the incident is plausible. But one of the key figures in the robbery, Buster Edwards, now released, whom we found selling flowers at Waterloo Station, thinks it unlikely that Savundra was in any way involved.

CHAPTER TWELVE

When in Doubt, Gallop

IF THE SECOND YEAR of F.A.M.'s existence was to be one of increasing unease for Cecil Tross Youle, it was to be an *anno mirabilis* for Savundra and Walker.

The formula of paying higher commissions to brokers than anyone else and charging motorists less than anyone else was proving irresistible. By the end of the first year the flow of money into Orchard House had reached a staggering £20,000 a week. While rival insurance companies and Lloyd's underwriters watched with frustration, F.A.M. became the fastest-growing car insurance firm in the country.

The frustration of the trade found its outward expression in a series of critical articles in insurance journals and telephone calls to the Board of Trade, urging them to take action against a set-up which was, in the opinion of many, palpably heading for disaster. Some companies took more positive action. The giant General Accident, advertising in the big circulation newspapers, warned the public of the risks they were running. There was a note of irritation in their message.

'There is no cheap insurance. As with everything else you get what you pay for. It is dangerous to seek the lowest price just to hold an insurance certificate . . .'

Officials at the Board of Trade watched F.A.M. with equal anxiety. They were to be criticised later for their inaction but the antiquated insurance laws made it difficult for them to intervene. Memorandums circulated inside the Board of Trade in 1963 show that F.A.M. was very definitely suspect, while at the same time confirming that officials felt they could not risk trying to force the company's hand.

Norman Nail, head of the home insurance division, was a wily company investigator with a nose for dubious operations. His main anxiety was to establish the size of F.A.M.'s assets and discover whether the company had a satisfactory method of estimating outstanding claims. His frequent telephone calls to Walker on these matters only served to increase his suspicions—not because Walker was unable to provide the answers but because he provided them with such alacrity. Nail was used to the directors of fast-expanding companies expressing confusion and having to ask for time to supply required statistics, but with Walker questions were, in Nail's opinion, answered with almost too much assurance.

Nail, however, felt himself to be a watchdog with no teeth. Before he could set the creaking investigative machinery of the Board of Trade in motion, he had to convince the Board's legal department that F.A.M. had a case to answer. Mere suspicion was not enough. And before any official enquiry could take place, the Board's decision had to be endorsed at Ministerial level. Nail knew that no purpose would be served by action which failed to produce conclusive results. That would merely strengthen F.A.M.'s position by making further enquiries more difficult.

It was against this background that Savundra pulled what he hoped would be a master stroke.

In December 1963, he telephoned the managing director of International Business Machines—Britain's foremost computer company—and told them that he wanted the most sophisticated system available installed in his office by the end of January.

I.B.M. said it was impossible. They estimated that it would take two years to install such a system properly. 'Ridiculous,' Savundra exclaimed. He could not wait that long.

In the end, by a mixture of charm and bullying, he got the experts to agree on a deadline of four months.

Thus there arrived at the offices of F.A.M. twenty-two-year-old John Waller, an enthusiastic and dedicated computer expert. Even today he can hardly believe his luck at being selected by I.B.M., whom he had only joined a few months earlier, for what was one of the most testing projects they had handled.

From the beginning, Waller, recently down from Cambridge where he had been a brilliant mathematician, hit it off with his boss. If this was due in part to Savundra's capacity to mesmerise his employees, Waller was also genuinely impressed by the speed of Savundra's mind and his ability to grasp complex mathematical concepts.

Working day and night, Waller developed a system which would make the computer do all the main underwriting calculations. Proposals were fed into the machine by means of punched cards and out would come the policy documents.

But there were snags. Waller himself says: 'The system was ninety-five per cent extremely good and five per cent horrendous.' There are others who would reverse the percentages.

The main difficulty was the sheer quantity of information which would have had to be stored if the system were to work exactly. It was impossible to programme it intelligibly with material on every different kind of car and driver. Colin Chance, a young scientist who helped set up the computer, commented: 'We just guessed our way through. We once produced a premium figure for a hypothetical one-armed West Indian bookmaker L-driver under twenty-five and it was £212 5s. [In those days an unheard-of figure.] With all the mistakes everything took three times as long to check as it would have taken manually.'

Then there was the problem of the policy holder who changed his vehicle or the type of insurance he wanted. Obviously these changes had to be done by hand, and the resulting confusion after cancellations and endorsements often led to inaccurate accounts being sent to brokers.

To some, the project, and others like it, has now become evidence of 'the great computer delusion'. Savundra, however, proudly declared: 'I have brought the fountain pen into insurance in place of the goose quill.'

He chose 8th June, 1964, his fifteenth wedding anniversary, for the unveiling of his new wonder. Jacquie, his adored daughter, now aged seven, was the guest of honour at the ceremony and it was she who pressed the button to start the machine running.

Shortly after the computer had been installed and had begun churning out its much-publicised 'instant policies', Savundra took another ambitious step. He acquired an eight-storey office block on the North Circular Road near Hendon.

It provided exactly the impressive background he needed, and he obtained it for the derisory rental of £36,500 a year for the first seven years—which worked out at only 12s. 6d for each of its 63,000 square feet. When it came to adapting the building to his requirements, however, no expense was spared.

The move to Jacqueline House (the building was renamed, of course, after his daughter), was more significant than a mere change in geographical location. Suddenly everything was done—and had to be seen to be done—on the grand scale.

Instead of the staff being huddled together, often two to a desk, as they had been at Orchard House, each department—computer, accounts, claims and so on—now had a floor to itself. There was a lavishly appointed canteen where all staff were allowed one free three-course meal a day, and there was even a floor devoted to an education department where induction courses were run for new recruits.

But outdoing everything in sheer luxury and ostentation was the floor at the top of the building reserved for Savundra and de Quincey Walker. It had a private lift, the use of which was forbidden to the rank and file.

Savundra's own office was impressive by any standards. To symbolise the allegedly world-wide influence of F.A.M. he had, on one side of the room, a polar bear skin representing the cold countries and on the other a tiger skin symbolic of those nearer the equator. When the tiger skin had first been delivered, he had noticed with dismay that the tiger's head was bereft of whiskers. Immediately he had one of his executives telephone the Zoological Gardens in Regent's Park, who supplied them for 1s. 6d each.

In pride of place above Savundra's desk, where no visitor could help noticing it, hung a photograph of himself apparently chatting warmly with Earl Mountbatten. He did not, however, make a habit of explaining to visitors how this picture had come to be in existence.

It was the result of a dinner at Torquay after the 1963 *Daily Express* power-boat race. Savundra tried to persuade Tommy Sopwith to introduce him to Mountbatten, whom he felt was just the sort of person he should know. Sopwith refused, but Savundra, after carefully briefing a feelance photographer to stand by in readiness, marched up to the illustrious Earl. 'I am very privileged to meet you,' he said. 'I served under you out East.' They shook hands. The camera bulb flashed. And that was the extent of Savundra's link with Mountbatten.

Perhaps the most impressive item of all in Savundra's office was a large, starkly beautiful crucifix which hung in a niche, softly lit by concealed lighting, and completely dominating one side of the room. But alongside religion was superstition. The whole floor was decorated in varying shades of green—a colour which, in defiance of the popular view that it was unlucky, Savundra regarded as extremely propitious.

The board room-cum-dining room, which opened off Savundra's office, was hardly less luxurious. Around the large, highly-polished table were chairs upholstered in white leather. One wall was taken up with an £11,000 electric mural consisting of a screen across which ever-changing colours swirled. Savundra used to call it 'my electronic goldfish bowl' and would seat guests in front of it, telling them it was relaxing.

Even the wash-room was fitted out to film star standards. Savundra shrugged off the £3,000 which it cost saying: 'My directors deserve a lavatory without cigarette stubs and dirty words all over the wall.'

The care he took with the details, in fact, suggested a philosophy he later expressed with customary shrewdness: 'If I offer whisky out of a cut-glass decanter which costs £5, it hides the fact that the drink inside costs only 42s.'

The board meetings which were held in these spendid surroundings were short and to the point. Savundra was the ring master and he cracked the whip. Invariably he would end with the injunction: 'Press on for more brokers! More premiums!'

By contrast, the frequent luncheons held on the top floor were leisured and lavish affairs. The table was oval to obviate problems as to who should be placed at the head but there was never any doubt as to who dominated the conversation. 'There are only three topics I allow to be discussed at my luncheon table,' he would tell his guests. 'Sex, religion and politics'—listing the three subjects traditionally barred in a gentleman's club.

The food, which was sent in hay boxes all the way from a restaurant in Sonning, was superb. The wines were expensive and the cigars Churchillian in size. Although Savundra himself ate sparingly and drank little, he revelled in the role of the open-handed host. His own favourite drink was American cream soda but during these office entertainments he would toy with a small glass of white wine while bottle after bottle was circulated amongst his guests.

The guests were an oddly assorted, but impressive, collection. They ranged from ecclesiastical dignitaries like Monsignor Asta to the famous economist, Cyril Northcote Parkinson, who once gave a lecture to the staff, and Herbert Hoover, son of American president. There were power-boat racers, computer experts, V.I.P.s from abroad, Generals, city tycoons and journalists who, Savundra used to say, would always be slipped £100 notes when they left the offices. This was probably an invention but it was the kind of thing he loved making secret boasts about. When one of his executives protested: 'You can't bribe journalists', his reply was: 'Don't teach your grandmother to suck eggs. I've bribed cabinet ministers in my time.'

Whoever the guests were and whatever their interests, they were never allowed to take their leave without first doing a conducted tour of the building and seeing Savundra's special pride, the wonderful computer.

As he showed it off he liked to remark modestly: 'The only difference between my machine and a machine which prints lavatory paper is that mine has money printed on it.'

Once, when giving an interview to a financial journalist, he gave it as his opinion that the worst insurance risk was coloured drivers. 'My computer tells me all the answers,' he said confidently and buzzed Waller on the internal phone.

'We don't have any figures,' Waller told him.

'Well, get some,' Savundra ordered.

Waller took a sample of a hundred policies and claims.

The sample came up with four coloured drivers, only *one* of whom had made a claim. On the other hand there were thirteen Irishmen among the hundred including *ten* who had claims.

Waller telephoned the information to Savundra.

'The position has just changed,' Savundra informed his guest as he replaced the receiver. 'The worst risks now seem to be Irishmen.'

The set-up at Jacqueline House certainly attracted world-wide interest.

Savundra sent Walker and Waller on a fact-finding mission to America but it turned into more of a publicity exercise. Waller says that American insurers were fascinated to find out just how the F.A.M. computer worked. I.B.M. even made a film of what they had come to regard as one of their most exciting developments and there was a constant flow of visitors from the Continent to see the mechanical underwriter in action.

As for his own staff, Savundra missed no opportunity of impressing them that they were privileged to be taking part in an exciting technological revolution and most of them believed it. As one executive put it: 'Savundra had the secret of leadership, the ability to make you feel that you are taking part in a great event.'

Despite all the splendours of the office block at Hendon, and despite Savundra's obviously dominating role in the affairs of F.A.M., he was legally still on the fringe of the company. If there had been trouble, he would have been able to extricate himself. But though there had been criticism of F.A.M.'s trading methods, there had been nothing to cause real anxiety. Indeed money was flowing in. And Savundra's egotism craved for the formal recognition that he was the genius behind the new company which had rocked the staid world of insurance. It would have been safer to stay in the shadows, but Savundra seems to have put completely out of his mind the possibility that there would be a day of reckoning, and to have come to believe in his own infallibility.

Whatever the motivation, he quite suddenly reversed his attitude towards the question of full and legal involvement in the affairs of F.A.M. Instead of shying away from the publicity, he began to court it. A month before the move to Jacqueline House he had had himself elected as vice-chairman of the company. To Tross Youle he explained that it was a step which he felt he was now able to take in view of the fact that King Badouin of the Belgians had finally granted him a full pardon for his part in the Belgian affair. This proved conclusively, he said, that he had been an innocent victim of an international conspiracy while serving the best interests of Nehru's Indian Government. As evidence he produced a letter from a firm of City solicitors, confirming what he said to be true.

Having effected this outward change in his status, he added to it in Jacqueline House by having all his correspondence proudly headed: 'From the office of Dr. Emil Savundra, Ph.D., D.C.L.'

The difference soon became visible in another direction—that of the life style of himself and his family.

He put his modest family house in Hendon Lane on the market and, before it was even sold, had moved his family into one of the grandest houses in Hampstead's Bishop's Avenue, which is popularly known as Millionaires' Row.

White Walls was a splendid Lutyens-style mansion set in almost two acres of ground with a floodlit garden and sun terrace paved in York stone. Behind its impressive double-front exterior it provided five bedrooms, three bathrooms and a suite of ground floor reception rooms, as well as a separate block to house the staff. It cost him £72,000 before the great property boom and he paid cash down— surely not the action of someone who regarded his days as numbered. In today's market the house would probably fetch in excess of £250,000.

He had scarcely taken possession of his new house before he was again on the telephone to I.B.M.

'My house has two television sets,' he told them. 'My new boat had twin engines. My company is going to have two computers.'

I.B.M. were quick to oblige the man who had become a favourite customer. Within weeks the new computer was installed, with an additional refinement. Both machines were now linked direct to F.A.M.'s main provincial brokers' office so that details fed straight into the computer from, say, Manchester or Birmingham, would result in the issue of a policy in precisely sixty-seven seconds. Nothing had been seen like it and even firms of brokers who had previously cautiously hung back, now jumped on the bandwaggon while Savundra, firmly mounted on his mettlesome steed, rode recklessly onwards.

CHAPTER THIRTEEN

On the Crest of a Wave

THE POWER-BOAT RACING CRAZE had its origins in America in the late nineteen-fifties. Its appeal in a country where money was the yardstick of social status lay in the fact that it was spectacular and could only be afforded by the rich, so that its devotees could demonstrate their daring and their wealth at the same time.

In Britain, it did not really become established until Sir Max Aitken, casting around for ways of boosting the circulation of his family paper, the *Daily Express*, decided to sponsor an off-shore power-boat race as something which could be built into an annual event and which would capture the imagination of the general public.

This new sport was tailor-made for Emil Savundra in his quest for social recognition. And for a man who liked to describe himself as 'God's own lounge lizard', stressing that he did not like work and was not cut out for it, the appeal was irresistible. Horse-racing might have been a possibility. But in that sport, publicity and glory tended to be concentrated on jockeys and trainers. Motor-racing was also excluded—it required too much skill. But power-boating enabled Savundra to mingle with the well-to-do men of action whose friendship, or acceptance, he desperately sought.

From the start the sport attracted such diverse characters as the roly-poly, holiday camp millionaire, Sir Billy Butlin, and one-time British bobsleigh champion Keith Schellenburg, the gambler Lord Lucan, and Tommy Sopwith, son of the famous aircraft designer, Sir Thomas Sopwith.

The first *Daily Express* sponsored race, which set the pattern for the others, took place in September 1961, over a course of 172 miles from Cowes to Torquay. Among the competitors there was an almost carnival atmosphere of light-hearted amateurism. Most of the craft taking part were little more than hotted-up motor cruisers and it was won by Tommy Sopwith at the far from impressive speed of twenty-two knots.

Savundra did not take part but he followed the race closely and formed the impression that if he set his mind to it, here was a chance of a real triumph.

At that time he had a thirty-five foot cruiser moored on the Thames at the Kingston Marina and one of the friends he had made through pleasure-boating was John Fleming, an ex-lieutenant commander in the Royal Navy, who ran a boating business in London. In early January 1962, Fleming received a telegram from Switzerland. It read: INTEND WINNING THE 1962 POWER-BOAT RACE. MEET ME AT EARL'S COURT BOAT SHOW. SAVUNDRA.

Fleming knew Savundra too well to be surprised. Savundra had been one of his first customers when he had opened his business, the Boat Showrooms, in Kensington High Street, and was a frequent purchaser of expensive gadgets.

Fleming knew next to nothing about Class I power-boat racing but if the free-spending Savundra was interested, it was time to do some homework.

The Earl's Court meeting turned out to be something of an anticlimax. Fleming took his client to various firms, capable of designing the sort of boat his client wanted. Savundra looked critically at their display stands, asked many questions and passed on. As Fleming was soon to realise, you worked for Savundra alone or you didn't work for him at all. At the Boat Show the established firms all had Savundra's potential rivals on their books. This ruled them out.

Later in the year Fleming received an excited telephone call. Savundra told him he had met the French Minister of Defence, who had introduced him to his brother. The brother designed boats—and had designed one specially for Savundra. The boat had been taken to Calais, and was being towed to Dover.

Shortly afterwards Fleming was taken to see Savundra's new boat. But instead of going to Dover, Savundra drove him to a boat yard in Isleworth on the Thames. There was a boat all right, but the name-dropping account of her origins, Fleming discovered, had been nothing more than typical Savundra blarney. The boat had, in fact, been built in Essex for the owner of the yard. In order to secure her Savundra had bought the entire yard as well. When they arrived she was being fitted out with bunks, galley stove, marine toilet. Three Chrysler engines had been ordered through what Savundra referred to as his Zürich office.

When later asked whether these had not been very expensive he remarked: 'The hull of a boat on its own is no good, unless you have a pet whale to tow it.' In fact, the office, from which his original telegram to Fleming had also been sent, really belonged to his Swiss lawyer, Dr. Paul Hagenbach. Once again it was all Savundra fiction.

Two months later the first *Jacquie S.*, named, as always, after his daughter, slid into the water at Teddington on the Thames.

From the moment Savundra had made up his mind to become involved in speed-boating he had read everything he could find on the subject and it was typical of him that he did not now hesitate to give practical expression to his new theories, however unconventional they might be.

The *Jacquie S.* was thirty-four foot at the waterline and was an unusually heavy craft with a very deep fin keel. It was Savundra's view that the disadvantages were outbalanced by the additional stability which this gave the boat in the rough weather conditions likely to be encountered in the Channel. By and large the experts who were invited to view his brainchild were impressed. As for John Fleming, his enthusiasm was unqualified. He gave it as his verdict that she was 'a great boat'.

Not everybody in Teddington was so impressed. Savundra would motor her 'slowly' down the river, but motoring slowly, when you have three Chrysler engines aboard, is difficult. He left a trail of fist-waving house-boat owners in his wake as crockery cascaded on to the floor of their saloons; and they must have come to dread the powerful throb of *Jacquie S.*'s engines, while he complained to Fleming that he was constantly being bombarded by claims for damages.

Jacquie S. was tested on a measured mile at Longbeach, near Gravesend. Assiduous in his search to get the best out of his boat Savundra constantly had the propellers changed in an effort to find the most effective combination. Everything was done in vintage Savundra style. Wherever the boat was handled—whether at fuelling stations or yards—lavish tips would be dispensed and attendants would be made to feel he was the most important customer they could have.

Three months before the race Savundra decided the time had come to move from the Thames—but not to Cowes. He was certain he was going to win and worried about the possibility of a sabotage attempt by jealous rivals. So he avoided fellow competitors and set up camp in Torquay.

Fleming, a true professional who had up to this point admired the professionalism of his client, was rather taken aback at the way in which Savundra now proceeded to treat the whole affair as a family festival. It seemed an extraordinary contradiction that someone who devoted so much of his time and money to getting everything right should not display the same singlemindedness when it came to practising for the race itself.

Instead, Savundra became absorbed in his family.

The evenings at Torquay revolved around Jacqueline. When the other children staying at the Imperial Hotel had long been in their beds, she would still be up, and the centre of attraction. Dressed in a different party frock each evening, her great delight was to take over from the conductor of the late-night dance orchestra while her parents, surrounded by the rest of the family, smiled indulgently, and other guests clapped politely.

The inadequacy of Savundra's preparations for the race did not become apparent until two days before the event, when the time came for the boat to be taken to the start point at Cowes. It was the first time that he or his crew had experienced conditions in the open sea and they hit rough weather. They kept the speed down but between the Needles and the Shingles Bank conditions got worse and they were subjected to a severe pounding.

The weather cleared sufficiently, however, for them to roar into Cowes harbour on full throttle so that nobody could be left in any doubt that this was a boat to be reckoned with.

Unfortunately Savundra's dramatic arrival on the field of battle was somewhat marred by an untypical oversight in his usual meticulous planning. No rooms had been booked for him in the Gloucester Hotel, which was the centre of all the social activity surrounding the occasion, and he was forced to find accommodation for himself and his entourage at a more modest establishment.

Almost immediately he was given news of a rather more serious setback. In the rough passage from Torquay one of *Jacquie S.*'s petrol tanks had been split open; and an inspection by the race scrutineers was scheduled for the following day. Unless everything was found to be in perfect working order his boat would be disqualified.

While Savundra tossed restlessly in his bed, his designer, Cyril Hughes, raced to London and back and then spent the rest of the night with his mechanic working against time to fit a new tank. They did not finish until after dawn.

By the time Savundra was due to attend the final briefing of competitors by Sir Max Aitken at the Royal Yacht Squadron, he seemed to have forgotten there had been a crisis. To the curious glances of other competitors, most of whom were having their first look at the dark, pudgy figure who had been hogging the pre-race headlines, he presented a front of almost brash confidence.

Later the meeting adjourned to Aitken's picturesque house on the waterfront for drinks, where Savundra boldly let his new acquaintances know that they were meeting the man who, in his own humble opinion, would become the greatest power-boat racer in the world.

The day of the race was overcast, with a stiff breeze and a heavy swell running. Last minute preparations were made and Savundra, Fleming and their mechanic climbed aboard the *Jacquie S.* Two fast naval patrol boats flanked the line of twenty competing craft as they headed towards the starting line. At 10 a.m. precisely the boom of the Royal Yacht Squadron cannon was answered by a mounting chorus of sound as throttles were pushed forward and twenty of the world's most powerful motor-boats set off on the choppy course to Torquay. The months of preparation were about to be put to the test as the patrol boats peeled off to the side and the race got under way.

Things started promisingly enough. Three boats streaked ahead in the early stages, one of them *Jacquie S.*, and as they approached the first buoy Savundra had a lucky break. The leading boat, *Tramontana*—driven by Jeffrey Quill, a former Spitfire pilot —suddenly veered off course and practically struck the third boat in the group, *Blue Moppie. Blue Moppie*, driven by two experienced American power-boat racers, Dick Bertram and Sam Griffiths, had to change course rapidly. *Tramontana*'s steering had momentarily gone, due to the excessive weight of an over-full fuel tank. As a result of this near-collision *Jacquie S.* was clear in the lead as she rounded the first buoy.

The triumph was short-lived and there was a touch of Laurel and Hardy comedy in what happened next. Savundra, never renowned for his good eyesight, was relying on Fleming to navigate. Fleming was glued to the compass. But the boat turned faster than the needle on the compass and *Jacquie S.* ended up doing a complete circle of the first buoy. They were lying in third place when the trouble really started.

A fresh wind was blowing on their beam as they raced south towards Nab Point, east of the Isle of Wight, and approached the next marker buoy. Fleming watched in horror as the boat immediately ahead, *Blue Moppie*, rounded it. She was now running straight into the teeth of the wind and, as she turned on the crest of a wave, she had leapt clean out of the water. Fleming yelled a warning above the roar of *Jacquie S.*'s engines but if Savundra heard he did not for a moment relax his grip on the throttle. Perhaps he had not even seen what had happened to *Blue Moppie*. At that moment, all his business worries forgotten, he was reliving the fine abandon of his adolescence in Colombo. A second later *Jacquie S.* took off in the most spectacular leap anyone who witnessed it had ever seen.

When *Jacquie S.* was being built, one thing above almost all else had become a fixation in Savundra's mind—the building of the right kind of seat. Most power-boat racers find it safer to stand, particularly if conditions are rough. But Savundra had insisted on special shock-damped seats, complete with stirrups and a safety belt. Unlike Fleming, he was not the right shape for racing. He preferred to sit.

The shock-absorber seats were not built to cope with this. As the boat crashed back into the water in a huge sheet of spray, Savundra crumpled up in pain. 'I've broken my back!' he screamed. Fleming grabbed the wheel as, still almost airborne, they shot past *Blue Moppie*. Through the spray Fleming saw Dick Bertram stare in disbelief and mouth the word: 'Christ!' Fleming pulled back the throttle. Savundra was out of action and moaning. The mechanic was in the stern, being seasick, and there was something wrong with the engine. As Fleming was shortly to discover, some of the tanks had split open and there were 200 gallons of petrol floating around in the bilges. Fleming fought to keep the boat steady and headed her towards the more sheltered waters of nearby Poole Bay; behind him Savundra had crawled to the stern and was gasping for a Pepsi-Cola—of which he always kept a plentiful supply in his boats. The mechanic was trying to open one for him with a hammer. Savundra, meanwhile, was gulping down blue pills from his pocket.

Fleming eventually had to stop *Jacquie S.* to see what was wrong. It was rough and he remembers Savundra croaking: 'For God's sake don't leave me— I can't swim.' There was one full tank of petrol intact, which was eventually connected to the engine, and they headed off to complete the course. Savundra perked up as the finishing line came in sight and took the wheel as they roared into Tor Bay. Unable to resist a theatrical gesture, he opened up the throttle and delighted his children by roaring across the finishing line at fifty knots.

Later, at a dinner held for the presentation of the cup, Sir Max Aitken paid Savundra an especially warm tribute. Then, as the other guests applauded warmly, Sir Max presented him with a silver salver in his appreciation of his 'outstanding sportsmanship'. (When a reporter asked him after the ceremony if power-boating was not an exhausting sport, quite incompatible with his history of heart trouble, he threw back his head and laughed heartily.) Savundra may not have won the prize he coveted; but he had certainly made his mark among the power-set.

There was another consequence, too, of that first race. Shortly after it Savundra gave a dinner party at Hendon Lane for everyone who had been closely involved with him over *Jacquie S.*

Fleming remembers it as a happy occasion. They had pre-dinner drinks in the luxuriously furnished drawing-room. Savundra was in his best form. Standing straddle-legged on a splendid tiger skin rug with his back to the fire, he dominated the conversation. Behind him, on one side of the fireplace, was a large photograph of him with Sir Oliver Goonitelleke, a former Governor of Ceylon, and, on the other side, another photograph of him with Cardinal Montini, before he became Pope.

Later Fleming was to mention to Pushpam that he, too, sometimes suffered from a bad back. He remembers her writing down for him the name of the man Savundra had been recommended to see—and afterwards had described in glowing terms. It was the osteopath, Stephen Ward.

To win the *Daily Express* trophy became more and more of an obsession with Savundra. He would dilate on his ideas and plans endlessly to anyone who would listen.

'It is like climbing the highest mountain without ever leaving sea level,' he would rhapsodise. 'It is the supreme achievement of beating the laws of nature, although doing fifty knots across Lyme Bay would be described by some people as certifiable insanity.' In another mood he would laugh at his own folly. 'Power-boat racing,' he would say, 'is like standing on the seashore throwing five-pound notes into the water.'

One of the people with whom he struck up a firm friendship was Donald Campbell, later to die tragically in *Bluebird* whilst trying to break the world water speed record. They spent hours together discussing the technical problems involved in going faster and faster. Campbell, whose ever-present problem was lack of money, had hopes that Savundra might be persuaded to become a backer but, although he would not say so to Campbell, Savundra had other ideas.

He wanted to break the world speed record himself.

At that time the acknowedged expert in power boats was Commander Peter du Cane, who ran Vosper's, the world famous firm of marine engineers in Portsmouth. His book, *High Speed Small Craft*, had become one of Savundra's bibles. He knew it almost by heart. And the heights to which he aspired became apparent during his first meeting with du Cane. It was Fleming who arranged it, and he remembers it vividly. They were ushered into du Cane's office, in a little cottage on the quay at Portsmouth. After the introductions, Savundra settled himself into a chair and announced matter-of-factly: 'I've got three ambitions. I want to win the *Daily Express* power-boat race. I want to break the world water-speed record. And I want to win the America's Cup for Britain.'

The second ambition interested du Cane the most. 'If you have the means,' he told Savundra, 'I can build the boat.' And at that meeting he told Savundra what might happen to *Bluebird* if Campbell were to achieve his ambition of breaking the 300-m.p.h. barrier. '*Bluebird* will simply take off,' he forecast.

It is doubtful, however, if du Cane would ever have entrusted Savundra with a potential world-record-breaker, even if Savundra had financed it.

It is generally agreed by people qualified to judge that Savundra had only two things going for him as a power-boater. Firstly, he had extremely strong forearms capable of holding a wildly-kicking wheel, and secondly, he was quite without fear. But his appreciation of the finer points of technique was noticeably lacking. Even his understanding of nautical good manners was held in some doubt. His weakness for showing off tended to manifest itself in his addiction to dashing past other boats, deliberately missing them by only a hair's-breadth. On one occasion, when he was out joy-riding in *Jacquie S.*, he spotted Sir Max Aitken in a sailing boat, struggling to make headway in an almost non-existent breeze. Savundra immediately set a course towards Sir Max, waving cheerfully. Furiously Aitken tried to signal to him to keep his distance as he fought to keep his boat steady in the heavy wash of *Jacquie S.* Savundra, mistaking the signals for a greeting, continued to circle the yacht in ever-decreasing circles as Aitken became more and more apoplectic.

The question of whether or not du Cane would ever have allowed Savundra to make an attempt on the speed record in a Vosper 'S' boat, was to remain academic. Savundra, for his part, never came up with the money.

Du Cane did make one practical suggestion which Savundra

immediately adopted. He advised the replacing of the three Chrysler engines which powered *Jacquie S.* with four Jaguars. These were duly fitted in Savundra's new boat-yard at Poole. He had dispensed with his old yard on the grounds that they had not come up with the right answer. Savundra never gave second chances, with the result that during the whole of his racing career he flitted from one boat-yard to another. By the time he finally quit, the story was current that every time he had a boat built, a yard went bust.

Savundra's participation in the 1963 race was to be even more memorable than that in 1962. None of the competitors or spectators present will forget his performance. It was as if Kenneth Grahame's monstrous Mr. Toad of Toad Hall had suddenly been let loose in a power-boat.

The publicity started early and Savundra lost no opportunity of impressing his Britishness on the world. His boat, he claimed, was unqiue in that it was British down to the last nut and bolt. Even the normally retiring Pushpam seemed to be enjoying the limelight. Playfully she complained to an interviewer that her husband only lived for his boat and slept with a slide rule under his pillow. 'I put him among the favourites,' enthused the correspondent.

Determined not to be caught out again in the matter of accommodation Savundra booked almost a complete floor at the Gloucester Hotel for himself, his family and his team; and to make sure that Pushpam and the children had the best possible view of the race from beginning to end he hired an aeroplane, piloted by ace test pilot Neville Duke, to circle overhead throughout the whole proceedings.

Much to his delight he found himself regarded very much as one of the lions. Quite apart from his ready acceptance by the other competitors, he found, when he went for a stroll along the waterfront, complete strangers would wave to him and shout words of encouragement.

It was something he loved to play up to. Where the others would button themselves up to the neck in windcheaters or oilskins before taking their boats out, he would cruise in a leisurely way close inshore, stripped to the waist so that the public could gaze in admiration at his great black torso and protruding stomach.

Came the day of the race and from the very first moment it was clear that Savundra was going to live up to his reputation. The four Jaguar engines certainly gave his boat immense power but it was obvious from the start that the revamped *Jacquie S.* was completely unmanoeuvrable. With four rudders to control, it soon became evident that it was quite beyond him to co-ordinate them all into steering the boat in the same direction at the same time.

Victim number one was boat designer Don Shead. As *Jacquie S.* shot away from the start she started veering violently from side to side and almost immediately struck Shead's boat with such force that both boats nearly overturned, pushing each other up out of the water at a crazy angle. Fortunately for the safety of Shead and his crew the boat was fitted with handrails. At the last moment he managed to sheer off and so avert total disaster. Savundra had taken aboard as an extra passenger Jack Knights, the *Daily Express* power-boat expert. Now all Knights could do was look over his shoulder to Don Shead and shrug apologetically as *Jacquie S.* shot off wildly in another direction.

All this was seen from above by Savundra's admiring family. There was more to come. Now more out of control than ever, *Jacquie S.* raced straight for the Needles lighthouse. Despite frenzied efforts to get her to alter course, she tore undeviatingly onwards to pile up on the rocks below the lighthouse. The solidly-built craft was barely damaged however, and Savundra, unperturbed, reversed and set off once again.

As he rejoined the race, most competitors took care to stay clear of him but not everybody in the Solent that day had sufficient speed to get out of the way of such a powerful boat. Especially vulnerable were the many small pleasure craft carrying spectators who had turned out to view the fun.

Mr. and Mrs. Ruffhead, with their two teenage boys were enjoying themselves on *Skip Jack*, a sturdy thirty-foot launch. That is to say they *were* enjoying themselves until they heard the sudden roar of *Jacquie S.* and turned to see her great shark-like bow, riding on the crest of a huge bow-wave, bearing down on them. They reacted with commendable alacrity, diving to either end of the boat as the *Jacquie S.* struck her squarely amidships. There was a sound compared by Jack Knights to 'a box of matches being trampled underfoot'. A moment later *Skip Jack* split clean in two. Minutes after that both halves slipped quietly beneath the waves.

Incredibly, no one was hurt. There were other boats close by and the shaken victims were soon pulled out of the water. Mr. Ruffhead later commented phlegmatically, 'We must be the only people alive to have been run over by four Jaguars.'

Savundra behaved with equal aplomb. Like Mr. Toad, he pushed his goggles up on to his forehead and surveyed the scene. 'Everyone all right?' he called cheerily before reversing off the sinking wreckage.

Jack Knights was not quite so calm.

'What on earth are you going to do now?' he asked helplessly.

'Go on with the race, of course,' Savundra answered promptly.

Jack Knights did not hang around to argue. He insists that the story of him plunging over the side and swimming for the shore is apocryphal, but he does not deny his relief when one of the spectator boats offered him refuge.

Savundra did not complete the race. Soon after the collision he hoisted the yellow flag signalling his withdrawal. *Jacquie S.* was not the only boat to drop out. *White Migrant*, owned and driven by Savundra's friend, Lord Lucan, had led in the early stages of the race before sinking—but it was Savundra who, by the manner of his exit, stole the headlines.

Back in the bar at the Gloucester Hotel, where the post mortems were held, despite the hilarity with which mention of *Jacquie S.* was greeted, there was a genuine admiration for Savundra's resilience and resolute cheerfulness. As someone was to remark much later, 'Whatever else he was, he was a bloody good sport.'

The following year Savundra was back again, this time with an entirely new boat, *Jacquie S. the Second.* Fitted with two marinised Ford V8 engines, she attracted a great deal of attention. The page devoted to readers' letters in *Motorboat and Yachting* was the forum for a heated debate on her merits and demerits and in the issue before the race she was accorded the front cover with an article inside in which Dr. Savundra expressed his supreme confidence that this time he had hit on the winning formula. Questioned on the wisdom of commissioning Fred Cross, who was an aircraft designer rather than a marine engineer, Savundra replied that it was because what he wanted was an aeroplane with the wings cut off. When he was accused of 'a lofty disregard for many of the accepted principles of boatbuilding', he fired back that in his opinion most boat builders were not even capable of passing an elementary maths exam, let alone designing a fast boat. 'Most of them go on guesswork,' he declared, adding, '*Jacquie S.*, on the other hand, has been put together like a precision watch.'

Generously, the editor of *Motorboat and Yachting* commented: 'It is the Doctor Savundras of this world, and there are precious few of them, who make the sport interesting.'

By and large, Savundra liked to keep his social and business life strictly apart. This was partly tactical, partly the Victorianism which made him believe that it was not gentlemanly to have to earn one's living. It was a rule, however, which his compulsion to show off occasionally caused him to break.

One of the men he admired in the power-boating world was Tommy Sopwith, but he also saw Sopwith very much as a rival. Whatever Sopwith could do, he had the urge to do better.

On one occasion he invited Sopwith to one of his lavish luncheons at Jacqueline House and afterwards took him on a personally conducted tour.

In the computer room there was, on one wall, an enormous chart recording the week-by-week income figures.

Sopwith, observing the graph rising vertiginously towards the ceiling, turned to Savundra and remarked drily: 'Oh, I see you must also own the room above.'

The rivalry between the two men manifested itself in a bet, almost in the Regency tradition, which was struck on whose boat would finish ahead in the 1964 race. The loser was to buy the winner the most expensive meal that could be devised. The steaks were to come from America and were to be flown over the North Pole, which, it was reckoned, improved their flavour. There was to be Sakhali asparagus flown from Japan and oysters from Australia. Wines would include a 1935 Margaux, Château di Cerce and Dom Perignon, the most expensive champagne, if not, in the opinion of many connoisseurs, the best.

Savundra had every reason to feel confident. Earlier in the season in lesser races *Jacquie S. the Second* (now being regularly crewed by Stuart Walker), had swept everything before her and the sideboard in his home gleamed with the cups and trophies she had won. This year, not only Savundra, but everyone else, expected him to win the big one.

He would probably have done so but for his own over-anxiety. His mechanic had checked and checked again but Savundra was still not satisfied. Cross-examining the mechanic on the night before the race he got the man to admit that there was one thing which had not been done. The ball bearing where the propellor shaft went through the hull had not been changed. Immediately Savundra ordered this to be put right. It was to prove a fatal decision. After five miles, with *Jacquie S.* holding a clear lead, the new ball bearing, not having been properly run in, caught fire. It necessitated a twenty-minute stop to effect repairs and with that the chance of winning was lost.

In spite of this misfortune, Savundra still finished a creditable fifth and only twelve minutes behind the winner. The only consolation was that he had finished ahead of Sopwith and won his bet.

Savundra's last race was in 1965.

The blame for the 1964 failure—for Savundra always had to blame others—he laid partly on his mechanic, whom he claimed had been guilty of sabotage, but he reserved the role of the major culprit for Ford's. Their 400-h.p. Interceptor engines, brought over from Detroit, had, he claimed, quite without justification, let him down.

Now, in his role of the free-spending millionaire, he set up his own company to build engines. Harry Westlake, a mechanical expert of great ability, was put in charge of the project with orders to build 650-h.p. supercharged turbo-jet engines which were to be one hundred per cent British. The were named Sea Unicorns and would have cost £5,500 in the open market.

Fitted with his new engines, Savundra claimed that *Jacquie S. the Second* was now so fast that she had broken two speedometers.

Alas, the day of the race was to prove another anti-climax. Despite desperate efforts, including constant changing of sparking plugs and even the gear-box, the mighty new engines failed to last beyond the Isle of Wight and Savundra was forced once again to withdraw. The Sea Unicorn experiment had cost him £60,000. These reverses only served to create in Savundra a sort of megalomania.

The 1965 race was hardly over before he turned up at Vosper's and commissioned Peter du Cane to build him a thirty-five-foot aluminium boat at a cost of £30,000. Then, deciding that he ought to have two boats, one for calm and one for heavy weather, he immediately went to a yard in Shoreham and ordered another.

But by the time of the next race neither *Flying Jacquie* nor *Speedy Jacquie*, as they were named, were in the line-up with him at the helm. Nor, in fact, was Sopwith ever required to pay for a Lucullan dinner party. Savundra had urgent reasons, unconnected with power-boating, for being out of Britain.

CHAPTER FOURTEEN

Caesar's Palace

SIMULTANEOUSLY WITH HIS ATTEMPTS to project himself as a sporting millionaire, Savundra sought recognition of another kind. F.A.M. now had a full-time legal adviser, Jimmy Newton, who was astonished one day in 1965 to be invited to accompany Savundra to lunch at the Buttery of the Berkeley Hotel. It was the first time he had received such an invitation and he was puzzled.

The meal had scarcely begun before the reason for it became clear. Savundra wanted to consult Newton on a matter so confidential that it could not be discussed in the office.

'How,' he asked, 'do I go about getting a knighthood?'

Newton was astonished and embarrassed, as it became evident that Savundra considered it to be just another business transaction. All Savundra wanted to know was how much it would cost, and to whom the money should be paid.

It took all Newton's tact to persuade Savundra that he would be well advised to wait until he was more securely established; and that anyway it was not a matter in which he could take the initiative.

Savundra accepted the situation with some reluctance but it was not long before his craving for recognition manifested itself again. This time he instructed F.A.M.'s chief advertising executive to prepare a long document, defining the contribution F.A.M. had made to the insurance industry. The purpose, it subsequently transpired, was to support Savundra's application for the Queen's Award to Industry. The application was duly sent off but that was the last that was heard of it.

At the same time, thrashing round for some concrete way of demonstrating his success to the world, he gave the most serious thought to moving the whole staff out of Jacqueline House and taking over a vast office block which had just been built at Stanbridge Park. It was only with the greatest difficulty that he was persuaded to abandon the idea, the only possible justification for which would have been to feed his ego by having the largest and most modern building in North London.

Faced with the Queen's perversity in neither granting him a knighthood nor even her Award to Industry, Savundra now applied himself in yet another different direction.

Harold Wilson had become Prime Minister in 1964 and made it clear early in the life of his administration that he was willing to seek advice and help from a wide range of leaders in the industrial field.

Savundra with his well-developed opportunism read the signs and decided that the time had come to draw the Prime Minister's attention to his own qualifications for being numbered amongst the favoured.

He saw his chance when, at the beginning of March, Mr. Wilson (as he then was) made a notable speech urging the need for industry to join in what he graphically described as 'the white-hot heat of technological revolution'.

The following day Savundra wrote him a letter which, in the admixture of obsequiousness and arrogant self-flattery, must be regarded as among his finer efforts.

It began:

'I have never till now had any Labour sympathies. Your recent speech on Television has convinced me however that your leadership is vitally necessary if this Country is to survive, let alone gain its former greatness.'

He followed this promising start by heartily endorsing every point the Prime Minister had made and then outlined his own contribution at F.A.M. to the great revolution:

'Using all the resources of skill and science and technology, we have ruthlessly modernised a traditional industry and it is the City Die-Hards, the Dinosaurs of the Modern Age, who are getting hurt. Of course the Dinosaurs are putting up a fight for survival and have descended to methods which are certainly anything but cricket to stamp out the menace to their very existence . . . the smaller, agile, streamlined Insurance Companies of the second half of the Twentieth Century, like ourselves . . .'

We have been unable to trace what, if anything, Mr. Wilson wrote in reply.

Meanwhile, at the F.A.M. headquarters, Savundra's switch from seldom-seen recluse to larger-than-life chief executive was in full swing. To his employees, he strove to be an almost God-like figure. 'When I appeared, everyone was expected to stand to attention,' he was later to say. 'It was very much a case of Hail, Caesar.'

'His word was law,' remembers one employee. 'He would come in with grandiose plans, wave his arms about and issue orders like a Bren gun. He always wanted everything done yesterday.'

His social secretary, Frances Lynch, recalls: 'He behaved like a film star. He created an air of terrible urgency about himself.'

His enthusiasm was infectious. He certainly had the capacity to create in people, however humble their task, the feeling that they were playing a vital role in important events. To quote Frances Lynch again, he made people, and particularly young people, 'drunk with the euphoria of going places'. Almost daily he would make a tour of the various departments. It was his custom to lead the way, expounding and gesticulating incessantly, looking for all the world like a mother duck leading her ducklings, with Tross Youle, flower in buttonhole and puffing a big cigar, slightly to one side of him and chain-smoking Stuart Walker on the other.

Visitors to his personal office remember him leaning back in his chair expounding on every subject under the sun while Walker, alongside, sat tensely upright, legs pressed together, lighting one cigarette after another and nodding his head vigorously at appropriate moments.

Although the aura of his presence was such that many of his employees felt they were expected to stand up and bow as he passed, there were a few who saw it all as something of a comedy. Privately they referred to Savundra and Walker as 'Gub-Gub and the Ghost'.

Another role which Savundra played with equal conviction was that of the benign *pater familias*. Tross Youle remembers him in this mood when one day in the boardroom he put one hand on his shoulder and the other on Walker's, saying: 'Tross, the world should be full of people like me with two fine Englishmen by my side. We could do great things. We could make the world a wonderful place to live in . . .'

More practically, at the end of 1965, he assumed the role of Father Christmas and ordered that all the staff be given a generous bonus. It was a gesture which cost F.A.M. £40,000. Then, still carried away by the Christmas spirit, he took the banqueting room at Grosvenor House for a grand staff party.

It was not, however, the traditional sort of office party at which the directors once a year demonstrate the common touch by mixing on terms of alcoholic camaraderie with their employees.

On the contrary, while the employees were eating the traditional turkey and plum pudding, Savundra and his directors were being served with a rather more epicurean repast in a private room; then, when it was judged that the time was ripe, he took them out to the top of the stairs which led down to the main dining room. There he acknowledged the spontaneous cheers which greeted his appearance by raising his hand in regal benediction before leading a dignified descent to mingle briefly with the more senior staff, and then being swiftly conducted to his waiting Rolls.

There were, however, those outside Savundra's immediate circle who did not fall so readily under his spell.

About the time that Savundra was writing to Harold Wilson, the Secretary General of the British Insurance Association, Mr. R.T.D. Wilmot, was preparing a memorandum for his chairman.

His purpose was to express his unease at the attitude the Press were taking as a result of Savundra's tireless efforts to promote the immense advantages he claimed for computerisation.

In particular, Mr. Wilmot complained, a 'young radical journalist' had telephoned him to get his reaction to an article he was preparing about the way that F.A.M. computers had drastically cut costs, and giving publicity to Savundra's statement to him that F.A.M. would command an annual premium income of £10 million within ten years.

Perhaps even more irritating to Mr. Wilmot was the journalist's stated conviction that F.A.M. were under 'very good management', a statement which he bolstered up by saying that 'Mr. Savundra was a personal friend of the Duke of Edinburgh and sailed with him at Cowes'.

'I spoke to him for about twenty minutes,' Wilmot noted. 'I tried to convince him that there was no magic in the installation of a computer and that I did not believe for one moment that F.A.M. had discovered a magic elixir which would enable them to outwit their more experienced competitors.'

Savundra, had he read this memorandum, would no doubt have dismissed it as the vapourings of one of the 'Dinosaurs of industry' but it does demonstrate the very serious reservations then developing in more conventional insurance circles about the mushroom growth of F.A.M.

Norman Nail of the Board of Trade was still watchful. His anxieties had been deepened by information passed to him by commercial sources overseas, relating to Savundra's past and in particular to his links with the Costa Rica coffee deal.

It was at this stage that Nail decided to pay a personal call on Dr. Savundra so that he could form a first-hand opinion about the workings of F.A.M.

There was no difficulty in arranging an appointment. Whereas before he had always had to deal with Stuart Walker, he now found that he was put straight on to Savundra himself. At their meeting, he found Savundra at his most charming. Far from appearing to have anything to hide Savundra took his guest on a detailed personal tour. Then he and Walker insisted that Nail should join them for lunch at a nearby restaurant.

There was only one slight hitch in an otherwise perfectly stage-managed occasion. Savundra proved a most hospitable host, and when it came to the bill, he turned to the waiter and airily told him to charge it to the company account.

'There is no company account,' said the waiter stolidly. It was Savundra himself who had laid down that under no circumstances were executives to charge up bills. Now he had hurriedly to explain this to Norman Nail lest he should be led to imagine that the company's credit was suspect.

Savundra used Nail's visit to complain that he was being made the object of unfair victimisation. He showed him a circular distributed by the Prudential Assurance which stated that F.A.M. was a near-insolvent business of the Brandaris type. (Brandaris was a short-lived Dutch cut-price insurance company.)

At the same time he produced an abject apology for the circular from the Prudential. 'It would have been worth £125,000 to me if I had taken them to court,' he claimed. 'I didn't do so because of the general upset it might have caused to my own expanding business. But just let me get something like this on the B.I.A. and I'll pull out everything I have.'

Nail's report stated guardedly: 'F.A.M. are trying, probably successfully, to build up a sound motor insurance business and if Savundra has any fraudulent and unethical plans they are not in evidence at present.' Of course, no report on a normal insurance company would have contained any mention whatsoever of the possibility of fraud.

Savundra was unperturbed by Nail's visit. He doubled his spending on advertising to drive home his modern approach with slogans like: 'F.A.M.: World leaders in computerised insurance' and emphasising the wonder of his '67-second policies.'

One of the problems which Savundra created for himself concerned his re-insurance arrangements, which up to this point had been very satisfactorily handled by a distinguished continental firm, Swiss Re-insurance.

Re-insurance is the method by which companies spread their risks. Much in the same way as bookmakers lay off bets so insurance companies make arrangements with other companies which specialise in re-insurance to cover risks over a certain sum. In the case of F.A.M. with Swiss Re-insurance the figure was £5,000.

The arrangement was running smoothly with the utmost goodwill on both sides until Savundra decided to gild the lily by asking Swiss Re-insurance to send a party to whom he could show off his business.

The outcome, far from enhancing his prestige, was disastrous. The Swiss arrived with their slide rules in their pockets and took advantage of the free access they were given to all departments. In spite of the lavish entertainment they enjoyed in the boardroom, they were not impressed. By their book the sums did not add up correctly. They returned home and wrote a report on their findings, which had the effect of sending Savundra into a rage. A specialist in vitriolic letters, he wrote back furiously accusing them of acting like 'drain inspectors' and terminating their contract. He does not appear for one moment to have stopped to consider whether the highly qualified Swiss might not have hit upon an inherent weakness in his trading methods.

Normally, for a respectable insurance company to part company with their reinsurers, would simply mean them shopping around for a suitable replacement. In Savundra's case, however, it presented a considerable problem. Firms specialising in re-insurance are among the most solid and respectable and the reputation of F.A.M. within the trade was not one that readily commanded respect. It is, therefore, rather surprising that Savundra did, in fact, manage to get his business taken on by a highly-thought-of underwriting firm in Lloyd's.

It was at about this time, presumably as part of his attempt to project the right image, that he decided the time had come for him to part company with his old ally, Bobby McKew. McKew, although Savundra would not readily have admitted it, had been for some time a source of irritation to him.

During the early days of F.A.M. McKew had probably been closer to him than anybody except Walker. They were the two men who saw him, on occasions, without his guard up, and both have tales to tell.

Walker remembers an afternoon when he and Savundra were walking along Park Place rather early for a business appointment. Savundra suddenly stopped at a door. 'I know a woman in here,' he said, ringing the doorbell. 'Just hang on a second.' The door opened and he dived inside, leaving his managing director to pace up and down the pavement. In ten minutes he reappeared again in good humour. Walker could not but admire the speed of the whole operation.

McKew had a similar experience. They had a short time to kill when Savundra said: 'Let's go to a brothel.' McKew who, when telling the story, likes to claim that he did not even know there were brothels in London, was then driven round to a house in Lancaster Gate where he and Savundra were ushered into a pleasant sitting room. Savundra was greeted like an old friend by the 'madam' who called him 'Eddie' and poured them both a glass of sherry. Suddenly Savundra was gone, only to reappear before McKew had finished his glass. 'You wouldn't have thought they would have had time to get their drawers off,' he says.

Towards McKew, however, Savundra's attitude now began to change. Possibly this happened because McKew, with his Irish sense of humour, could not resist any opportunity to take a rise out of the man he had affectionately nicknamed 'the Black Pope'.

McKew's sense of humour was not always in the most delicate taste. It will be remembered that he did most of F.A.M.'s printing, which had come to include Savundra's own personal needs. On one occasion Savundra asked him to have some sacred cards engraved depicting the Virgin Mary surrounded by angels. McKew persuaded the engraver to substitute his own face for that of the Virgin Mary. Savundra was deeply affronted.

One day he called Walker into his office and told him that he no longer wanted to have McKew as a shareholder. The reason he gave was that he could not have associated with the company someone who had a criminal record.

McKew's first reaction was to refuse to sell his £6,000 holding. Walker was sent back with a cheque for £20,000 and eventually this was accepted—but only when a new E-type Jaguar was thrown in.

Savundra's determination to preserve the image of the business tycoon of integrity and brilliance was almost paranoiac. Even when handling day-to-day problems, where it was necessary to summon an executive meeting and give his decision, he would have in front of him on his desk an impressive array of pieces of paper covered with neat mathematical workings which would indicate the many hours he had spent in arriving at the correct solution. Faced with this evidence no executive would challenge the great man's judgement.

Not even Savundra's closest friends were allowed to introduce a note of levity when in the office. Donald Campbell, who generally had a greater licence than most, discovered this when Savundra introduced him to his social secretary, Frances Lynch. 'Oh darling, what lovely eyes you have,' said Campbell. Savundra looked at him stonily.

'Miss Lynch does not like rubbish like that,' he snapped. 'She does have lovely eyes, but that is not the point.'

Outside the office both Savundra's and Walker's life styles became ever more opulent. In the garage at Savundra's Bishop's Avenue mansion there was a Rolls-Royce, two Aston Martin DB5s and a 3.8 Jaguar. The Rolls-Royce, one of a series of five which he owned during this period, carried CD number plates (to which of course he was not entitled) which enabled him to park in restricted streets and lessen the risk of collecting a ticket.

The gardens, which were kept immaculate by the services of a full-time gardener, featured such exotica as two large wrought-iron elephants, while a towering radio aerial bore witness to his passion, second only to power-boating, as a radio ham.

Visitors to White Walls speak of the vulgarity of the interior, which had a garish colour scheme, an abundance of white leather furniture and a huge ivory-and-gold piano in the drawing room. But none could complain of the hospitality. Emil and Pushpam would make themselves entirely responsible for the comfort of their guests. Once seated at the dinner table no one was permitted to move. The host and hostess generally included on the menu the traditional curry with gold leaf on top, and personally served every dish and poured every glass of wine. They even lit the guests' cigarettes and cigars. There were no servants in evidence—only Emil in a gold jacket and Pushpam in a colourful sari.

None could deny Savundra's generosity and it was not all done from a desire to impress. Apart from his lavish entertaining he was an easy touch for anyone who wanted to borrow money. 'They've opened a vein in my arm,' he would complain to Walker. 'They're going to bleed me dry.'

The main beneficiaries of his generosity were, however, his family in general and Jacqueline in particular. Much of Frances Lynch's time in the office was spent in arranging the delivery of unexpected gifts. If Savundra wanted something special he would go to any length to procure it and gifts were flown from all over the world to mark family occasions. Miss Lynch's efforts in this respect did not go unrewarded. Having fulfilled some particularly difficult request, she would come to the office the following morning to find an expensive box of chocolates or bottle of perfume on her desk.

As the premiums flowed in to the F.A.M. treasury, Savundra's own personal expenditure grew in proportion. He bought the white grand piano which cost £2,400 from Harrods, where for some reason he had no fewer than three accounts, and over £16,000 was spent on alterations to White Walls. He lavished so much attention on White Walls that he never found time to visit a house on the Thames at Old Windsor which had been bought, as a weekend retreat, with some money sent to England in 1960 by Sir Chittampalam Gardiner.

If Stuart Walker's own way of life did not quite match up to Savundra's extravagance, it certainly could not be described as modest. He had the historic Old Manor House at Hampton Court, which had undergone considerable modernisation since the days when it had been the home of Christopher Wren, resident there from 1706–23. It had six bedrooms and three reception rooms. In one of the several bathrooms was a six-foot-square mosaic tub and there was an elegant pillared walled garden stretching down to the banks of the Thames, where Walker planned to moor a motor cruiser which he was hoping to buy. He also had another large house in Hastings, set in its own secluded grounds. Its only historic claim was that it had once been a nudist colony and Savundra, fearing, he claimed, that his family might catch sight of nudists flitting between the trees, would never visit it.

Of course all this cost both of them a great deal of money, but Savundra had another weakness which was a bigger drain on resources than anything in the domestic sphere.

He once said, 'Some people collect stamps, or dogs. I collect companies.' It was nothing less than the truth.

There were eventually to be thirty-two of them based at Jacqueline House. Many were 'book' companies with no operational function, like the holding company Jacqueline Securities which was the major shareholder in the Fire, Auto and Marine Insurance Company. It was also a major shareholder in Fire, Auto and Marine Insurance Brokers which had, in turn, been formed as another book company for the sole purpose of creaming off 5 per cent commission on all premiums submitted to F.A.M. Conveniently the only shareholders in Jacqueline Securities were the Savundra family and Walker. Then, as a tax 'evasion' he formed Jacqueline Properties, which on paper owned White Walls so that all work on the house and garden could be charged against the company and therefore be done tax free.

Although this web of companies caused a lot of work, not to say confusion, for F.A.M. executives, they did not harm Savundra's own financial situation. Indeed, they did the opposite. Executives in the building were not the only people to be baffled—Savundra had always used confusion as a trump card and he knew the value of creating a labyrinth of such legal and financial complexity that it would defeat the endeavours of any official investigators.

There were some companies, however, which were less incestuous. The Sea Unicorn project, which he set up specifically to build engines for his power boats, was an example. It was a concern without profit as an end product. It was simply a money spender. Then again, there was another whole series of companies unconnected operationally with insurance out of which he did hope to make substantial profit.

Savundra had a weakness for mechanical gadgets. He was also a natural salesman and it has often been said that the easiest person to sell anything to is a salesman. Therefore, the two scientists who presented themselves one morning at Jacqueline House for the purpose of selling their mechanical gadget to Savundra were undoubtedly on an easy wicket. Messrs. Steel and Vigeis had an idea for a new type of burglar alarm. It worked on a laser beam principle, so that when the beam was broken, an alarm would be triggered off. Some of the devices were more sophisticated and involved flashing lights and silent telephone calls to a local police station. All the scientists needed to produce these appliances was £25,000.

Savundra took the bait. Immediately he involved himself in a flurry of company-forming (the operation in Savundra's opinion called for no less than three companies named respectively Photo Electric Development, Photo Electric Research and Photo Electric Securities) and before the gratified Mr. Steel and Mr. Vigeis had time to catch their breath, a factory had been taken over at Shoeburyness and a staff of twelve women hired to manufacture the alarm.

There was only one problem. The designs had not yet been completed so for several weeks the ladies arrived punctually at the factory, knitted all day and duly collected their pay packets at the end of the week.

Finally the first Alertocalls, as they were called, came off the production line. Getting rid of them, however, was another matter. One was displayed for a time in an Oxford Street shop and a few were sold to small businesses, but that was all. Closer at hand, the idea appealed to the ever-loyal Stuart Walker, who had installed at the Old Manor the most sophisticated model, which was supposed to ring an alarm in the local police station.

It could only have happened to the accident-prone Walker, but the day after the system was installed burglars broke in. They loaded their van with the twelve-foot long dining-room table and a set of

Chippendale chairs while the alarm remained obdurately silent. It did not even protest when Walker's uncle happened to call. The burglars simply knocked him on the head and carried on with their furniture removal. Savundra compensated Walker for this misfortune by presenting him with two guard dogs to replace the alarm, but this episode did nothing to dampen his enthusiasm for the activities of Mr. Steel and Mr. Vigeis.

Now he agreed to back them in the development of a proximity fuse for ballistic missiles. This was another laser beam device which worked on the principle that it could be set to make a rocket explode at any desired distance from a target. For this new project a retired army officer, Major-General Sir Bertram Ralfs, who had chanced to apply for the job of F.A.M. Personnel Officer, found himself recruited as chief executive.

Filled with enthusiasm for his new idea, Savundra flew to India to offer it to Mrs. Indira Gandhi as a protection against the Pakistanis— for 'sabre-rattling' as he called it. Once again he was wearing his favourite hat as saviour of the Third World. His idea was to produce a special 'Woolworth version' for the Indians but obviously nothing could be done until the weapon had been properly tested.

Trials were planned to take place at the army base at Fort Holsted but they never came off. Costs continued to mount until the whole project became too expensive, even for Savundra. It was shelved but not before, in the estimation of Jimmy Newton, approximately £160,000 had drained away.

There were other ventures which were equally unsuccessful—most hairbrained of all, perhaps, being the idea of insuring smokers against lung cancer. For a time this became THE BIG IDEA. When Joseph Gordon, who joined F.A.M. as a barrister and eventually became general manager, attended his interview, Savundra used the occasion for a soliloquy on the subject: a floor of Jacqueline House was to be devoted to medical research . . . he was going to do great things for British medicine.

No one could persuade him that the idea was a non-starter. As Joseph Gordon put it: 'If a smoker admits the possibility exists of getting lung cancer he will not take out a policy. He will give up smoking.' Nobody, in other words, admits that they might be committing suicide—as eventually became evident when Savundra employed a market research firm to test the idea.

Champion Assurance, however, a sister company of F.A.M., which was set up to handle general life insurance, had a happier history. It was run almost single-handedly by a highly efficient and qualified insurance expert, Clive Brewer, from its beginnings in 1964 and by the time the whole Savundra edifice collapsed it had 400 customers on the books. As the name suggests, it aimed at projecting a sporting image and there were plans to obtain the services of stars like George Best and Ted Dexter to feature in an advertising campaign.

There was one other scheme beside Champion which had all the potential of becoming a fertile oasis in Savundra's desert of wild ideas. It was based on the belief held by most insurance companies that garages are apt not to play straight with them. When a garage knows his customer is on an insurance claim there is a danger that the estimate will be exaggerated. Savundra's answer was a simple one: to own his own garages. When F.A.M. crashed, he had two—one in Horsley in Essex and the other in Chiswick in Kent. The plan was to establish a countrywide network. The garages would not only handle F.A.M. claims; they would also act as brokers' offices. Thus everything could be done from a central point.

Other schemes, at least for a company like F.A.M., were not so practical. There was a Pay-As-You-Drive Plan—by which customers could pay for their premiums by instalments, like Pay-as-You-Earn income tax. But the potential convenience for customers was far outweighed by the amount of excess paperwork laid on the shoulders of the F.A.M. staff. A few drivers did opt to use the scheme but on the whole it was ignored.

Then there was a plan to offer postal orders in competition with the Post Office. This was to involve the issuing of coupons to newsagents and tobacconists—in Savundra's scheme of things a permanent flow of cash was envisaged, plus the extra advantage of fall-out money from coupons lost or never handed in. The snag was to convince businesses all over Britain that F.A.M. coupons were a fair substitute for Post Office orders.

One final potential scheme must be mentioned, if only because it was typical of Savundra's brazenness. In March 1966, Savundra paid a call on his acquaintance from the days of the Costa Rican affair, Franz Hacke-Prestinary, who no longer held the post of Costa Rican consul, and was living in a flat in the Cromwell Road. So well had Savundra covered his tracks in the Costa Rican swindle that Prestinary, who had dropped out of the negotiations, believed when Shiv Kapoor stood alone in the dock at the Old Bailey that it was he and he alone who had been guilty of the fraud.

Prestinary now conducted research for businessmen interested in the Costa Rican market and Savundra had no difficulty in persuading him of the benefits which would accrue to his countrymen by the introduction of cut-price insurance. Prestinary put the wheels in motion for F.A.M.'s expansion abroad but the idea turned out to be another non-starter.

While Savundra was absorbed in all these schemes, however, good and bad, a slow but inexorable fuse had begun to burn under F.A.M. The company's postbag no longer consisted almost exclusively of eager applications for the wonderful cut-price policies.

The claims were beginning to come in.

CHAPTER FIFTEEN

The Cottage with the Green Shutters

AMID THE PLETHORA OF companies there was one which, far from being a mere appendage to F.A.M., was the very lynchpin of Savundra's empire, Its aim, not so well publicised as that of the others, had little to do with the paying of claims.

In January 1963, Savundra flew to Zürich for a personal meeting with the Swiss lawyer, Dr. Paul Hagenbach, who had been instrumental in providing the first capital for F.A.M. by setting up a company for his client, Count Maxim de Cassan Floyrac.

Dr. Hagenbach, a grey-haired man in his early sixties who walked with a pronounced limp, had a lifelong record of association with foreigners eager to take advantage of the facilities offered to investors in Liechtenstein, a country with a well-earned reputation as a tax-dodger's paradise.

This tiny principality wedged between Switzerland and Austria has an area of only sixty square miles and a population of around 15,000. Apart from the one main village (which has no railway station or airport) and an abundance of green fields and cows (its only natural resource is grass), Liechtenstein's visible assets are Europe's biggest false-teeth factory and, perhaps appropriately, a firm which makes the world's smallest adding machine.

Its most famous product, however, is an invisible one. The country is an international financial centre which possessed in 1963 a total of 20,000 limited companies.

It was this, of course, which interested Savundra. Liechtenstein offers an obliging selection of advantages to the tax-oppressed—the silent partnership, the limited company in single ownership, the secret trust. But the company with the most magical qualities of all is the Anstalt.

The Anstalt has no members, shares or shareholders. The legal minimum for the board is one. And the directors, however many, do not in fact direct anything. All power in the company is vested in the Founder, and the document defining the Founder's Right can be passed to anyone else at any time. There are only two restrictions: the company cannot carry on its business inside Liechtenstein and it cannot be used for an illegal or immoral purpose. Apart from that the licence is all-embracing and most Liechtenstein directors do not even know who the real owner of their company is, let alone what is their line of business.

For what Savundra had in mind, which was nothing less than the transfer of F.A.M.'s cash to his own pocket, this was a situation which was eminently suitable.

The standard way of setting up an Anstalt, the most malleable corporate device in the world, is through a lawyer like Hagenbach, to whom this type of business was routine. 'After all, this kind of work is a Swiss lawyer's daily bread. For what I did I received legal fees and that was all. I was never an associate,' he was later to explain.

Savundra was in touch with Hagenbach again only days after that preliminary meeting. He suggested that instead of setting up a new company, they should buy up an existing one. Hagenbach agreed and soon came up with the grandly named Merchant Bankers and Trust. It original owner, an American, had died and it was for sale: total capital 10,000 Swiss francs, approximately £800.

Acting on Savundra's instructions Hagenbach bought it with money sent from a numbered account in Switzerland and then organised the necessary 'board'. Despite the enormous scale of company business in Liechtenstein its organisation is in the hands of a tiny proportion of the population. Almost the entire 'company trade' at that time was cornered by ten lawyers and fifteen professional company directors.

Some of the lawyers were directors of 2,500 companies each but the professional directors, who offered a specialised service, had fewer clients and it was into the hands of a member of one partnership that Hagenbach put Merchant Bankers and Trust.

Dr. Oswald Buhler and Dr. Rudolph Wiederin were typical professional directors. Lawyers by training, they worked as a partnership from a pretty yellow-painted chalet in the picturesque village of Mauren in the foothills of the Alps near the Austrian border. Hagenbach kept up a close relationship with them for the express purpose of supplying his clients with trust directors. Buhler at the time was already looking after 250 such concerns but for Wiederin, who was learning the business, the figure was nearer 50—and it was Wiederin who became the one-man board of Merchant Bankers and Trust.

Savundra did not have to make much of a financial sacrifice for the privilege of employing him—professional directors at that time rated the modest fee of £80 per annum.

Later in 1963 the name of Savundra's new company was changed to Merchants and Finance Trust, because its original name was too similar to that of another Liechtenstein-registered company. Then, at the beginning of 1964, M.F.T. was filed in Companies House in the City of London as a foreign company operating in Britain and Stuart Walker was appointed as manager and sole representative in London.

The stage was now set for the redistribution of F.A.M.'s income via Merchants and Finance Trust, so as to put it out of reach of British creditors and make it available for any purpose Savundra and Walker might decide upon.

Years later, detectives, lawyers, accountants, journalists and financiers were to wrestle for months with the jigsaw puzzle relationship between F.A.M., M.F.T. and their actual owners. But basically, the method used by Savundra and Walker to syphon F.A.M. cash into their own pockets was a fairly simple one.

As has already been pointed out, insurance companies are relatively free to move their spare cash abroad. Savundra once said: 'In England, an insurance company can invest in anything.' And that was not far from the truth.

What he did was to switch the bulk of F.A.M.'s funds to M.F.T., where, of course, Savundra and Walker had total control of their disposal.

So far as the F.A.M. chairman, Tross Youle, and the other directors of F.A.M. were concerned, M.F.T. was a merchant bank charged with the investment of the insurance company's funds and they were content to leave such matters of high finance in the hands of Savundra, whom they recognised as the expert. They did not realise there was nothing to stop Savundra and Walker drawing out as much as they pleased from the F.A.M. account, for their personal use.

The way the money was 'windmilled' makes it difficult to be accurate about all M.F.T.'s activities. By the end of F.A.M.'s life almost one million pounds appeared to have been transferred into this 'bank'—and from there to other destinations. Some of it was handed out to Savundra's friends and colleagues in small personal loans—a kind of 'Savundra Slush Fund'. About £108,000 went on F.A.M. and F.A.M.-related companies. Some of it went into the abortive Photo

Electrics scheme. But the bulk of it went to Savundra and Walker. A close study of the accounts reveals that they collected more than £603,000—in the same proportion, roughly, as Jacqueline Securities shares were divided, the greater part going to Savundra.

At the trial there was to be a good deal of argument as to how much actually went into their pockets. Days seemed to be spent bandying around heady figures, several witnesses being led through financial labyrinths of daunting complexity. Savundra's defence counsel was once, with a touch of exasperation, to wonder whether there was not between the accountant and the layman 'an impenetrable barrier'.

The cause of the headaches was principally the way F.A.M.'s share capital was issued. Tross Youle held a small percentage of these shares—5,500. Jacqueline Securities held the rest and by the end of F.A.M.'s life it was claimed that 500,000 authorised shares had been fully paid up. This was not true. Tross Youle had paid for his allotment but Savundra and Walker had paid for less than half of theirs in cash borrowed from M.F.T. The others—about 248,000—were shown as having been bought in cash, but in fact the deal was only a paper one. To create the illusion of a larger holding and increased company capital Savundra and Walker added (in stages) a collective total of £248,000 on to M.F.T.'s debt to F.A.M. and £248,000 on to their debt to M.F.T. In other words no money had changed hands but Savundra and Walker had pretended to borrow money and pay F.A.M. in order that they could mark their shares as fully paid up.

For the purpose of describing these complicated financial manipulations we have bracketed Savundra and Walker together as if they were equal architects of the whole scheme; it is clear to us, in considering these transactions and in the light of future events, that Savundra's role was that of manipulator-in-chief. It was after all his golden rule that not even his closest associates should hold all the pieces of the jigsaw and unlikely that he made an exception in the case of Walker. Indeed, there is considerable doubt as to whether Walker was well enough equipped to understand the implications of the whole set-up. Certainly he did not appreciate the dangers he had put himself in by allowing himself to be made 'London manager'.

Savundra was a master at creating smoke screens and ingenious attempts were made to give M.F.T. the colouring of a genuine merchant bank. Some money drawn from it was, in fact, paid back in as 'fresh capital', after being channelled through Kuwait, in the Middle

East, and Switzerland, so as to make its origins difficult to trace. Thus the appearance given was that M.F.T. handled other sources of income besides F.A.M. premiums.

Savundra had moved swiftly once the foundations for his private arrangements to deflect money into his own pocket had been made. Hagenbach was instructed to open a numbered account in Zürich on behalf of M.F.T. Then, at intervals, sums of money purporting to be 'fresh capital' were paid into this account. Hagenbach never knew where they came from as no sender was ever named. He would be told by the Union Bank that a certain sum had been paid into M.F.T.'s account by another Swiss bank—which effectively concealed where the money originated. At least £33,000 was transferred in this way. Savundra was thus compounding the protection he had in his Liechtenstein trust by exploiting to the full, once again, the secrecy of the Swiss banking system.

The fact that F.A.M. was re-investing with a merchant bank—even if its ownership and stakes were always kept a mystery—was enough to satisfy the directors. But if M.F.T. could pass muster with an uncritical board, there was to come a time when the company investment policy would have to face a harsher scrutiny. F.A.M. was an exempt private company—exempt, that is, from publishing its accounts in Companies House. After two years, however, F.A.M. would have to satisfy the Board of Trade about its financial position and if loans were being made to the directors, they would have to appear in the books.

Through M.F.T., however, Savundra was able to conceal these loans from the Board of Trade as well as his board of directors—but in case there should be any difficulty, he took a precaution in February 1965, just before presenting the audited accounts to the F.A.M. board.

He and Walker drew up a 'legal agreement' which purported to replace and consolidate all previous agreements—although there is no evidence that any of these existed. This agreement contained an astonishing series of paragraphs. They were witnessed by Herr Wiederin—who of course had no say whatsoever in how M.F.T. used its funds. His signature was merely a formality.

The new agreement provided that F.A.M. money should be lent to M.F.T. at a flat rate of four per cent and lent in turn to Savundra and Walker at three per cent. Later this was not to strike everyone as terribly astute banking practice, although of course it had its advantages for the beneficiaries.

Other aspects of the loan agreement were even odder. Loans made by M.F.T. pursuant to the terms of the agreement, for example, could not be recalled for twenty years.

Further, under paragraph five of the contract: 'Payments of principal and interest under this agreement shall be made by the borrower to the bank at its London office or, in the event of the closure of the London office, to its office in Liechtenstein.'

And to whom should the payments be made? To none other than Savundra and Walker, the owners of the 'bank' . . .

In fact, the 'bank' only consisted of a brass plate in Zürich, a ledger entry in Liechtenstein and a plaque and a ledger on the fifth floor of Jacqueline House in London.

F.A.M. executives might be told that it was re-investing the company's reserves in stocks and shares and government bonds. Dr. Wiederin might assume, as he later made clear, that a company calling itself Merchants and Finance Trust was in the business of financing merchants. At the time he would certainly have been surprised to find out what he was actually directing. Neither he or his partner, Buhler, knew that their tidy cottage, with its oak-panelled sitting room, its collection of hunting prints and its bright green shutters, was technically the headquarters of a company through which hundreds of thousands of British motorists were being deceived. M.F.T. was no investment company but the vital point in a remarkable financial merry-go-round.

CHAPTER SIXTEEN

Warning Signals

THE FIRST OUTWARD SIGN to anyone apart from Savundra and Walker that all was not well with the insurance giant of Jacqueline House came in March 1965, when the chief accountant, Leslie John Cocke, was ordered to restrict payment of claims to £10,000 a week.

For some time the premium income had been dropping from its peak of £40,000 a week and at the same time the amount of claims had been steadily growing. When the order to restrict payments came, the claims department had been paying out between £15,000 and £20,000 a week and profitability had almost entirely disappeared.

Inevitably the restriction caused a ripple of unease to run through the building. Soon the unpaid claims started to pile up. At first they were contained in files but as the number grew they were piled into shoe boxes on the floor of the claims office.

Leslie Cocke had another reason for unease. He had been working on the trial balance sheet, now being urgently demanded by the Board of Trade. This had to show a surplus of £50,000 on the trading figures or ten per cent of the premium income, whichever was the greater. In 1964 the income had been £2,203,363 so the margin required was in the region of £220,000. The actual figure which showed up on the balance sheet was barely £90,000.

Leslie Cocke had been one of the few people employed by F.A.M. on the initiative of Tross Youle. He was a fellow member of the R.N.V.R. Club and a highly qualified accountant. He was now the only person in the firm besides Walker and Savundra himself who might, through preparing the accounts, represent a threat to Savundra's plan to outwit the Board of Trade. Savundra's solution was to have Cocke sacked.

To achieve this he called in Tross Youle. Cocke, he told him, was not loyal and was no longer in touch with affairs. Worse, he had lost control of the firm's accounts and, alleged Savundra, had actually 'lost' a £10,000 two and a half per cent Government Bond. Savundra put it down to drink—on which, he said, Cocke relied. The time had come when he could no longer afford to retain him.

It was Tross Youle, whose office was little more spacious than a large cupboard by comparison with the magnificence of Savundra's work space, who was given the embarrassing job of having to sack his friend.

Twenty-seven-year-old Alan Hatherall was promoted from the job of Cocke's assistant to chief accountant; but if Savundra thought he had got rid of a potential trouble-maker in favour of someone more malleable, he was mistaken.

Hatherall was a sober, hard-working and conscientious young man with a strong belief in the ethical standards of his profession. He was the exact opposite of the volatile and at times bombastic Savundra.

Now he took over where Cocke had left off and his trial balance sheet confirmed the one drawn up by his predecessor. It showed that, without doubt, the company was insolvent.

At this stage, conveniently for Savundra, Hatherall got married and went off on his honeymoon. While he was away, Arthur Conway, F.A.M.'s auditor, turned up to check the balance sheet. Conway, of the Chancery Lane firm of accountants, Fisher, Conway and Fenton, was accompanied by one of his partners, Arnold Dinnen.

Together the two men made a careful study of the position and, at a meeting with the directors in the great boardroom, duly declared that the required solvency margin had not been achieved.

Savundra was at his smoothest and most persuasive. There had been, he assured them, a mistake. Opening his attaché case, he produced two documents. One was a three per cent Government Bond with a face value of £510,000 15s. 10d.; the other was a letter on Merchants and Finance Trust writing paper. Both were passed to the auditors. The letter read:

This is to confirm to you that the credit balance of the Fire, Auto and Marine Insurance Company in our books on April 30, 1965, was £77,660 7s 5d. We also confirm that we have purchased on behalf on Fire, Auto and Marine Insurance Company and in their name £510,000 15s. 10d value of 3 percent Savings Bonds, 1955–1965, for the sum of £500,000, stock certificate in respect of which is attached hereto. This last mentioned item is not reflected in our books as an asset held by us.

Signed on behalf of the Board,

J. S. Martin.

In fact, as it later transpired, there was no such person as J.S. Martin.

The auditors were told that they might keep the letter but as soon as the stock certificate had circulated round the table it was slipped back into Savundra's attaché case. He had to keep it, he explained, as he might want to realise it at short notice.

Conway and Dinnen had no reason to be suspicious. They accepted the stock certificate as evidence that the company was solvent and duly amended the trial balance sheet to show an additional £510,000 as assets.

When Hatherall returned from his honeymoon, he at once noticed the staggering alteration to the draft he had prepared and marched in to see Savundra. Where had the new money come from, he wanted to know, and where was the accrued interest which must surely also appear in the accounts?

Savundra swept his concern aside. The stock certificate, he said, had been bought from the Bank of England. As for the interest, it had 'gone back' where it came from. Hatherall took this to mean M.F.T. but he was far from happy about the situation. He guessed Savundra had negotiated a short-term loan abroad, using the money to buy the Government Bond. Once the auditors had caught a glimpse of the certificate (conjectured Hatherall) it could be resold, having served its purpose. The money could then be returned to the lender, the whole operation having cost only a small interest payment.

On 26th August the final accounts were drawn up and submitted for signature. Savundra, Walker and the unsuspecting Tross Youle duly signed and they were sent to the Insurance Department of the Board of Trade. For Norman Nail there was no lever to enable the start of an investigation. Indeed, the accounts showed a healthy surplus to requirements of almost £400,000.

Not that he was happy. For almost a year he had suspected the company was not steering a legal course but there had been nothing he could do. And when he expressed, as he frequently did, his doubts to Savundra, he was met with bland assurances. 'Oh, we don't get many claims because we only take on the best business . . . and such is my confidence in the company that I'm even prepared to back it with family trust funds.' This last sentence, if one thinks of Merchants and

Finance Trust, must surely come near the top of the chart of Savundra's euphemisms.

The first sentence, too, was an evasion. Quite apart from the fact that it simply was not true—there were, by this time, hundreds of claims coming in—the idea that F.A.M. was getting the best business was, and always had been, a false one.

The theory had been that the offering of cut-price insurance would produce such a huge flow of business that brokers would be able to be selective with regard to what risks they accepted.

Savundra, however, although he himself was genuinely anxious only to handle low-risk business, had reckoned without the profit motive of the insurance brokers and agents. Many brokers were people of high integrity, but virtually anyone could act as an insurance agent and not all these part-timers were over-scrupulous in seeing that their customers' interests were properly safeguarded. There were those, too, who failed to mention, when submitting proposal forms to Jacqueline House, that the driver in question had had an accident or was in some other way a bad risk. Worst of all, there were those who were patently fraudulent, hanging on to 'no claim' premiums and only submitting policies on which F.A.M. was liable to pay out.

In Jacqueline House, in late 1965, the general feeling of unease grew. As his department became swamped with unpaid claims, Maurice Howard left. He was replaced as claims manager by a man who had been the company's chief engineer. His job had been to see that the estimates for repairs by garages bore some relation to the actual cost. He and his staff had had the responsibility of sorting out the genuine claimants from the sharp practice boys. Now, in his new capacity, he was to find that many genuine claims were being stalled.

He pressed Hatherall and Hatherall pressed Savundra. At first Savundra said he would go to Switzerland and arrange for the transfer of funds from Merchants and Finance Trust to the Bank of England but nothing came of his promise.

Hatherall now wanted the paper assets to be sold. Savundra used his bullying tactics. 'I'm twice your age and experience,' he would snap, 'leave the financial aspect of things to me'—or, on another occasion: 'That cupboard over there is full of balls I've cut off. Do you want yours to join them?'

Hatherall, while admitting that his position was unenviable, says, 'Most of us were young and relatively immature and a bit scared of him.' However, he persisted in talking about the need to liquify assets —and soon fell out of favour for good. One week he authorised the payment of a greater number of claims than the limit laid down by Savundra and there was a considerable row. 'I have run the financial affairs of governments, so mind your own business,' Savundra shouted, adding his favourite set-down: 'Don't get into the ring with heavyweights.'

Hatherall had not proved at all a satisfactory replacement for the unfortunate Cocke, so he too had to be moved out. There were no grounds on which he could be sacked but Savundra pushed him into the job of company secretary and brought in as accountant an even younger man, Cecil Jager.

The one thing which Savundra seemed unable to comprehend was that there would come a time when the flow of money would dry up. For ten years he had lived the life of a tycoon. His great house in Bishop's Avenue, his cars and his speedboats all bore evidence to his financial genius. He seems to have deceived himself into believing that all problems would go away, that the bonanza could go on for ever.

He was less successful at deceiving others at Jacqueline House. Rumours that all was not well with the company's finances persisted. By March 1966, morale was at such a low ebb that Savundra summoned all the senior staff to a meeting in the boardroom.

There was, he assured them, nothing to worry about. The company's financial structure was sound. All the reserves were tied up in blue chip investments. Indeed, F.A.M. was so solid that they could comfortably survive for a whole year even if not another penny was received in premiums and, of course, there was no likelihood of that.

Altogether it was a masterly performance. Most of the doubters were convinced. Alan Hatherall was not. He both distrusted and disliked Savundra and by now he was convinced that F.A.M. had serious difficulties.

About this time he came to hear about Savundra's adventures in Belgium, though he was given the name Savundranayagam it was the final provocation. Hatherall quit F.A.M., but not before giving vent to his feelings about the man who had employed him. He told Savundra: 'A. I don't like the way you treat people, they never know where they are with you so they aren't safe; and B. I don't like the way you run your business.' He did not make an outright accusation of dishonesty, but his remarks were not of the kind Savundra was used to hearing in his office.

Also before leaving, Hatherall mentioned his discovery to one or two of his colleagues in the office, telling them Savundra had a criminal record and the only sensible thing to do was to get out. None took his advice, but one was bold enough to ask Savundra about the report.

'Ah,' he said. 'Savundranayagam. That is another man. I am always being confused with him. But he is already dead.'

During April 1966, as the time approached for the second audit in the company's history, the auditors again began to make pressing demands to see the accounts.

Savundra himself drew up a draft balance sheet. It showed that the £500,000 certificate had disappeared. In its place was a portfolio of shares which included major holdings in Great Universal Stores, Burmah Oil, Simon Engineering, Beaverbrook Newspapers and the Distillers Company. (Savundra forever made it plain to his auditors and accountants that he would only invest in British Government stock or top—blue chip—British companies.) The total value was more than £800,000. By a curious coincidence the total amount of reserves now apparently 'banked' with M.F.T. was £877,606.

The pressure on Savundra had become considerable. It seemed to the F.A.M. executives that the money was quite clearly there—the problem was that it was tied up in paper assets. All the executives were convinced that if these were liquified, the company would be in no difficulty; all that was needed was ready cash to pay claims; they could not understand Savundra's reluctance to obtain it.

But in the face of their combined insistence, his reaction was simply to talk obscurely about the absolute necessity of keeping the reserves intact; if we sell them, he said, we liquidate the company. His listeners were not yet in a position to appreciate the irony of his words.

So Savundra stubbornly continued to take any course except that which would have been the obvious one had his claims been true. Cecil Tross Youle, who had wide contacts in the City, had been sent on a tour of merchant banks in March to try to raise fresh capital. Predictably, it was not a fruitful exercise. With him he took a set of draft balance sheets which showed, under the heading of securities, the new blue chip stock. Some bankers showed interest but having studied the mysterious shareholdings which did not seem to produce any income, they politely showed him the door. Indeed Tross Youle's efforts did him personally more harm than good. Much to his chagrin one prominent banker whom he was to approach later cut him when they met. He obviously thought the innocent Tross Youle had been deliberately trying to deceive him.

Appeasing the auditors again was Savundra's next big hurdle. They wanted to see the actual certificates.

Most of the pressure of fighting the defensive action fell on Stuart Walker. It was made clear to him that as managing director it was his job to deal with auditors. His way of dealing with them consisted at first in a good deal of stalling: the certificates were in Zürich, he said, where M.F.T. kept them, there were delays in getting them over . . .

Eventually, at the auditors' insistence, a meeting was fixed at Jacqueline House in mid-April. When they arrived, they were shown securities worth £34,487. Walker was not there and when he did arrive he explained that there were other securities worth £800,000 in the safe. The reason he was late, was that on the way to Jacqueline House he had remembered that he had left the key at his home . . . on returning to pick it up he had unfortunately been unable to find it. Savundra was meanwhile at his home taking no part in the proceedings.

The auditors left, but the effect of all the confusion had been to worry them and when, on 22nd April, the certificates were at last available for inspection, they took particular care to note down their numbers.

The arrival and departure of the certificates was indeed a mysterious affair. They were presented to the auditors by Stuart Walker, who claimed he had found them on arriving home at Hampton Court the night before the audit, pushed through his letter-box in a sealed envelope.

Barely had the auditors left Jacqueline House when, Walker went on to claim, 'a little man, about 5 feet 9 inches, with fairish hair and a thin face' appeared and collected them, saying that he was sending them back to Zürich. One thing is certain—they were never seen again.

For the moment, however, the temperature had cooled somewhat in the office. The trial audit had gone through smoothly enough so there seemed to be no immediate danger.

But it was not many days before the pressure to sell the shares again mounted on Savundra. The claims were still inexorably building up.

It was at this stage that Savundra had a bright idea: he would go to America and raise fresh capital. The attraction of America was that it was fresh territory; the banking fraternity were not so hidebound as they were in London. Accordingly, pausing only to pack £5,000 in cash for expenses into a suitcase, he set out for New York on 10th

May. His contact was the prominent New York lawyer, Emmanuel D. Margolies, whom he had 'met' in the course of his ham radio activities. In F.A.M.'s heyday Savundra had frequently laid on special lectures for his staff and one of the men he had invited to come over and speak was Margolies.

Once in New York Margolies introduced him to leading bankers and insurance tycoons, but none was as responsive as Savundra had hoped. The director of the Insurance Company of North America went so far as to write to Stuart Walker saying that he had met Savundra and found him 'charming and dynamic . . . just the kind of person we would like to do business with', but as usual negotiations broke off when Savundra raised difficulties about the close examination of F.A.M. books.

Things had certainly not gone as Savundra expected. Even his incurable optimism must have been evaporating. His reaction was typical. He had a heart attack. Immediately he flew back to London, and sought refuge, as in a previous crisis, in a room in the London Clinic. He claimed that during his three weeks in America, Dr. Charles Friedberg, one of New York's leading cardiologists, had diagnosed that one of the arteries pumping blood into his heart was blocked. His condition was made more serious by the sugar diabetes he had contracted ten years earlier. He had been told, he announced firmly, that if he wanted to stay alive, he would have to give up business and take up fishing.

From his strategic position at the Clinic Savundra could claim inaccessibility whenever the situation demanded it, but he could also use the place as an operational headquarters.

From the Clinic he wrote to the chairman of Vehicle and General Insurance Company and offered to sell F.A.M., enclosing a draft balance sheet of accounts. The reply was terse—and predictable. 'In order that my board may make a detailed appraisal of the situation, I shall be grateful if you could arrange to let me have . . . a schedule of the investments at cost, totalling £903,029.' None of Savundra's cunning had deserted him, as his next letter showed. The straightforward request was evaded and the Vehicle and General chairman given the impression that if he did not move fast, his chance of acquiring a valuable property would be gone for ever. Savundra wrote:

> In view of the very advanced state of another negotiation I am conducting, I have been told that my continuing any negotiation with you would be regarded with much disfavour. In these circumstances I must withdraw from my negotiations with you while

thanking you for your courtesy, unless you are willing at this stage to make a firm offer at not less than £3 per share for 500,000 fully paid shares of £1 each, subject to auditors' reports, of course. I have no intention of trying to organise an auction but I had in my own mind decided to sell F.A.M. for not less than £1.5 million and the first party who agrees that will get the company . . . if this proposal is of interest perhaps we could meet again and figure out any details.

But it was not to be; and a similar attempt to woo Legal and General met with the same frosty response, despite an enticing hint at the bottom of Savundra's letter to the effect that F.A.M.'s profits had not yet been added to the draft documents.

One side effect of the forlorn bid to get rid of F.A.M. was a furious telephone call from Tony Hunt, the managing director of Vehicle and General, to Norman Nail. He and Savundra had always regarded one another with a veiled distrust. Now Hunt was out for blood, as he told Nail. 'This bloody rogue, Savundra . . . Can't you do something about him? He's got no money. He's queering the pitch for the real pioneers.'

It was clear that no potential purchaser was going to risk any money on F.A.M. until he had been given the answers to two vital questions: Where is the interest return on the portfolio of shares, which should be nearly £10,000? And if you have these reserves, why don't you liquify them instead of asking us to bail you out?

F.A.M. was entering its final days and while Stuart Walker, pale and gaunt with the strain, was trying to think of ways of stemming the all-engulfing tide of claims, Savundra stayed on in his sick-bed, first at the Clinic, then at his home, White Walls.

Sometimes F.A.M. executives would telephone him asking advice, but he seemed unable to concentrate on business. One man who kept in regular touch was the solicitor, James Newton, and he remembers one episode which highlights the bizarre drama going on in the background as F.A.M. tottered on the brink. He had been lunching with Donald Campbell at Leatherhead. Campbell, always a firm friend to Savundra, had been recently drawn into a business venture linked with F.A.M. He had been trying unsuccessfuly to contact Savundra and was worried. Newton tried telephoning him then and there, from Campbell's house, and Savundra himself answered.

'I am in bed and all alone,' he whispered hoarsely down the line. 'They have left me all alone.'

Immediately Campbell insisted on driving to London to see him.

Savundra's imposing £100,000 home in Bishop's Avenue, Hampstead.

After the crash of FAM he took his weekend retreat in Ousley Road, Old Windsor, off the market and moved in.

His business affairs looking gloomy, Savundra is rushed to hospital with acute bronchitis diagnosed.

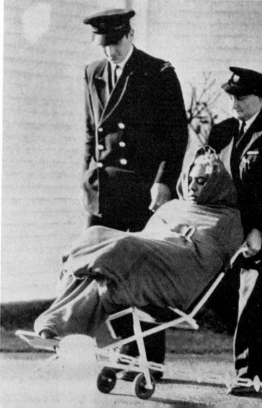

Hard times—Savundra signs on at the local employment exchange.

After his visit to the employment exchange, Savundra spends some of his three pounds' daily allowance from his wife on a modest sandwich lunch in Regent's Park.

An hour later he arrived at White Walls with Jimmy Newton. They rang the bell and waited for what seemed an interminable time before there were a series of scuffling and scraping noises from inside. Then the plethora of locks and chains attached to the White Walls front door were undone and Savundra opened it, wearing only his pyjama trousers, and promptly collapsed in front of his two visitors on the step. Newton and Campbell together carried him up to bed and rang the doctor. Before they left he appeared briefly to regain consciousness and managed to whisper a few words.

'I've got no money . . . next year my children won't be able to have strawberries for tea.'

CHAPTER SEVENTEEN

Exit

SAVUNDRA HAD FINALLY REALISED before his trip to America that if he failed to raise additional capital, the whole edifice would collapse; but he had no intention of collapsing with it.

Quite the contrary. As F.A.M. crumbled, he was already planning a phoenix which would rise from the ashes. In March 1966, he formed a completely new insurance company called Transway—a name he had picked up from watching his favourite television programme, 'The Power Game'.

Stuart Walker claims Transway was to have been the first really streamlined motor insurance company, issuing a certificate within seconds of an order and providing the motorist with a card which, in the event of an accident, would entitle him to a settlement cheque on the spot, immediately his damaged vehicle had been inspected. In the opinion of Jimmy Newton, Savundra was trying to attract trade from the Rolls-Royce end of the market, and the impressive line-up of directors would certainly seem to bear this out. Among them were Donald Campbell, Sir John Langford-Holt, the Conservative M.P. for Shrewsbury, the Hon. Maurice Howard, and the Earl of Lucan.

But however glittering the surface, the primary aim of Transway was obviously to replace F.A.M. when that company finally collapsed. In Norman Nail's words, it was to be 'Savundra's bolt-hole'.

The first step was to rent an impressive suite of offices in Pall Mall and furnish it luxuriously. The authorised capital was again to be £50,000 in £1 shares. Langford-Holt, Jimmy Newton, Maurice Howard and Donald Campbell were to be given 500 shares each on blank transfers, as were three F.A.M. executives, who were to move to the West End to head the administrative staff. Lucan was to have £2,500 fully paid-up shares. The balance of 44,500 shares was to be issued to another brand-new company called Interstate Trust. A revealing memo from Savundra at the time shows himself and Walker as owning one share each—but his green pen has subsequently been drawn through the lines referring to these and the two extra shares became part of Interstate Trust's holding.

Thus, when F.A.M. collapsed, the leading *dramatis personae* would not appear in the front line of the new structure.

When the mystery of the Interstate Trust shares was eventually probed, Stuart Walker attributed the holding to London solicitor, Richard Medley. Medley, in turn, admitted that the shares were registered in his name but made it clear that he did not buy them with his own money. He was, of course, merely the registered holder of the shares.

To complete the similarity of the *modus operandi* of Transway to F.A.M. there had to be a bank. Merchants and Finance Trust, of course, would shortly have outlived its usefulness. But in Savundra's scheme of things the making of money fast depended on having a place to which it could 'disappear', and the easiest method of achieving this was setting up an 'offshore' bank. The word 'offshore' has come to mean areas in the world where the financier is not subject to the stringent regulation of business found in most Western powers. The countries concerned are mostly tiny, and Liechtenstein is a classic example. Others where men can conduct their operations in a vacuum between tax authorities, as it were, are the Channel Islands, Bermuda and British Honduras.

Savundra decided to establish his new bank in the Channel Islands, and secured the services of a young man in Guernsey to act as his counsel. Mr. Vic de Graham Carey was a newly-qualified advocate; he was also the grandson of the late Sir Victor Grey, the island's bailiff (civil head) from 1936 to 1945. On 22nd February, 1966, young Mr. Carey walked through the narrow, winding street of St. Peter's Port to the Guernsey Royal Court building and registered the resoundingly-named Security Bank of London Ltd. As in Liechtenstein, the formalities were minimal. It was simply a matter of making a brief registration to accord with Guernsey law. The directors listed were Savundra; Walker; Paul Hagenbach, the Swiss lawyer; E. Margolies, Savundra's American friend; and Graham Dorey, de Graham Carey's partner.

The object of the Security Bank of London was to receive the expected rush of premium money from Transway and invest it. It would have a London office—indeed, like M.F.T. it was only registered abroad—but unlike M.F.T. it would offer private banking facilities—current accounts, deposit accounts, etc.—as well.

Meanwhile the most urgent problems which faced Savundra was the severance of his links with F.A.M. He had to get out before it was too late. Only if he could establish that he was not associated with F.A.M. when it failed would he avoid being sucked into the morass. He formulated his escape plan.

In the third week of June 1966, he summoned Walker to his house. He told him he was a sick man and would have to go to his Swiss clinic to rest. He also added that it was difficult for F.A.M. to raise money while he was the boss—people were prejudiced against him because of his colour. There was another problem, too. A book had just been published (*The Gnomes of Zürich* by T.H. Fehrenbach) which referred to his involvement in the old and (he'd hoped) long-forgotten Belgian affair. It was a gross libel on him, he told Walker, but he felt that it might also affect the raising of the necessary capital to save the company. He was still quite convinced that the money would come from America but it would probably be an advantage if he was disassociated from the affairs of F.A.M., if only on a temporary basis.

Now he proposed that Walker buy him out of his shareholding and go it alone. He was sure the company was still a viable proposition and Walker could see it through its difficulties. The raising of capital would have to be done by someone with maximum authority, and sufficient time and energy to devote to the task. His health was so poor he had no alternative but to sell and leave—it would be in the best interests for him. And, of course, he would come back shortly, when his head had cleared and he felt better, and help sort things out. It would be easier, then. The fuss would have died down. He realised that Walker did not have a great deal of liquid cash, so he would sell the whole of his shareholding for the laughably small figure of £2,529—providing Walker took over Savundra's debts to F.A.M. of £488,285.

At last Savundra had realised the chips were down and he must kiss farewell to his dreams of power-boats and all the dozens of other ideas—from offering three-wheeler cars a special insurance package to covering yachts and small craft and running a prep. school for learner drivers—he had mapped out for the future. His instinct for self-preservation had fully surfaced and it told him that the time had come to get out and throw somebody else to the lions—his closest colleague, Stuart de Quincey Walker.

Incredibly Walker agreed to the proposition. Possibly he was misled by Savundra's insistence that money would be made available from America but he should surely have known Savundra well enough to realise that if this was a genuine possibility, the last thing Savundra would do would be to resign. The most likely explanation is that, like practically everyone else associated with Savundra, he was mesmerised.

What Savundra was, in fact, saying was: 'You have the business. If it survives, I will return and reap the benefit. If it fails, you can carry the can.' To sell such a proposition required skill of the highest order, even allowing for Walker's trusting loyalty.

Savundra officially resigned from the board of Fire, Auto and Marine and all his other associated directorships on 22nd June. Three days later he flew to Switzerland.

Before he went he had made it abundantly clear to anyone who needed persuading that he was, in fact, a very ill man. He had phoned Nail at the Board of Trade to tell him. 'I may die. I have sold out to Walker. He has the responsibility now. But I don't want to let down all those poor people who insured with us, and my staff . . .'

Journalists who attempted to contact him were given the impression that he was in too delicate a state to concentrate on an interview. Jimmy Newton was present during one of these conversations and he listened as Savundra croaked breathlessly down the telephone about his heart. But when he hung up he was grinning. 'My God,' he said, 'I should have won an Oscar for that one.' Newton was taken aback. In all his time working for F.A.M. he had never seen Savundra drop his guard quite so completely.

It was to prove a salutary lesson, however. About a week later Newton spoke to Savundra on the telephone at the Hirslanden Clinic in Zürich. Now that Savundra had severed his connection with F.A.M., he wanted Transway to start operating. He knew this was impossible until the Board of Trade had been convinced that the company had a paid-up capital of £50,000. To achieve this he tried to persuade Newton to inform the Board of Trade that he, Newton, had £50,000 of Savundra's money 'in his client's account'. Of course, Newton, having the trusteeship of none of Savundra's money, refused, but the request demonstrates Savundra's brazen attitude. It did not occur to him that he was asking a lawyer to risk his professional reputation by telling a blatant lie—or, if it did, he regarded it as nothing more than a simple favour to a friend.

The Hirslanden Clinic, as might be expected, was another of Europe's five-star hospitals. Perched on a hill, it overlooked the outskirts of Zürich. Cheapest rooms cost at that time £12 a night;

Savundra, however, paid the top price of £25 for one of the best in the building.

Back at Jacqueline House Walker had frantically stepped up his sales campaign, apparently oblivious of the fact that the increase of premium income would have to be on a gigantic scale if there were to be any hope of saving the stricken ship.

Teams of selling agents drove round the streets of Cardiff and Glasgow, both fertile districts for cut-price insurance, bearing huge placards which proclaimed: 'This car is insured with the cheapest insurance company in Britain? Is yours?'

It may have boosted sales, but it was like trying to put out a forest fire with a bucket of water.

At the same time Walker put out a statement, both to brokers and the Press, saying there was no cause for panic, and there would be no trouble in meeting claims; he was confident the company would remain in business. And at this stage the Board of Trade still felt unable officially to admit to their suspicions. 'From the information available,' said a spokesman laconically, 'there appears to be no immediate danger of insolvency.'

As a final last-ditch move Walker had announced that F.A.M. was going to increase the cost of its premiums by thirty per cent from 1st July.

Ironically, this turned out to be the very day F.A.M. stopped trading. At the end everything happened very fast. It was soon apparent that Savundra had got out just in time.

On 26th June, only a day after he had left, F.A.M.'s latest young accountant, Cecil Jager, telephoned Tross Youle and asked if he could visit him. If Jager had been worried before, the departure of the company vice-chairman at a moment like this had made him much more so.

He arrived at Tross Youle's pleasant country house near Henley with Joseph Gordon, the barrister who had a few months before become general manager of F.A.M.

'The company is in terrible debt and we are all very suspicious,' he told Tross Youle. 'We are certain there is something terribly crooked going on.'

Tross Youle was deeply shocked. He was so little aware of the true nature of the situation that just one month previously he had written to Cecil Jager, pointing out that in accordance with his agreement he was entitled to take up another 2,500 shares in F.A.M. and asking for his account to be debited accordingly.

Even now he was unwilling to believe Jager's announcement that a collapse was inevitable. He was, however, sufficiently alarmed to consult a barrister friend, Bill Mars-Jones (now a High Court judge). Mars-Jones's advice was brief and to the point. He told Tross Youle to get expert advice, and put him in touch with the distinguished firm of City accountants, Cork Gully & Co., specialists in liquidation.

Next day a senior partner in Cork Gully, Mr. Gerhard Weiss, arrived at Jacqueline House. It was a routine matter—simply a case of an insurance company finding itself in financial difficulties.

Mr. Weiss wasted no time. When he discovered that the company's securities were being held by M.F.T. in Zürich, he at once demanded that they be produced. Walker agreed to fly that day to Switzerland to bring them back.

What Walker expected to achieve by visiting Zürich is difficult to guess. Perhaps he simply wanted to buy time. On this trip he visited Hagenbach, who made it clear that the share certificates were the property of M.F.T. Indeed Hagenbach made him sign a deposit receipt confirming that this was the case.

Next Walker visited Savundra at the Hirslanden Clinic where, unwittingly, he tightened the noose round his own neck still further. When Savundra heard that his former partner had signed a receipt for Hagenbach, he grew highly emotional. He made Walker sign a statement saying he had acted entirely on his own authority. The statement read:

> I, Stuart de Quincey Walker . . . solemnly declare that all and any deposits of money made by Fire, Auto and Marine Insurance Company either by me or by any other person/s with any of the bankers to the company including the place of business established in London by . . . Merchants and Finance Trust. . . . of which I have been the London manager, was so deposited either by me directly or under my specific instructions and authority to do so. I furthermore solemnly declare that all and any payments made by Merchants and Finance Trust Company were made with my specific authority and under my direct orders.

Exactly what happened at this extraordinary meeting—one of the last between Savundra and Walker—can never be known. It was undoubtedly melodramatic. Walker says Savundra maintained that his name, at this juncture, had to be kept in the background. His past (he was now forced to admit) would not bear scrutiny; if he was associated with F.A.M. it might jeopardise the injection of new money from the States and thus the company itself. Besides, Walker could not escape the fact that he *was* London manager of M.F.T. Walker remembers Savundra telling him: 'You're the only friend I've got', and then stumbling out of bed, taking the incriminating statement which he had prepared from his dressing gown pocket, and thrusting it into Walker's hand with the words: 'For my sake, Stuart, please sign this.' Walker did, and then, spellbound by the mixture of Savundra's arguments and the emotion with which they were delivered, flew sadly back to London.

Savundra, when faced with this account of events, attributed it to Walker's 'vivid imagination'. But he admitted that he felt Walker, by signing the document, had clearly confessed his guilt.

Walker reported to the Board and to Weiss that there was no chance of getting the shares back for the purpose of realising them. They were all tied up in a ten-year loan. He brought out a letter from Hagenbach, which spelt everything out all too clearly. It read:

To: Fire, Auto and Marine Co. Ltd.,
Attention of the Managing Director, Mr. S. de Quincey Walker.
London.
Dear Sirs,
   I am instructed by my clients Merchant and Finance Trust Company to advise you that they cannot agree to your request to make available to you any funds against your fixed deposit arrangements made with their London place of business, though without prejudice they will endeavour to find you a source of ready finance to help your fluidity position.
   Furthermore I am instructed to inform you that they have endeavoured in accordance with your request to make available to you as was done last year for a limited period and solely for the purpose of your audit the quoted securities you require, registered in the name of your Company, on the strict understanding that these securities are at all times the property of my clients and will be returned to them after presentation to your auditors.
   They further confirm their ability and willingness to comply with all and any of their legal obligations at all times.
          Yours faithfully,
               Dr. Paul Hagenbach.

Weiss was flabbergasted. So were F.A.M.'s directors. The news that the assets were tied up on a time deposit seemed to them incredible. In such a volatile business as insurance, where an avalanche of claims can take a company unawares at any moment, it is a basic maxim that investments must be quickly realisable into liquid cash—within a month, at the longest.

But if Hagenbach's letter was the first explosion to rock the framework it was only a hint of what was to come the next day, 29th June.

It will be recalled that the company's auditors had taken careful note of the details of the shares alleged to be held by M.F.T. and now Jager started to check up. *It took one morning on the telephone to confirm that the share certificates were forgeries.*

Lawyer John Stitt recalls receiving the news as one of the most dramatic moments of his professional career. His firm had been for some time employed both as Walker's personal solicitors and to act in difficult claims cases for F.A.M. He had a great personal liking for Walker and when he heard of F.A.M.'s difficulties had cut short his holiday and returned to London to try to help, rather than delegate the matter to a subordinate.

He was discussing with the late Maurice Finer, Q.C., the best way of presenting the winding-up petition, when he was called to the telephone. It was Jager to give the news of the forgeries. Suddenly an unhappy but by no means unique situation of a company being in financial trouble had become a gigantic case of fraud.

On the same day Nail visited Jacqueline House. He had with him an official letter from the Board of Trade demanding immediate clarification of the situation. At a board meeting held at Jacqueline House at 10 a.m. on Monday, 4th July, Weiss reported that Fire, Auto and Marine was insolvent and, more guardedly, that 'there were certain irregularities in the investment portfolio'. There were two alternatives, he told them. Either the company itself would have to file a winding-up certificate or the Board of Trade would be forced to do so. The latter course would be slower and costlier. Immediately the board agreed to adopt the first course and a Press statement to that effect was issued the same day.

The F.A.M. executives had of course suspected the company was in trouble. But they had all assumed they were dealing with a disastrous, but quite straightforward, case of civil debt when suddenly, as John Stitt put it, 'the criminal element flashed in.' It was later to become clear, of course, that the £500,000 bond shown to the auditors the year before had also been a forgery. In thinking Savundra had 'borrowed' it, Hatherall had been over-generous. But, as he puts it: 'If you don't live in a world where you anticipate fraud and somebody shows you a Bank of England certificate you assume it is genuine.'

News about the forgeries had not yet reached below boardroom level of Jacqueline House. Most of the staff believed that, in spite of all the rumours, the difficulties were only temporary. A deputation of the more senior employees informed the board that they were willing to take a cut of a month's pay, if it would help. Further down the scale the girl punch-card operators offered to forego £2 a week. The immense loyalty of the staff to their amiable Ceylonese doctor was touching but it was to no avail. The company was now in the hands of a liquidator in the person of Mr. Weiss. It was Friday and payday. Most of the staff were told not to come back on Monday.

The emotions of a crowd in a tense situation are fickle and when Weiss's assistant announced over the intercom that almost 450 people had lost their jobs, hopefulness and loyalty turned to anger. Pandemonium broke out. Furious staff members hurled typewriters out of windows; coffee machines were smashed, desks and safes ransacked and papers scattered all over floors. Some items, including company documents, were stolen or given away to passers-by in the street. One executive said melodramatically that it was like the fall of Saigon.

Meanwhile, Cecil Tross Youle, alone in his office, insulated from the hubbub all around, phoned his wife. 'The company is crooked,' he told her, 'we have gone bust and all my investments have gone.' Then he wandered through to the splendid boardroom. Standing on a table in the corner was a relic of happier days—a bottle of Dom Perignon champagne. He opened it and helped himself to a glass. At that moment Weiss bustled in.

'What's all this drinking?' he demanded.

'What would you do in the circumstances?' Tross Youle replied. 'You'd better join me.'

'I can't do that,' said Weiss, but he permitted himself a smile.

Tross Youle himself took the winding-up petition for F.A.M. to the Law Courts, then went to El Vino's in Fleet Street, where he ordered another bottle of champagne. The chairman, at least, was going down with flying colours. While he did so Cecil Jager and general manager, Joseph Gordon, went to the Fraud Squad.

On 2nd July, the day the liquidation of F.A.M. was announced, Walker again flew to Zürich where he witnessed a head-on confrontation between Hagenbach and Savundra in the Hirslanden Clinic.

Hagenbach says that it was at this meeting that Savundra told him where M.F.T.'s money was really invested—in twenty-year loans to himself (£380,000), Walker (£220,000) and other individuals and enterprises in England (£400,000). He says his reaction was one of total disbelief: 'This is crazy. In Switzerland this would be considered illegal. I don't know British insurance law well, but I cannot believe that an insurance company could be permitted to invest its reserves in long-term loans to its directors.'

'In England,' said Savundra, 'an insurance company can invest in anything.'

The picture of Fire, Auto and Marine as Britain's fastest growing and most revolutionary insurance company had shattered into a thousand fragments. And it did not take long before the Press began to study the pieces.

The *Sunday Times* and the *Daily Mail* led the way, and the *Sunday Times* published the result of a week-long investigation on Sunday, 10th July. An Insight reporter, following a hunch, had come to the same conclusion as Cecil Jager—that the only solution to the puzzle of the unrealisable assets was that they were forgeries. Where Jager had only needed to know that one or two of the certificates were forgeries before having ample evidence with which to present the Fraud Squad, the *Sunday Times* wanted everything cut and dried. It was already late afternoon on Friday, 8th July, and they needed proof if they were to have their story ready for Sunday. Harold Evans, managing director, telephoned the chairman of Burmah Oil and told him of the *Sunday Times'* suspicions. The Burmah chairman came straight back to London, and as Evans telephoned the other alleged issuers of shares on the F.A.M. list (G.U.S., Simon Engineering, Distillers, Beaverbrook Newspapers), other company chiefs all over the Home Counties' stockbroker belt hopped into company cars and drove through the night to their offices and records. The resulting discovery, of course, was that *all* the certificates were bogus.

In Zürich, however, the key witnesses kept a curtain of mystery drawn round the affair. In his clinic Savundra had himself guarded as if he were in a fortress and no Pressman could reach him personally or by telephone, cable or letter.

The only statement he did make was about his heart condition. In fact, so determined was he to prove that it was genuine that he issued a press release, saying his latest attack had been 'confirmed by electro-cardiograms taken independently by the greatest cardiologists in the U.S.A., England and Switzerland.'

Dr. Hagenbach, too, was unhelpful. He seemed to know little about M.F.T. and he denied that he had any knowledge of the connection between it and F.A.M. Gerhard Weiss also wanted to talk to Savundra. Almost immediately after the crash of F.A.M., Weiss had officially been appointed liquidator of the major part of the Savundra empire and he began a long and difficult investigation. He flew to Zürich, where Hagenbach told him he did not even know who owned M.F.T. but thought he/she lived in North Africa. He claimed that he only carried out instructions—it was not for him to worry whether the intentions behind instructions he received were proper or improper.

Weiss now went to Liechtenstein.

The tiny principality of Liechtenstein is run from one building, Government House, in the capital village of Vaduz. The ground floor is devoted to enquiries and administration, the first floor houses the Parliament, the second the Prime Minister's office, the third the police, and the top is given over to company records.

Because there is no railway station at Vaduz, Weiss had to get there from Switzerland by taxi. He called on the chief of police and told him that he had come to investigate the affairs of Merchants and Finance Trust. 'I know,' he said, 'that it is against the law in your country not only to breach the confidentiality of your bankers and lawyers but to request someone else to do so. Before I break the law, therefore, I'm telling you I'm going to do it.'

The police chief did not seem overconcerned. He gestured vaguely towards a pile of paper on his desk. 'We have already had an enquiry about this company,' he said. 'In fact I intended to deal with the matter this afternoon.' His intentions, however, were rather belied by his inability to find the right file, which was eventually located at the very bottom of the heap.

To make amends he invited Weiss to accompany a policeman who would go to see Herr Wiederin that same afternoon. The trip did not prove fruitful. Wiederin, in shirt-sleeves, met him in the garden of his green-painted chalet, which served as a house-cum-office, and they talked for an hour. Wiederin knew nothing about the company he was supposed to direct and had, in fact, already written himself a letter resigning from its board in the wake of the news from England. If there was little he could tell Weiss, he did at least produce copies of the loan agreements Savundra and Walker had drawn up.

For Weiss the trip to Switzerland and Liechtenstein was one of the first steps in an enquiry into F.A.M.'s vanished money which was to last ten years.

CHAPTER EIGHTEEN

Flight to Ceylon

ON 9TH JULY, 1966, Savundra disappeared. The reporters keeping a constant vigil on the clinic in Zürich, hoping to obtain an interview, had been given the slip. He had simply vanished. He had told no one where he was going. Finally, one caller met an office-girl who had seen him leave quietly through a side door. He had asked her if she could smuggle him out secretly ('to dodge some bloodhounds baying at my door') and she had shown him into the back streets where a black car was waiting to whisk him away. The girl gave her interviewer a guileless but revealing footnote to her description. 'It was rather strange, for although he had been admitted with a severe heart attack he was looking very well when I saw him. His stay seems to have done him a lot of good . . .'

In fact, as it soon emerged, Savundra had gone straight to the airport and caught a B.O.A.C. flight to Ceylon under the thinly disguised incognito of S. Nayagam. Simultaneously, Pushpam, who had been staying near him for a few days in Zürich's most beautiful hotel—the five-star Bellerive on the tree-lined bank of the lake—flew back to Britain.

The purpose of Savundra's flight to Ceylon was to put himself temporarily at least out of reach of the tentacles of the F.A.M. investigation. But when he landed at Colombo, there was a bizarre episode.

As he walked down the gangway of the aircraft he spotted a group of armed soldiers and policemen with dogs waiting at the bottom. Horrified, he collapsed, with an (undoubtedly genuine) heart attack.

By the time he was revived, however, he discovered he was not in jail but in an upstairs bedroom at his sister-in-law's house. The sol-

173

diers had come not to arrest him but one of his fellow passengers, Major-General Richard Udugama, the disgraced commander of the Ceylonese Army, who had led an unsuccessful coup against the Ceylon government six months previously.

Despite this unexpected hitch on his arrival, it was three days before Savundra's whereabouts were discovered. Then reporters began to lay siege to the house.

One such was Len Adams of *The People*. On 14th July, a Friday, Adams was looking forward to a holiday, when a phone call came through from his editor summoning him to an emergency conference in the office. The holiday would have to wait. Savundra was known to be in Colombo and *The People* wanted an exclusive interview.

With the help of the paper's top crime reporter, Roy East, a list of questions to be put to Savundra was worked out and later that Friday night Adams found himself on a plane bound for the East.

Once in Colombo he checked in at a huge Victorian monolith of an hotel in the town centre. He found he was not the only British journalist there and his colleagues immediately told him he had made a wasted trip—Savundra had annnounced he was not seeing anyone. There were guards at the gate of the house with shotguns, who had been ordered to fire on any intruders on sight.

Adams went down to the hotel swimming pool, had a swim and planned his strategy. He had met one Ceylonese journalist when he arrived at the hotel, Kalin Fernando, who seemed more ready to co-operate. Fernando himself had been cold-shouldered by Savundra and had told Adams straight away that he was a 'slippery' customer.

After his swim Adams sought him out and said he had decided to telephone Savundra. It went against all his instincts—it being much easier to put down a phone than slam a door—but at least there was the chance of speaking to him that way.

The first attempt at telephoning ended in thirty seconds. Adams got through to Savundra's sister, Mrs. Page, who made her position very clear. 'Dr. Savundra is a sick man,' she said curtly, 'don't call again', and she hung up.

Adams went to the bar, had a drink, and after an hour called again. It was a long shot but this second phone call had better results. On the other end of the line, it seemed, was one of the house servants. Adams was given the message: 'Ring at 9.30 p.m.'

It was a case of third time lucky. This time, to Adams' amazement, the easily-recognisable voice of Emil Savundra came over the line straight away. 'Hello, who's that?' Adams reminded him they had met, once before, at a press conference. Then he tried to persuade Savundra to meet him.

'There are so many conflicting stories,' he said. 'My editor feels it is only fair that you should be given the opportunity to clear them up. It is obvious you feel you've been maligned.'

The last line, at least, elicited a favourable response and got Savundra on to something which was rapidly becoming one of his favourite subjects. 'I have been ruined by the gutter press of Britain,' he said—the prelude to a long, impassioned diatribe on the evils of newspapers, interspersed with references to the state of his health.

'Well, at least I will be able to tell my readers how ill you are,' said Adams.

There was a pause. Eventually Savundra said: 'I will see you at 10.30 for ten minutes.'

Accompanied by Fernando, Adams travelled by rickshaw to the 'Millionaires' Row' of Ceylon—Barnes Place in the Cinnamon Gardens district of Colombo. Savundra's sister-in-law lived in a house with a supreme court judge on one side and a government minister on the other.

The house was huge and surrounded by dense jungle foliage. Armed guards with Alsatians waited in front of imposing steel gates. They allowed Adams to pass but told Fernando to wait. Adams went up the long drive and rang the bell. After a brief conversation with a woman in a sari, he was ushered up a flight of stairs and into a vast bedroom by two men in white coats.

Savundra, looking flaccid and pale, lay propped up on pillows on a massive double-divan bed. The room was fragrant with the scent of exotic perfume. A fan whirred softly overhead.

A moment or two passed and then Savundra opened his eyes and slowly reached out for a large bottle of pills resting on a thick red volume of Company Law. 'I am a sick man,' he whispered hoarsely. He eased himself up into a sitting position, pulled the pale green sheets around him and swallowed a number of pills. Then he clapped his hands and the servants in the room vanished. 'Before we start, let's get something straight. What I'm going to say must go on record . . . Mr. Adams, give me your credentials.'

Adams handed over his Press card. Savundra clapped his hands again. This time three servants entered, one of them carrying a portable tape-recorder. They were followed by Mrs. Page and her teenage son. Switching on the tape-recorder Savundra asked Adams to affirm his presence by speaking into the microphone.

Then, solemnly, he said: 'The time is 11.00 p.m. on the 15th of

July, 1966, and I am stating as follows to Mr. Leonard Adams, an official representative of *The People* in the presence of two witnesses—Mrs. Page and Master Page.

'I am considerably distressed, my health seriously affected, and my dignity and reputation injured by the publication of various news items in a newspaper called *The People*.

'I state that said publications are clearly defamatory and their imputations and innuendos false, even though parts of them may be quotations from other newspapers and other documents in other parts of the world.

'I intend taking legal action to the utmost limits of English law unless immediate amends are made by you.

'I finally instruct you to desist from any further publications of similar nature concerning me.

'End of mandatory notice delivered verbally and completed at five minutes past 11 on 15th July, 1966.'

When the recorder was switched off, Adams told Savundra he would relay his message to London. 'You will probably find they have been served with a writ already,' Savundra replied—a correct assumption. 'It may surprise you, Mr. Adams, but I am in receipt of all the newspapers from London. Nothing escapes my eagle eye.' And once again, as on the phone, he launched into a long attack on the Press, referring to them as 'the gutter-snipes of creation' and 'jackals feeding on the carcasses of the afflicted'. All this from the man who had once boasted that he liked to slip journalists £100 presents when they came to visit Jacqueline House.

At intervals, one of the servants would approach his master to plump up the pillows.

Adams was worried. The week before *The People* had printed a long article on Savundra, calling him 'this man of evil.' He wondered if Savundra thought he was a con-man who had got in to his room under false pretences.

Savundra finished and waved a hand. Everybody vanished again, leaving them alone. There was a pause. Overhead the large electric fan rotated slowly. The temperature outside was eighty-six degrees Fahrenheit.

'Now, Mr. Adams, I intend to shoot you,' Savundra said quietly. 'I have a pistol under my pillow and I am going to use it. Under Ceylonese law it is permissible to shoot intruders below the knee and that is what I propose to do. I consider you an intruder.'

As he elaborated on the effect a shot in the knee-cap would have, Adams reflected that he was dealing with a man who was obviously

Savundra is brought to trial at the Old Bailey.

Norman Nail of the Board of Trade.

Mr. and Mrs. de Quincey Walker with their solicitor, Mr. Fior (centre).

shpam and Emil during a recess in the hearing.

Judge King-Hamilton at the Old Bailey.

Judge Aarvold, Recorder of London.

"Is your cell insured against fire? Is your get-away car covered? What about that yacht you want in the Caribbean?"

Jak's cartoon in the *Evening Standard* of March 8th, 1968 comments on Savundra's sentence of eight years' imprisonment.

Home again—Emil is reunited with Pushpam on the day of his release.

sick and who seemed capable of doing what he had threatened to do—and even of digging up some obscure Ceylonese law to justify it.

'What the hell am I doing here?' Adams thought. 'I should be having a quiet picnic back home among the Surrey woods.'

'Dr. Savundra, hold on,' he said, 'I know you are a sick man, but I didn't create the situation you find yourself in. I have come to you as the representative of thousands of English people, who are crying out for some straight answers. As I said on the phone, the reports which have appeared have been second-hand, or garbled. I thought it was only fair to come direct to you . . .' The only thing seemed to be to go on talking, to try again and gain time. If Savundra did produce the gun, what could he do? The door seemed too far for escape that way. Would it be best to fall flat on the floor?

After about ten minutes he broke off, his throat dry. 'Dr. Savundra,' he said, 'have you got a glass of water?'

For the first time, Savundra smiled. He poured a glass of lemon juice from a jug besides his bed and handed it up. 'Mr. Adams,' he said, changing his mood in an instant to that of benevolent uncle, 'I like you. You are the first man I have spoken to who seems to appreciate my situation. You have been very patient. I think you understand how I am suffering.

'Ever since last week I have been hounded from pillar to post by so-called journalists. I have had enough. I don't want to see anyone any more. All I want is a complete rest so that I can return to London some day and scourge these filthy muck-rakers, as Jesus Christ scourged the money-changers in the Temple. And when I have done, they won't know what hit them. They have made my family suffer and they will suffer too.'

He took a drink from his glass of lemon juice. Adams remarked on the bottle of brandy at his bedside. 'Is that part of your medicine, too?' he asked.

'Unfortunately, no,' said Savundra with a faint smile. 'My only sustenance is forty pills a day and three injections up the tail.' He flourished a hand in the direction of the bedside cabinet, where there were more than twenty bottles of tablets.

'You see these bottles,' he said. 'My doctor says it is a wonder I am still alive. I need all these pills to keep my poor heart going. You can take it from me that if I was not stricken when I was, you would not be here hounding me. I was all set to expand F.A.M. through the length and breadth of Britain. We could not go wrong and, even if I say so myself, I was the man responsible for the success.

'When I moved to the company, I built it up to a fantastically successful business. Then I realised, after some time, that we were paying claims at the rate of £10,000 a day—yet our established brokers were bringing in only £250,000 per month. All the firm needed was fresh capital.

'I can assure you, Mr. Adams, I had plans to raise the money and carry on more successfully, but the hand of God struck me down. I could have done great things for the English people.'

He fell back on the green sheets and asked his visitor to excuse him for a few moments. Then, after taking another pill, he went on: 'Something went wrong with the firm after I pulled out. And now, all you damned Englishmen are trying to crucify me because I got away, leaving another Englishman holding the can. But you can tell your bloody countrymen this. I shall never help them again. They have picked my brains for too long.

'Now the country can go bust for all I care. In future, all my energies, God willing, will be devoted to building up my homeland, Ceylon.

'We have a culture to be proud of and we will rise again.'

Adams asked him when he would be returning to Britain.

'My first reaction is to say never,' he replied. 'But that is not true. I promise you that those who have done me injustice will bitterly regret they ever heard my name.'

At this point Savundra's sister glided into the room and rebuked him for talking too much. Turning to Adams, she said: 'I must ask you to leave now.'

Adams got up. 'I will report to the English people how sick you are, and I hope you will not now be persecuted.' He offered to shake hands.

Savundra said: 'I bid you good night,' and lay back on the pillows, closing his eyes.

But as Adams left, the familiar voice followed him down the stairs. 'I will have a drink with you in London,' it called faintly.

Shortly after the Adams interview Savundra agreed to see another Pressman, Arthur Cook of the *Daily Mail*. On this occasion the interview evidently did not end so peaceably. His own account of it, issued to the local Press (and hotly denied by Cook), claimed that Cook had seized him by the throat and shouted: *'You tell me what you did with the £384,554 15s. 6d. you stole. I want your confession now.'* Savundra said he was so incensed that he forgot his serious medical condition and hit Cook over the head with the drawer from his bed-side table. Then he chased him out of the room. At the top of the staircase he alleged Cook turned and shouted: *'Let him tell me what he did with the money, the bloody black crook.'* Savundra's statement added: 'I distinctly remember this last imprecation of his . . . before I collapsed in a heap with a coronary spasm.'

His disillusionment was all the more bitter because of his one-time enthusiasm for all things English. He had liked to call himself 'the original black Englishman' and continually reiterated his passion for his country of adoption. 'Black I may be,' he would say to his power-boating friends, 'but I think it is a damn poor show when an English-man has to go to America to get an engine for his boat.'

Now, beleaguered in his sister's house in Colombo, he was quoted as saying: 'I am thoroughly ashamed that I ever, as a matter of expe-diency, accepted, held and used British nationality.' Shortly after wards he applied to the Ceylon Ministry of Defence and External Affairs to regain his citizenship of Ceylon. Abruptly he was told that he must give a convincing reason why he ever gave it up in the first place before they would even consider it.

It was not only the British Press who were interested in Savundra's intentions. The British Foreign Office were concerned about attempts he might make to avoid extradition. A confidential internal memorandum introduced the subject as follows: 'I expect you will have seen our telegrams about the homing flight of *Rara Avis Zey-lonica* alias Dr. Savundra, whose activities have been so widely chronicled in the British and foreign newspapers of late . . .'

The writer also says that he had had news of Savundra in Ceylon 'enlivened by splendid reports of an alleged gladiatorial encounter between Savundra and the *Daily Mail* correspondent, Mr. Arthur Cook, as a result of which and on police advice Mr. Cook staged a tac-tical withdrawal to Singapore.' Finally, he observes, 'Meantime, and perhaps not surprisingly, uncorroborated rumours reach us that Savundra (who is married to the sister of Mr. Cyril Gardiner, the chairman and managing director of the Galle Face Hotel) is (pre-sumably as a means of bringing his ill-gotten gains to Ceylon) offering financial participation in a number of local ventures such as an hotel-building project, the purchase of American aircraft for Air Ceylon, etc., etc. . . .'

Despite this touch of levity the Foreign Office were determined that Savundra should be brought to trial in Britain.

In spite of his repeated statements that he would not see anyone from the Press, Savundra could not, in fact, resist the challenge.

Deserted by all but his family and closest friends he had an urge to try and justify himself in the public eye.

One journalist who interviewed him did so when his ex-Commanding Officer in the Ceylon Engineers, Colonel Fernando, then an extra A.D.C. to the Governor General, was present. Most of his comments were addressed to the Colonel.

'What can one do, sir?' he said, gesticulating excitedly. 'One thing you taught us, sir—do your bloody job. If you can't do your bloody job, get out.'

And again: 'The honour of the regiment is at stake, sir. Your faith in me and the faith of a few like you must be upheld.

'Of course I will go back and fight. How could they think otherwise. Is Britain so broke that she can't wait four weeks, six weeks, eight weeks for a man to recover his health? In that country they let a dog rest to mend his leg. They could at least extend a similar courtesy to me.'

Ceylonese newspaper reporters, too, pressed for interviews with their country's most notorious son. The yarn he spun one of them was that he had worked his way up from assistant manager to the post of deputy chairman; then, recently, he had found that two and two in the company's figures added up to 5½ and, as any good businessman might, had felt it was time to sell. 'I sold my shares to Mr. Walker for £340,000 . . .' he explained. The reason the company had eventually collapsed was that others had ganged up against it.

On another occasion he said: 'Perhaps it is time the true facts of all the cases I was involved in were known,' he continued, 'and if they are, the repercussions—I am not exaggerating—will be felt in a good many parts of the world. I have held the can long enough for too many people. But perhaps I should have the true facts known only post-humously, else I may become posthumous minutes after the facts are known.'

He left his Ceylonese interviewers with an impression of dazzling verbal skill. One paper was quite rapturous: 'What amazed us was the lightning quickness with which his brain worked. Asked a hot question, he would avoid it so brilliantly that his answer would leave you thinking that he had, in fact answered the question.'

At this time, too, his cardiograph and X-rays showing the delicate condition of his heart became permanent props—capable of being produced to convince anyone he was a sick man.

Meanwhile in England, the rumour was going round that Savundra did not have a heart condition at all and had just run away. Loyally Walker retorted: 'All I can say is that he must be a very clever man indeed to have fooled the many specialists who have examined him.'

At the same time Walker was doing his best to hold things together. 'There is nothing wrong with *my* heart,' he declared, 'I am ready to help the Board of Trade or Scotland Yard.'

Tross Youle was also putting as good a face on matters as possible.

'The failure of the company,' he said in July, 'is really quite a straightforward issue. The company was going well, going like a bomb really. Our premiums were low, but not ridiculously low. One of our main factors was certainly our belief that it was necessary only to have a London head office. It was a grave mistake not to have representatives and offices in the provinces.'

Tross Youle also spoke of £4,000,000 expected from an American company. Like Savundra, he blamed the Press.

'Had stories not broken out in the Press we could have expected that money to pay off the claims. There has been tremendous loyalty from the staff. Many have come along to ask if Mr. Walker and I start in business again, will we let them know. I am afraid this will not be so. Mr. Walker is the most honest man to every degree but we won't go into business again together. After a thing like this it is better to break away.'

CHAPTER NINETEEN

The Return

WHATEVER TROSS YOULE AND Walker believed, there was no doubt how the public felt. The rumours which for three years had been whispered in business circles were at last public knowledge. There was much angry speculation about how a man with Savundra's past could do what he had done.

'People in Britain probably knew a bit about the good Dr. Savundra,' commented *The Economist* wryly, 'so why did 400,000 car drivers not get to hear of it?' Was it something to do with a tradition in British business circles which said: 'Don't tell anyone, least of all the papers?' Or was it due to the tradition in British newspaper offices which said: 'Don't print a word, he's got a good lawyer?'

In the House of Commons Mrs. Barbara Castle, the then Minister of Transport, warned motorists insured by F.A.M. that they must immediately take out new policies. Many, however, were unaware that they were no longer covered. As a demonstration of judicial sympathy, one offender was let off with the nominal fine of 5s. The crash came in the middle of the holiday period when many policy-holders were abroad and not in touch with the daily news. Others had effected their insurance through garages or brokers and were in many cases unaware of the name of their company.

When an insurance company failed at that time there was no redress for the customers. Unlike a member of the public who suffers loss through the professional negligence of, say, a solicitor, there was no corporate body to take over the responsibility. The Motor Insurers Bureau, which is jointly financed by all motor insurance companies, would pay out claims to third parties injured by an uninsured driver—but the driver himself had no cover.

Thus the F.A.M. crash brought misery in its wake. Out of 400,000 motorists on the books there were 43,000 with outstanding claims. Some of them were tragic cases like Mrs. Amy Wilson from County Durham. Her husband was killed in a car crash and F.A.M. was due to pay her £1,250 in compensation. Her husband had only been earning £18 a week and there were no savings and no house. When F.A.M. failed to pay she was forced to go out to work, although she was not really fit to do so. Another crash widow, Mrs. Agnes Morgan, found herself trying to live on her pension of £4 10s. a week when her unpaid entitlement from F.A.M. for the death of her husband was £1,000. And these were not isolated instances.

There were others forced to reinsure, however, who were better able to speak up for themselves than elderly widows living far from London.

Outside Jacqueline House there were extraordinary scenes as crowds of angry motorists besieged the building demanding to have their claims paid or their money back. Security men on the double doors had to struggle to keep them out. One woman, mother of two Mrs. Mary Wightman from Essex, managed to slip through the cordon and stage a six-hour sit-in protest.

While the public besieged Jacqueline House the Press were keeping a round-the-clock watch on Pushpam and Walker. White Walls was virtually under siege. Savundra's gardener stayed on full-time to deter callers, trimming lawns during the day, sleeping in at night. On the gravel driveway stood two rarely-used motor cars—a fawn Jaguar and an Aston Martin. At first Pushpam would have nothing to do with the doorstep journalists who pounced on her every time she made an appearance, but as the days passed she became more friendly.

'I am very worried about my husband,' she told one. 'I have booked a call to Ceylon. Please let me know if you hear anything before I do.' She added that her husband was under terrible strain and might well have committed suicide, had it not been for the family's Catholicism.

Even the most hardened observer developed something akin to sympathy for the loyal wife, and when a brawny man in his shirt-sleeves got out of his car and shook his fist in the direction of the house, shouting: 'Come on out. I want my insurance money!' he was sharply told by the doorsteppers to clear off.

Walker's time was spent between the Board of Trade and the Press, when he was not locked in his office or his house wrestling over the problems with which he had saddled himself. At last the truth dawned on him. But not until he had heard confirmation that Savundra was in Ceylon—and had not returned to Britain as he had hoped—did his intense loyalty begin to wear thin.

'I can see all too clearly who has been left holding the baby. I am the mug,' he told one journalist.

But not all the meetings he attended were so official. Ever since the early days of F.A.M. Savundra had sought to cut his ties with the underworld. With money pouring in he had wanted to establish a way of life in which his former dubious associates had no part. It was an attitude which was not generally approved of. Now gangster chief Billy Hill summoned Walker to come and see him. 'I never thought he smelt right,' he said, referring to Savundra. 'I am going to give you some advice. I know this man and I tell you that you must destroy him before he destroys you.' He went on to warn Walker that unless he firmly pinned the responsibility on Savundra, he would surely go down with the sinking ship. Frank Prater, who had helped Savundra in his impecunious days, also tried to help Walker.

His solution was simple. 'Go to the office', he told him, 'and get the bloody books. That's all you have to do.' Without the books, he explained, the Board of Trade would be helpless. All the evidence would be removed and the investigations would grind to a halt.

There was a further advantage to the Prater plan. With possession of the books Walker would be the only person in a position to collect the outstanding premiums owed by brokers all over the country. Some estimated the amount at something like £1,500,000 but more conservative estimates put it at £500,000. Just the same it was a lot of money.

Walker was aghast. To do anything so obviously deceitful was not in his nature—even to save his own skin. Exasperated, Prater begged him to give someone else the office keys and tell him to collect the books. Walker would not budge.

'Walker was no real con-man,' Prater says today.

A more conventional proposal to save the day came from a Dr. Benjamin Cohen, Brighton financier, one of the minor characters who flitted across the stage at this time full of bright ideas—saving companies, apparently, being something at which he specialised. A long statement of his record and plans arrived in the Jacqueline House boardroom. He would house the company temporarily in Brighton, it seemed, and take it on a 'no cure no pay' basis. No one appeared particularly impressed and he faded off the scene. A Mr. Michael Knowles, who ran a company called Irish American, also made advances with a view to a take-over. This last association would have been unlikely to do the company much good, Irish-American itself being about to crash, but in any case Arthur Cheek, the Official Receiver, was remaining resolutely of the opinion that new life could never be breathed into the corpse of F.A.M. As Walker put it: 'Only a miracle can save us now.'

On his own account Savundra had, as he thought, one last trump card to play. He sent a cable from Ceylon to the Prime Minister, with copies to Barbara Castle and Douglas Jay, then President of the Board of Trade, suggesting the nationalisation of car insurance including, of course, his own company.

The winding-up meeting of Fire, Auto and Marine was held on July 24th, 1966. The Fraud Squad were already investigating Savundra's empire and after the company was wound up the Board of Trade also mounted an enquiry under Section 165 of the 1958 Insurance Companies Act. This provides for the appointment of an inspector if fraud or misfeasance is suspected. The Board of Trade had come under much heavy fire for their failure to uncover the facts of F.A.M. before it was too late, but their reasons for delay have already been explained. The fact was, as Savundra had been known to say, anyone could drive a horse and cart through the 1948 and 58 Companies Act—if the Board were to wrongly suspect fraud or misfeasance, they could be taken to court for grave defamation.

Gradually some of the facts became clear. F.A.M. had a total deficit of almost £3m, out of which £300,000 was owed to the 43,000 policy-holders who had outstanding claims. The exact figure F.A.M. was owed was to take a long time to establish as the accounts, mainly because of the computer, were in a chaotic state. The estimated figure of £1,500,000 due from brokers turned out to be a wildly optimistic figure: what had happened was that many brokers had been sent incorrect statements. Because of the computer's incapacity to handle changes, some of these demanded money for policies which had been cancelled—one broker's statement showed £600 as owing instead of the correct figure of £20; in another case a demand for nearly £400 was eventually withdrawn and £10 accepted as settlement.

Some accounts sent to the larger brokerages revealed even more serious exaggerations—in one case £13,000 instead of £5,000. One top broker, Frank Briscoe, reflected the general feeling among the more established firms when he criticised F.A.M. for the way its accounts contained duplications and charges for policies which had been cancelled and which often did not include credits due.

An even more unfortunate by-product of the fallibility of the computer system, from F.A.M.'s point of view, was that inaccuracies in accounts became well-known to the less scrupulous brokers, many of whom anyway were notoriously tardy in settling their accounts, who used it as an excuse for even more delay. Further, there were private

motorists who cashed in by sending in completely false claims—
knowing that F.A.M.'s books were so disorganised that they would be
quite likely to collect. Indeed many succeeded.

In mid-November, the Official Receiver, Mr. Arthur Cheek,
passed a ten-page report to the President of the Board of Trade. He,
in turn, sent it straight to the Director of Public Prosecutions for a
decision on whether criminal charges could be brought. The police,
however, were very far from completing their investigations and no
immediate action could be taken.

The man at the centre of the storm was still in Ceylon but less than a
month after the completion of the Cheek report he was on his way
back to England. He had decided to return.

For many, his action of voluntarily stepping into the lion's den
poses an insoluble puzzle. True, he would shortly have had to leave
Ceylon with the expiry of his temporary visa, but there are various
countries in South America which do not have extradition treaties
with Britain where he could have found refuge. So *why* did he come
back.?

Some say the clue is to be found in his vanity. Yet the reasons go
deeper than that. Savundra was a gambler who always believed he
would win—whatever the odds. Who was to say he could not do it
again?

To stay away from Britain might have been prudent. But to return
was the ultimate challenge, and in his eyes not to return would have
been an admission of guilt and weakness. He had fooled governments
before. And after all he had opted out of F.A.M. *before* the crash.
Things had only gone wrong after the hand-over. So back he came.

One problem he did not have to anticipate on his return, incidentally, was that of personal re-insurance. Emil Savundra was not
himself one of the 400,000 policy-holders of Fire, Auto and Marine.
The certificate for his maroon-coloured Rolls-Royce was in the name
of Co-operative Insurance Company.

Typically, his return was far from a straightforward operation.

He had prefaced it some time earlier with a letter to the Official
Receiver, the main purpose of which seems to have been to demonstrate that some of the world's most eminent doctors had insisted he
be treated lightly. The letter said:

> I confirm to you officially that I suffered a coronary thrombosis
> in May this year, confirmed by Dr. Samuel Oram, Chief Car-
> diologist, King's College Hospital, London, Dr. Alec Wingfield,

Chief Cardiologist, Willesden General Hospital, Dr. Charles Friedberg, Chief Cardiologist, Mount Sinai Hospital, New York, Dr. Edward Partinope, Chief Cardiologist, New Jersey Hospital, and various other eminent cardiologists, every one of whom has confirmed the diagnosis categorically by reason of the electrocardiograph and other findings. The result is that *I am suffering from severe angina pectoris* which will be no doubt vastly aggravated by cold, strain, effort and anxiety.

Despite these health problems, Savundra, immaculately dressed in a dark suit, white shirt and blue tie, boarded an Air Ceylon VC 10 at Colombo airport bound for London, via Karachi and Rome. He told reporters: 'I have an appointment I intend to keep.'

The appointment with Mr. Cheek was fixed for 9th January, 1967.

Savundra spent two nights in Rome at the Lux Hotel, a second-class establishment near the railway station, and then vanished. He left the hotel without breakfast, announcing that he was going to the City Air Terminal, but the airport had no record of a departing passenger called Savundra.

Reporters were convinced that his return to England was a hoax. However, he reappeared two days later in a small hotel near St. Peter's. On 17th December he drove to the air terminal, not to resume his journey, but to meet his family whom he had asked to join him in Rome.

White-haired and with a pronounced limp, he was unusually amiable towards the reporters who surrounded him. In his hand was the inevitable small attaché case. 'This is not full of money, you know. It contains winter woollies for the children. I myself have not got a penny. All I got out of the insurance business was a heart attack.'

Clearly he felt no apprehension about his appointment with Mr. Cheek. His spell in Ceylon had completely re-established his old self-confidence.

'I will conduct a symphony orchestra,' he declared. 'I will write the score and the authorities in Britain will have to play under my baton.'

Then he announced he had decided to stay in Rome over Christmas with his family. 'They are more important to me than the whole British public. We will go to London in the New Year. We will stay together now and only force will part us.'

The date of his appointment, 9th January, passed, however, and still he lingered on in his small forty-shillings-a-night *pension*. His heart was playing him up again. Visitors were shown copies of his cardiograph and hospital bills as 'proof' that his condition was genuine. A new appointment was fixed for 23rd January.

Surrounded by his usual battery of pill bottles Savundra now issued a challenge to the B.B.C. He would, he claimed, appear before a television 'jury' to explain his actions. His fee would be £100 per second and with an hour's programme earning £360,000, he would donate the proceeds to F.A.M. to pay out to disappointed creditors.

'A hundred pounds a second' became the cry whenever he was asked any question regarding F.A.M., although he would talk as freely as ever on his two pet subjects—his health and the obnoxiousness of the Press.

Then, to everybody's surprise, he stepped out of his *pension* one morning and caught the plane to London. It is a measure of the close surveillance under which he had been kept that the fact that he was heading for London became known and such a large crowd was waiting for him at Heathrow that the police had to escort him through the barriers.

Peter Earle of the *News of the World* was one of the journalists to meet him. They were old acquaintances.

Dressed in a Savile Row suit and carrying a rolled umbrella, Savundra strutted across the tarmac towards the airport bus. 'I am poor as a church mouse now,' he proclaimed, 'and I wish to demonstrate my poverty by riding on humble public transport.'

'My dear Doctor,' said Earle, 'you have really torn the seat out of it this time. Not even you can beat this rap, and you have beaten some in your time.'

'Nonsense,' snapped Savundra, 'I am like General MacArthur. He said: "I shall return" when the Japs drove him out of the Pacific. And I, the great Savundra, am returning in likewise fashion.' Then he smiled. 'I've had fifteen pills already today. They are nitroglycerine, you know. I feel I am going to explode at any moment.'

As usual he was vociferous on the subject of the Press. Asked why he thought the Press had been persistent, he replied by pulling up his coat sleeve to expose his coloured skin. 'That is why,' he said. 'Why else would they have hounded me so much? There have been other insurance scandals recently and they have not received the same treatment.'

One thing he was determined to demonstrate was the fact that he was broke. 'If I cannot get a job,' he declared, 'I shall demand my rights as an Englishman who has paid his taxes and demand national assistance for my wife and five children.'

He was as good as his word. After a day at White Walls in a state of siege, with the wrought-iron gates barred and his faithful gardener on guard, the man who one year before had been living like a millionaire emerged at 10 a.m. on Monday, 16th January, got into a friend's car and was driven to the Labour Exchange in Regent's Park Road.

The spectacle of Dr. Emil Savundra painfully climbing the stairs, followed by a crowd of photographers, to the yellow-painted vacancy section on the first floor was described by one newspaper as 'the oddest sight of the year so far'.

Savundra found himself sixth in the queue. 'It's nothing to wait three hours,' a fellow unfortunate told him, but he was lucky. The manageress of the Employment Exchange accorded him V.I.P. treatment. As he was ushered down the corridor to her private office he walked past posters urging him to 'Drive a London ambulance', take 'a secure job as a postman', even, ironically, 'Enjoy a brighter future with the Prison Service.'

His visit did something to restore his faith in Britain. The interview lasted seventy minutes. Afterwards he said: 'They could see the impossible situation I was in and went out of their way to be kind. They took my coat, gave me a cup of tea and offered me a cigarette.

'I told them that I could not dig roads but my doctors say that I am fit for light sedentary work. Perhaps with my experience I can be of some use to the country's export trade. They filled in the necessary forms for me and promised to make all the arrangements.

'Damn it, this is the only civilised way to behave. This is cricket. This is what the Union Jack is all about.'

As he passed the queue of fellow applicants on his way out, one of them stood up respectfully. It was his former gardener at White Walls. And in the crowd outside one woman who had been a policy-holder with F.A.M. said: 'I know him. He was such a nice gentleman. I do hope he gets a good job.'

Another bystander was less sympathetic. Taking off his hat with a sweep, he shouted sarcastically: 'Let's have a whip round for poor Mr. Savundra.'

Determined to demonstrate his poverty, Savundra walked from the Exchange to Regent's Park, stopping to buy a sandwich on the way ('My wife gave me £3 this morning for small expenses'), which he proceeded to eat sitting on a park bench, feeding the crumbs to the pigeons. It made wonderful press material.

Making his way back to White Walls on foot, however, he met an old acquaintance to whom he confided the real humiliation he felt at having to 'sign on'. He spoke of his loyal wife and wonderful children.

'I used to have many friends, but not one has come near since my return. In a situation like this you find out who are your fair weather friends and who are your foul weather friends. Last year I got 650 Christmas cards. This year I had two. They were waiting for me when I came home. One from my gardener and one from the man who holds the burglar alarm keys. Apart from my family I am completely deserted and alone.'

It is not surprising that Tross Youle and the other F.A.M. directors should now be steering clear of the man to whom they had once been devoted. It is not surprising either that men like Lord Lucan and John Langford-Holt, director of Transway, with whom he had once been friends, should be acting in a similar manner. Like F.A.M.'s directors, they felt they had been betrayed.

Transway and the Security Bank of London folded quietly, but not without one odd episode. When the bank was wound up, a typical example of the confusion which forever seemed to be associated with Savundra's dealings came to light. It had been stated that the nominal capital was £2,500,000 and paid-up capital £150,000. Apparently a clerical error had been made. The shares were worth a shilling each—not a pound. So the paid-up capital was really only £7,500.

Savundra's closest associate of all, Stuart Walker, was not in a position to meet him on his return. He had temporarily left the country.

First, in the midst of his round of meetings with officials and the underworld, Walker, with an odd sense of timing, married in secret. His bride was a pretty twenty-five-year-old blonde fashion designer called Carol Filer. The wedding took place at the Register Office close to his Hampton Court home with only his own and the bride's mother present. Immediately after it the newly-weds went to Holland on a protracted honeymoon.

Before leaving Walker had picked up £20,000 as an advance payment on the sale of his house. Now, with his career as an insurance tycoon in ruins, he returned to the only world he really understood. In Holland he chartered a sixty-foot converted barge called the *Vrouw Aleida*. She was fitted with twin diesels and had a cruising range of 1,400 miles.

He then set off through the French canals for the Mediterranean. Walker, too, was pleading poverty. Pitiful reports of the honeymooning pair filtered back to their friends in England. 'I have just

£200 left in the world,' Walker went on record as saying. 'I could survive the winter if the winter is not too long.' From Nice a postcard
arrived for a friend reporting that he and Carol were having to collect
empty wine and milk bottles to sell in order to buy food.

One friend who did not have an opportunity of proving his loyalty
in the hour of need was Donald Campbell. On 4th January, 1967,
whilst Savundra was dragging his feet in Rome, Campbell died on
Lake Coniston in a final attempt on the world water-speed record.

CHAPTER TWENTY

Trial by Television

SAVUNDRA'S ENCOUNTER WITH THE Official Receiver finally took place on 23rd January. On the following afternoon he received a writ for £386,534.

At the same time Walker, who had by now returned to London, was served with one for £216,762.

What upset Savundra most of all at this time, however, was not his writ but the attitude of the Press and the public. Whenever he appeared anywhere a crowd would gather and there was always somebody to hurl abuse. And the publicity accorded to his visit to the Labour Exchange had sparked off yet more criticism.

Why, asked a Labour Member of Parliament, was an unemployed company director taken into a private office while five men were left waiting in a queue? Why was he allowed to be photographed on the premises with an official?

Most of all Savundra was hurt and appalled by his private mail. A David Hawkins of Hadlow in Kent wrote to offer him a job as a petrol pump attendant to 'give him a chance to talk with any former policy-holders' and there were other sarcastic suggestions from anonymous writers.

'You should find new work sweeping the roads,' declared one un-signed effusion, postmarked Ealing, 'also your wife washing floors.'

Another read: 'It is only in a shamefully overcrowded country like this that you would be allowed to set foot in. The Germans had an answer for people like you. We do not like your face here.'

One writer threatened his life: 'I will get you and if I can't get you I will get your family.'

Savundra commented: 'In spite of the few savages which you still seem to have left, I am convinced that Britain does not consist of bar-

barians. I am worried, however, about racialism. It is a horrible thing now creeping into Britain.'

It was a restatement of his belief that if he could only get face to face with his critics he would win them over to his side.

Emil Savundra's fateful decision to confront David Frost on television was taken on the spur of the moment.

He had been watching, along with eight million others in Britain, the 'Frost Programme', having just returned to White Walls after a week at Barnet Hospital. The programme happened to feature a sketch on motor insurance. One of Frost's team, Barry Cryer, had picked up the idea from watching a commercial about Northern Assurance, which showed a man leaning over a castle wall saying 'Insure with us' and thumping the wall to show how solid it was. Cryer had a desk built, with all its legs sawn through. He sat behind and, assuming a Ceylonese accent, began to extol the merits of cut-price insurance. 'I advise you to buy insurance companies,' he said, thumping the desk, which promptly collapsed.

At the end of the show the studio telephone rang and one of Frost's researchers answered it. A buzz of interest went round the room when he was heard to say, 'Yes, Dr. Savundra . . . Yes . . . Yes.' Director Steve Minchin remembers that the immediate thought in everyone's minds was that the skit had upset Savundra and that he was ringing up to complain. In fact, quite the contrary was the case. 'Oh, I'm glad you enjoyed it, Dr. Savundra,' the researcher was saying. His listeners exchanged astonished glances, and then someone said: 'Try and get him on the programme.'

So the question was put: 'Well, if you enjoyed it so much why don't you come on the show?'

Savundra put up only token resistance. He said he would have to think about it, but ten minutes later he was on the telephone again, agreeing to be interviewed.

Perhaps his motive in ringing up the first time had been precisely to be made such an offer. In any case once it had been made it could not be refused. It had become another challenge and even now, in what seemed to everyone who knew him a reckless decision, his nature triumphed over logic. He still felt he could come off best after any confrontation; and this was a chance of achieving at one fell stroke what he most wanted—to put across his own personality to a huge public.

Now he told the organisers of the programme: 'I only cross swords with the real masters . . . and since David Frost is a real master I will cross swords with him.'

And so it was immediately arranged—for the next week. This time there was no question of a demand for £100 a second. A fee was discussed but Savundra refused. 'anything you would normally pay, send to a children's charity,' he told them. (It would have been 45 guineas.)

David Frost was at the time Britain's top-rating T.V. personality. His interview programme was compulsive viewing, and his mixture of charm and abrasiveness was either loved or hated by millions.

The news of the coming confrontation between Savundra and Frost created immense interest. It would be a memorable clash of personalities in which neither party could afford to appear the loser. It was Frost, however, who had the shuffling of the pack.

He arrived at the Rediffusion studios at Wembley Park sharp at 10 a.m. on Friday, 3rd February—the day of the show. He was on the crest of the wave. The night before he had pulled off an astonishingly successful interview with the then Foreign Secretary, Mr. George Brown (now Lord George-Brown). The morning papers were full of it. One of them cynically described it as the 'best party political broadcast of the year'.

Frost had managed to put George Brown so much at his ease that he dropped the defensive air he so often adopted when being interviewed and came across with all the spontaneity of a man chatting over a social drink with his friends. The studio party given afterwards was euphoric with Frost and Brown indulging in an orgy of mutual congratulations.

The considerate and sympathetic treatment accorded to George Brown was not, however, to be repeated in the case of Emil Savundra. From the very beginning Frost decided that Savundra was to be given a rough passage. It was not a fencing match which was being planned but an assassination. At the conference on the morning of the broadcast his first question was: 'Who have we got to confront him with?'

His staff told him that most of the studio audience was composed of victims of F.A.M.

'Right', he said to researcher Jeanne le Chard, 'are they really mad at him? We'll need to have someone who is going to break down that lovable avuncular front of his. And by God, will he be all lovable if he can.'

There was some dismay when it was learned that the average

member of the audience—mostly garage proprietors—had only lost something in the region of £80. In Frost's view this was not enough to create a sense of outrage. Then at the last minute it was learned that there were a couple of widows of crash victims who had not been compensated.

The trap was set. Now there remained an afternoon of suspense while they waited to see whether their victim would appear, or whether, at the last moment, he would opt out. It was only minutes before the programme was due to start that Savundra arrived at the studios in a black, chauffeur-driven limousine. He was immediately surrounded by reporters and an angry crowd. There were shouts of 'Lynch him, lynch him', as police struggled to keep the demonstrators at bay.

Two plain clothes detectives, who had been mingling with the crowd because of a rumour that Frank Mitchell, 'The Mad Axeman', who had recently escaped from Dartmoor, would be one of those appearing, lined up on either side of Savundra and escorted him to the studio.

Inside the atmosphere was electric. The mood of the hand-picked audience changed from nervous expectancy to something nearer hysteria as Savundra, immaculately dressed as usual, stepped on to the studio floor and seated himself next to David Frost.

The programme which followed is now part of television history.

It started quietly enough with Frost giving a brief resume of Savundra's career and some broad details about what had happened to the premium income of F.A.M. There was some almost light-hearted banter about Savundra's claim to be a secret agent for the Vatican—and then the interviewee made his first mistake.

In reply to some attempted heckling from the audience he snapped: 'I am not going to cross swords with the peasants. I came here to cross swords with England's greatest swordsman.'

If he intended to flatter Frost with this remark, it fell lamentably flat. Instead, by calling the audience peasants, he intensified the feeling against him. Savundra, too, in reacting to the heightened animosity in the studio, perceptibly hardened and any trace of charm disappeared in the supercilious attitude he adopted for the rest of the programme.

Those who knew Savundra well realised that he had not intended the word 'peasant' to be as insulting as it was taken to be. In Ceylon it was applied to a social class, but it did not imply stupidity or boorishness.

Savundra had grown to use the word without grasping its full derogatory meaning.

'Nobody is a peasant,' said Frost. 'They are the people who gave you money.'

'They have given me nothing at all'.

This elicited and angry chorus of 'Oh yes we have' from the audience, and it was suggested, sarcastically, that should Savundra return the money he had been given, he could gladly have back his policy documents.

To give Savundra his due, he remained remarkably calm as point followed damning point. Occasionally he would snatch off his horn-rimmed glasses and wave them menacingly at Frost as he made some emphatic denial but on the whole of the two, it was Frost who was the less collected.

The animosity towards Savundra, however, mounted. It reached its peak when the two widows in the audience were singled out, almost it seemed by chance. One alleged that when her solicitor tried to contact F.A.M., there were constant delays, that they kept 'messing us about', would not meet the full claim, and kept offering, instead, £500. The woman said she had been left with three children to provide for.

Savundra asked her when the accident had happened. It was nearly two years previously.

Why, then, asked Savundra had the solicitor let the case hang around for two years. 'The only possibility,' he said, 'is that there was a material undisclosure and that the company offered you a £500 ex-gratia.'

The woman strongly denied this. Savundra came back with: 'You don't know about it, do you? I thought the poor gentleman was dead.'

Another widow claimed that when her husband was killed, she was supposed to receive £7,000. The claim was settled in April, 1965, but the cheque was held up until June 'when, of course, it bounced'.

Savundra: 'All these and other heartrending stories which I have heard make me realise only too well that my selling out was the wisest thing I ever did.'

Voices: 'For you. What about us?'

Only at this stage did Savundra really bite back. Towards the end of the interview Frost had openly accused Savundra of being concerned in a 'fake deal' and challenged him to explain how, by his resignation, he had removed himself from all moral responsibility.

With the two men leaning forward in eyeball-to-eyeball confrontation, so that their foreheads almost touched, Savundra
launched himself into a violent attack on the British democratic process, which, he insisted, was to blame for what had gone wrong with
F.A.M.

By the time the interview had ended Frost was quivering with
indignation and the audience tense with anger.

Savundra too was shaking with rage. While the audience stood and
booed, he strode off the stage, ignoring reporters and shouting:
'Audience fixed! Audience fixed!' His black car was waiting and it
lurched off into the night, illuminated by popping flashbulbs. Back in
the studio the audience, thoroughly delighted by the performance,
were chanting: 'Good old Frostie! Well done Frostie!'

Once again, David Frost had provided riveting viewing. But the
programme was to be severely criticised as 'trial by television', and as
injurious to the processes of justice.

Savundra was arrested exactly a week after his appearance on 'The
Frost Programme'. The case against him had not been fully prepared
but after seeing the television interview the Director of Public
Prosecutions had telephoned the Fraud Squad and said that action
must be taken straight away.

Savundra was arrested not at White Walls, but at his other home—
the white-painted house in Old Windsor which he had bought in 1960
but hardly ever used. He had moved there the day after 'The Frost
Programme'. White Walls had been let to a Moroccan princess for the
incredible sum (in those days) of £100 a week.

He had left White Walls furnished, taking with him only his silver
packed in the boot of his Rolls. At Old Windsor he said: 'I want to be
near Runnymede, where the Magna Carta was sealed, so that I can
contemplate the birthplace of English justice.'

His contemplation was not to last for long.

At 6.20 on the evening of 10th February he returned home after
visiting friends. As his beige and maroon Rolls-Royce turned into the
gravelled driveway, a black Hillman Minx, parked in the street outside, started up and pulled in behind him. Out of it got Detective
Chief Inspector Albert Overall and Detective Constable Thomas.
Savundra invited them inside where they showed him a warrant for
his arrest and cautioned him.

'I said "What is the charge?" ' so (Det. Chief Insp. Albert Overall) read it out. It just didn't make any sense so I wandered back to my study table—this is a very tiny cottage— the distance would be about three feet—and picked up a scrap of paper and said: "Would you mind telling me the charge again?" and he read it out slowly so that I could write, in green ink, as he should remember if he cares to, but my hand was shaking and I couldn't write very well, and I wrote as best I could, and then when I had finished writing I looked at it and I couldn't read certain words, and I said would he mind reading it again . . . Then Mr. Overall asked if he could go through my papers. I said "Certainly" . . . and he went through every paper on my writing table, went through my filing cabinet section by section by section, and through every file . . .

I was so flummoxed. I was grabbing at the telephone trying to get hold of my solicitor, who was unfortunately busy showing a prize pup at Crufts, which I am glad to say won . . .'

When asked if had anything to say, Savundra replied: 'I wish to say nothing at this stage.' He made a few hasty telephone calls before being driven off to Ealing Police Station.

As they left, they passed Old Windsor's local P.C., who had cycled up while they were in the house and was now standing guard at the gate.

At the Ealing Court, Savundra, under his full name of Savundranayagam, was charged that:

1. On a day in July 1965 at Jacqueline House, North Circular Road, Willesden, he uttered a certain forged valuable security purporting to be a certificate evidencing a holding of three percent Savings Bonds, to the value of £510,000 15s. 10d., knowing it to be forged.

2. That at Jacqueline House between 1st July and September 4th, 1965, being a Director of Fire, Auto and Marine Insurance Co., with intent to defraud, he was concerned in making a false entry in a balance sheet forming part of the accounts of the said Company for the year ended April 30th, 1965, purporting to show that on April 30th, 1965, the said Company held British Government Securities to the value of £540,000.

From the charges, it was evident the police had not completed their full case. There was, as yet, no mention of the certificates forged for the 1966 audit.

At 10 a.m. the following morning Savundra appeared before the

Ealing magistrate. Wearing a camel hair coat, white shirt and maroon tie, he arrived by Black Maria. Almost at the same moment Pushpam arrived by Rolls.

Savundra's counsel, Mr. Ian McCulloch, at once applied for bail. At the same time he spoke about the possibility of contempt proceedings being brought against a prominent 'television personality'. His client, he went on to say, had made a voluntary submission to the Board of Trade and, with his roots in England, was hardly likely to attempt to flee the country.

'It is monstrous,' said Mr. McCulloch, 'now that these investigations are going on that there already should have been a trial by television.' He also criticised the *Sunday Times* which had printed a transcript of the interview.

But the plea for bail failed and Savundra, who had smiled briefly at the magistrates when the proceedings opened and winked once at his wife in the gallery, listened expressionlessly as Inspector Overall gave evidence. The inspector was not convinced the defendant would remain in the country now that he was faced with criminal charges of a particularly serious nature—and more serious charges might be preferred. After twenty-one minutes the hearing was over. Savundra was remanded in custody.

During his appearance the public gallery had been crowded and more than a hundred people had gathered outside the black iron gates of the court in the hope of catching a glimpse of him . . . but he was escorted by police out of a back entrance.

Only a handful of people remained in court to hear similar charges against Stuart de Quincey Walker, who had also been arrested the night before and remanded in custody.

One person who was there, however, was his new wife, Carol. Dressed in a fur-trimmed sheepskin coat over a white two-piece, with her flowing blonde hair tied by a brown scarf, she sat, occasionally glancing up at her husband.

Hearing he was refused bail, Walker turned from the dock towards the court cells and pursed his lips as if to blow a kiss to her as he left.

Now, for the two accused men, there came a long wait. The prosecution at later hearings withdrew their objections to bail but it was to be almost a year before their case was completed. For the first time in his life Savundra lived quietly. Occasionally he could be glimpsed, strolling round Old Windsor with his wife or attending a school function with one or two or his children, but for the most part he remained hidden behind the closed gates of his house.

Newspapermen could find little to keep the story alive. There were occasional paragraphs about new opulent tenants from Morocco or Saudi Arabia at White Walls, which provided an excuse for mentioning Savundra, and reports of postponements of the proceedings. Otherwise nothing.

It was not until September that Scotland Yard gave notice of new charges to be brought. One was concerned with the forgery of the share certificates and another, in more general terms, which alleged 'that between February 1963 and August 1966 they conspired together and with other persons to defraud people taking out insurance policies with Fire, Auto and Marine'.

Savundra had another spell in hospital with his heart trouble but a few days before the trial was due to begin on 10th January, 1968, he was announcing: 'I am ready, willing and able to go to court to stand trial and vindicate myself before the world.' Bubbling over with confidence he said he would be spending the final weekend 'tying the bows and knots and putting the cherry on the cake of my defence. I shall see this trial through even if it means going to court on all fours'.

The evening before the trial he appeared on the B.B.C. programme, '24 Hours'. It was filmed at Old Windsor, and this time he was careful to keep off F.A.M. Instead, in a philosophical mood, he talked of life and death: 'Believing as I do that death is only the beginning, I can say for myself that, as happen to all human beings, I am on the final run . . .' Asked how he had spent the long months awaiting trial he said blandly: 'I have done nothing. Abso-bally-lutely nothing.'

In fact, he had made elaborate preparations to conserve his health through what he knew was going to be a long ordeal. Two Harley Street specialists had prescribed a total of twenty-two pills a day for diabetes and his heart condition. Every morning before leaving for the Old Bailey he counted out the pills from a plastic bag into an elegant heart-shaped container which he carried with him into the dock. He was also anxious that the sittings should not last long. 'I have been told by my doctors to rest after five o'clock and be in bed by nine,' he announced. 'I hope the court does not intend sitting late, otherwise my snores might interrupt the proceedings.'

CHAPTER TWENTY-ONE

Trial by Jury

THE WINTER OF 1967/68 was a bad one. Life in London was constantly disrupted by snow storms which played havoc with the traffic and taxed the patience of commuters. The morning of Tuesday, 10th January, was a particularly bad one and the heavily-falling snow caused long tail-backs and made thousands of people late for work.

The snow also held up the start of the year's first major criminal trial at Court No. One in the Old Bailey. Several of the participants were very late, among them the judge, Alan King-Hamilton, who lived in Finchley, and the prosecuting counsel for the Crown, John Buzzard, who had to drive up from his home in Edenbridge, Kent.

One person on time was the principal defendant. Savundra had left his home so early that he was at the Old Bailey just after 9 a.m.—an hour and a half before the trial was due to start. What he had called 'my famous Rolls-Royce' in his T.V. appearance of the previous night had been left behind and a friend had driven him from Old Windsor. He walked across to the court with his glasses in one hand and his briefcase and brolly held aloft in the other, reminding a small crowd which had gathered of a Chancellor leaving Downing Street with a Budget Day box full of secrets—an appropriate posture, perhaps, as it had recently been facetiously suggested by a member of Her Majesty's Opposition in Parliament that Mr. Callaghan was making such a mess of the job that it might benefit the country more if he was replaced by Savundra . . .

At the Old Bailey he had a long wait. As the morning wore on he sat on a bench outside Court No. One holding himself erect and clutching his briefcase and looking absolutely composed. He had taken his ration of pills for the day and was feeling 'as well as I ever do'. Inside the court there was a buzz of speculation as everyone waited for the proceedings to begin. Huge bundles of papers lay on solicitors' tables. About twelve people waited patiently in the public gallery.

It was 2 p.m. before the court assembled and then it proved, from the point of view of public interest, to be a false start. In fact, it was to be Thursday before Mr. Buzzard opened his case because Tuesday afternoon was devoted to legal arguments, and on Wednesday the judge had another engagement.

Pushpam had said, shortly before the trial: 'Emil's mistake was that he went into business at all. He should have been a lawyer. The law is in the family. He is the son of a barrister and four generations of our family have been chief justices.'

Savundra, whose days as a law student had not been productive, smiled. But it was a lawyer's role, rather than that of a prisoner, which he tried, with considerable success, to assume throughout the trial. He paid elaborate respect to the judicial procedures and to the judge, to whom he bowed low and solemnly whenever occasion demanded it. When he left the dock each afternoon, he shook hands with a smiling policeman who unlocked the gate for him with the deference of the doorman of a plush hotel.

People in court had to keep reminding themselves that this was the accused. He somehow seemed to be honouring them with his presence.

Mr. Buzzard spent two days on his opening address, talking about the 'remarkably simple device' by which Savundra and Walker had stolen £600,000 of money from motorists' premiums. Simple the device may have been but it must have all seemed very confusing to the jury. Mr. Buzzard jumped with grasshopper unpredictability from complicated letters to accounts and company documents collected together into four folios of some 600 sheets of paper each.

Judge Alan King-Hamilton was also ever active. When not leafing through his papers, he was taking notes with a finely sharpened pencil in a huge red leather book. Day by day the blue-bound transcripts of the proceedings piled up on the Judge's desk, until eventually it seemed as if he must disappear behind them. He rarely interrupted proceedings, but his long, thin face frowned in concentration as Mr. Buzzard ploughed patiently through his sums.

'I'm not going to repeat myself, or the other way round, I'll try not to repeat myself . . . but I think it's £5,000. I haven't bothered to do my arithmetic but it's four thousand and one thousand and I think that's five thousand . . . I don't want to weary you with this, members of the jury, but on page 12 towards the top on July 17, do tell me if you don't understand . . .'

After a few minutes and some head-scratching by the jury, a humble clerk whispered up to him, 'Oh dear, page 13, quite right, now on page 13 . . .'

There was something timeless about it all. Outside it snowed steadily and traffic rumbled past, but none of this intruded. As one correspondent observed, the ageing clerks, scribbling furiously, and the battery of wigged counsel might have stepped out of Pickwick's famous court with 'all that pleasing and extensive variety of nose and whisker for which the bar of England is so justly celebrated.'

If Savundra's trial by David Frost had been short and violent, his trial by jury was conducted in the unhurried atmosphere of British justice. Frost had used the weapon of surprise. Now Savundra was to be slowly and relentlessly tracked down through a bewildering labyrinth of documents and figures.

Mr. Buzzard gradually picked his way through the exhibits, describing the setting up of the bank in Liechtenstein, Savundra and Walker's use of it, the production of forged stock to conceal the fraud, and the documentation of the loans . . .

'It may be the defendants thought that if they passed the insurance money into their own and other pockets via M.F.T., and went through all the documentation and bookkeeping to show that it was a banking transaction, they might be lucky enough to evade their responsibilities.

'But the law is not such an ass. The criminal law looks at the substance rather than the letter.'

The prosecution started calling their witnesses late on Friday afternoon. Savundra's power-boating friend, John Fleming, talked of the impression of great wealth Savundra always exuded and agreed with counsel that he was 'a man of tremendous personality'. Peter du Cane talked of Savundra's ambitions to win the Cowes-Torquay race and his 'money is no object' attitude. Tross Youle described some of Savundra's most ambitious ideas—like installing a direct line from Jacqueline House to the New York Stock Exchange. He also talked of his vanity.

'Did he regard himself as something of a genius?' asked Rudolph Lyons, Walker's Q.C.

'Yes,' said Tross Youle. 'Savundra considered himself among the world's greatest geniuses.'

Witnesses were still being called by the prosecution at the end of

January. A different side of Savundra's character was described by
Cocke, the accountant he sacked, who said he was outspoken, 'sometimes downright rude'. Then Hatherall, Cocke's successor, took his
place in the witness box, confirming that he had never seen the
£500,000 Government Bond.

Savundra's counsel, Sebag Shaw, a small man with a brilliant reputation, suggested that £500,000 in the bank might look better than
£500,000 in Government securities. 'It might depend on the bank,'
he added.

Judge Alan King-Hamilton made one of his rare interruptions. 'It
might also depend on the Government,' he said. There was a ripple of
laughter in the court.

On 8th February, Savundra eventually took the centre of the stage.
Even before that, during the first weeks of the trial, his personality
had seemed to dominate proceedings as he sat silently in the dock,
most of the time hunched in thought. Now he was to have the star
role. As reported in one newspaper: 'The podgy figure in the suit of a
City gentleman took the rostrum at the Old Bailey and with majestic
sweeps of his slender brown hands gave his final performance before
the hyper-critical eye of justice.'

Three days previously the bail which he and Walker had secured was
withdrawn, a common practice in a long trial when the prosecution
case is coming to an end. Savundra was later to claim that this had had
a profound effect on his mental state and on the outcome of the case.

When he stepped into the witness box, Judge King-Hamilton (who
had just decided to extend court hours by thirty minutes a day—'in
some little way, it may help to back Britain, I don't know') told him he
could remain seated because of his health. 'Thank you, my lud, thank
you.' Savundra bowed obsequiously. He began his evidence quietly,
telling the court he was forty-four, married, had five children, had
been 'born British' in Ceylon and come to Britain first in 1950. These
domestic details were not queried and in the afternoon Sebag Shaw
had him expounding his conception of insurance.

'To put it shortly, I thought of the computer,' he said. 'I had the
idea of making the computer do what these super-sophisticated
human species—the underwriters—do in their closed closets.'

Sebag Shaw wondered whether he wasn't expressing himself rather
graphically. 'I'm sorry, sir. I'm under medication but I will do my
damnedest.'

When asked if throughout the operation of his company he had ever done anything wrong, he leaned forward and said loudly, thumping the witness box with a clenched fist: 'Emphatically, no.'

'Did you at any time knowingly use or utter documents that were not genuine or true?'

Savundra thumped the witness box harder and his reply was louder: 'Under no circumstances at all.'

'Were you ever knowingly a party to putting forward any balance sheet or other record of account which contained a false entry or false assertion?'

'Again, emphatically, no.' For the third time Savundra hit the witness box and his voice was even louder and more indignant.

The next day he told Sebag Shaw his reason for leaving F.A.M. was the orders of his doctor, who said that he must get rid of this company and all other business activities or he would have the option of learning to play the harp.

'That is a picturesque way of saying you would put your life at risk?'

'Yes.'

When urged to answer questions more briefly, he replied: 'It is very difficult to be an Anglo-Saxon when one is not.'

The question of the forged £500,000 Government Security was raised. 'I believed then, I believed up to the moment of my arrest, I believed until the charge had been read out for, I think, the third time and I had written it down and had had a chance to look at it in writing to see exactly what it meant, that it was a genuine stock certificate.' The man responsible, he claimed, had been Stuart Walker.

Rudolph Lyons, Q.C. for Walker, took over towards the end of Savundra's second day in the box.

'Have you taken tranquillisers today or pep tablets?' he began.

'This depends sir, on what you call tranquillisers or pep tablets.'

'That is not a very helpful answer, is it?'

After some preliminary sparring about Savundra's degrees, Lyons suggested that the money Savundra invested in F.A.M. was 'the sort of capital a back-street grocer might start with'.

'I don't know what your back-street grocer might have, sir, but that £1,000 is a fortune out East.'

Savundra's treatment of Lyons alternated between amused tolerance and sudden flashes of anger. Awkward questions—about M.F.T., or his treatment of Walker, or his view of himself—would be shrugged off, as with infinite patience ('I suggest, sir, that the question is not worthy of you,' he would say, closing his eyes and butterflying his long fingers in the air. Or, shaking his head sadly: 'I'm afraid your instructions are hopelessly wrong, sir'; or, 'I suggest, sir, that you must re-inform yourself about this matter').

There were moments when the studied eloquence disappeared: 'Stop trying to bulldoze me, you're too heavy . . . I was conducting affairs for the same reason as you are appearing here today—for a fee.' When Lyons suggested that Savundra's 'lively imagination' had enabled him to substitute Walker's actions for his own, he shouted: 'I suggest, sir, you have been paid to use your imagination yourself.'

The judge frequently had to intervene, telling Savundra not to be offensive to counsel. He warned him 'You are not doing justice to yourself or your cause by embroidering, or trying to fence with counsel, and by trying to be clever.'

Savundra jumped to his feet and bowed low to the judge. 'You have cut me down to size pretty effectively, your lordship . . .'

'Sitting there in Court No. One,' wrote Peter Earle of the *News of the World*, 'I marvelled at his cleverness and fatal stupidity.'

As the trial progressed everyone tended to become more relaxed. The jury, at first awed like new boys at a public school by the solemnity of the proceedings, now greeted each other every morning like old friends. Only Savundra and Walker in the dock, the one ever-active and unpredictable, the other pale and impassive, continued stolidly to ignore each other.

Up in the public gallery were the two wives, Pushpam's vivid saris lending a splash of colour to the sombre surroundings. Now her husband was spending his nights in the cells, she was in the habit of bringing fruit and chocolate for him each day—which he often distributed among other prisoners in the cells—and taking away his dirty laundry in a Harrods bag.

Bemused by Savundra's florid verbal jousting, by the mapful of faraway places mentioned ('I am surprised we should be playing geography at this expensive rate and in his lordship's time', said Savundra ironically when asked whether he *really* thought Tangier was in the Middle East), by wearisome statistics reeled off hour by hour, and by the constant mention of Steinway grand pianos and vast houses and power-boats, the reporters in court had to keep reminding themselves of what was actually being discussed. It all seemed remote and unreal.

LYONS (counsel for Walker): Dr. Savundra, over the years . . . you've been involved in some very large commercial transactions, have you not? . . .

SAVUNDRA: As an agent of certain governments I have been

engaged in various matters of a major nature.

LYONS: The one I have mentioned was oil for China, was it not?

SAVUNDRA: It was.

LYONS: How much was it? Was it an amount of oil worth almost a million dollars?

SAVUNDRA (with a dismissive wave of the hand): We are now treading into an area which may make me fall foul of the Official Secrets Act.

LYONS: You say you have been a secret agent for governments . . .

SAVUNDRA: I don't like the word secret, it smacks too much of James Bond and there are no blondes around.

SEBAG SHAW (Savundra's counsel): If he were a secret agent he had better remain secret so far as his agency was concerned, that is what I suggest . . .

LYONS: Did you tell Mr. Tross Youle you have been an agent for the Vatican?

SAVUNDRA: I have not told Mr. Tross Youle that I have been an agent for the Vatican because I have not been an agent for the Vatican . . .

LYONS: Have you handled Vatican funds in foreign countries?

SAVUNDRA: I have had that privilege.

LYONS: Did you tell Mr. Tross Youle that you had had business dealings with national leaders such as with Nehru and Nkrumah?

SAVUNDRA: Both statements are true.

Savundra was clearly going to say little of value about his past under cross-examination by Lyons. There was illuminating moments, however.

'Have you ever given a thought to the people who became uninsured in 1966 and did you try to do anything to help clear up the mess?'

'Of course I have given thought to them. For a start the T.V. companies made such a noise about it—the very rich T.V. companies—that when they offered to interview me I gave them a written offer to run the first-ever trial by T.V., with me in the dock.'

'How does that possibly answer my question?'

'I gave them an offer to pay the liquidators, so as to alleviate the misery caused by the collapse of the company, if they wanted to run a trial by T.V. lasting as long as they liked. My offer was that they should pay £100 a second and this would go to alleviate the distress.

'They took up the challenge and offered to pay £60,000 for an interview and I agreed. This seemed to call their bluff and they withdrew.'

'This would not have helped very much.'

'No, but three hours at £100 a second would have very much.'

'Is this the only way you had in your mind to help people who suffered from the crash?'

'There was no other way I could help.'

'Where did you get the idea that you were worth £100 a second on television?'

'I am not worth £100 a second and I did not expect that amount. But just as you are entitled to request your brief be marked at a certain fee, I am entitled to request that I am paid a certain price.'

Lyons reminded Savundra that he had, after all, spent the months after the company had crashed in Ceylon. 'I do not set the pound note above the value of the heart,' Savundra rejoined. 'I stayed there until I knew I could face the bull-baiting I would have had to face when I returned to the so-called civilised countries of the West.' Besides, he stressed again, before going he had transferred his holding in F.A.M. to Walker, thus ridding himself of total legal responsibility.

Savundra also talked of his love of forming companies and his earlier plans to transfer F.A.M. money to a bank in America because 'those of us with some foresight could see what was going to happen here. I had more faith in the American economy'.

He was asked about the world he moved in. Was he a friend of Max Aitken's, for example? Savundra shook his head sadly. 'That is a question you must ask *him*. I cannot vouch for the terms of friendship.' Had he not told Walker he was on friendly and first name terms with millionaires and men of title? 'I wouldn't know if they were millionaires or merely putting it on until I saw their bank balances. And I was on first name terms even with my gardener.'

'Walker treated you as a financial genius,' said Lyons.

'He treated me as a friend. I haven't seen him doing a pooja, as we say out East,'—and, rising from his seat in the witness box, Savundra held his hands together chest-high as though in prayer and bowed his head in Eastern-style greeting.

Savundra never stopped antagonising Lyons, despite the judge's rebukes. He could not stand losing an argument. There were outbursts about Frost-style tactics and repeated suggestions that Lyons was behaving as if he were in a boxing ring. The discussion about first names led to a confrontation when Savundra was asked about a letter he had written to Tross Youle. He said it should not have been mentioned: it was in first name terms so it was a private letter.

'But yesterday you said you called even your gardener by his first name.'

'Yes, I did. But I wouldn't call you dear Rudolph, would I?'

Judge King-Hamilton intervened. 'Apologise to Mr. Lyons.'

Savundra rose. 'I apologise,' he said, giving a waist-deep bow. 'I am rather dopey this morning. It wears off during the day.'

Talking about Walker's character, Savundra suggested he was a decent man who had become dissipated, lazy, greedy and unreliable.

He made great capital, for example, out of the house in Hastings. This, he said, had been bought with an M.F.T. cheque and was a nudist colony.

'I suggest that is utter rubbish,' said Lyons.

'I beg your pardon, sir, he had to be there every weekend to chase away the nudists who used to go there to sunbathe, thinking it was still a nudist colony. One day I went there with my wife and children for lunch. I am glad my wife was not embarrassed by the presence of any nudists.'

Savundra denied that he had dominated Walker throughout the history of F.A.M. When Lyons suggested, for example, that the only instance where he had had to face criticism was over the extravagant expenditure on a directors' lavatory, the reaction was sharp.

LYONS: Didn't Mr. Walker say 'You can build a house for £4,000'?

SAVUNDRA: If Mr. Walker said that, sir, he was talking to himself, soliloquising inside the lavatory.

LYONS: You often abused him, did you not, just as you are doing now?

SAVUNDRA: No, sir, it is not my practice to abuse people except when they go out of their way to irritate me. I am the easiest and most tractable person in the world to get on with as anybody will confirm.

Savundra also insisted Walker had had the control of M.F.T., but claimed that he himself had had to handle quite a lot of paper work towards the end. 'I discovered the absolute necessity of taking over some work after Mr. Walker started coming later and later every morning and asking for more and more Alka-Seltzer.'

The picture he painted of M.F.T. was a masterpiece of imagination. Mysterious Egyptian men and women flitted across the scene, the chief one being a Sultan Achmed Mohammed Pasha said to be Walker's most influential friend. It was the death of Sultan Pasha, Savundra said he gathered, which prevented M.F.T. from lending money at the critical moment, thus precipitating the downfall of

F.A.M. Nothing could be done until Pasha's estate had been wound up . . .

Just the same, he claimed, Walker had been longing to take over F.A.M.

'What was his reaction to the proposed sell-out?'

'He was delighted, sir. He was licking his lips with glee. He said something to the effect that now I had resigned and he would be able to get the new capital the company would be able to expand enormously.'

If, asked Lyons, there was capital to come in—ten million dollars, according to Savundra, from the First National Bank of Boston—why had he sold his shares? Why not just resign and withdraw from participation in the business?

'Some people are born to sit in the driving seat,' declared Savundra, 'and others to ride in the dicky. F.A.M. was my baby and I no longer wished to have anything to do with it or any money in it when it was under somebody else's control.'

Lyons wondered whether his game was not to try and make Stuart Walker the 'fall-guy'.

Savundra replied: 'I know what that expression means—I have read cheap literature before. If you are suggesting I am the Big Bad Wolf and Walker is Little Red Riding Hood, you may as well take him back to the Baby Bunting stage.'

The cross-examination by Mr. Lyons was to end in another outburst, Savundra accusing Lyons of trying to confuse him and wear him down, while at the same time insisting: 'I am not asking for quarter, never having asked for quarter in my life.'

Mr. Lyons was followed by Mr. Buzzard, who took Savundra methodically through the details of F.A.M. It was Buzzard who explored most thoroughly the reasons why Walker had been made managing director of the company. First, however, he elicited a highly colourful picture of Walker at sea off North Africa, being chased by destroyers and smuggling arms. The object, said Savundra, was 'political upheavals in that part of the world'. He went on to claim that he had received a good reference for Walker from a diplomat in the French Foreign Office.

BUZZARD: How did he give Mr. Walker a good reference?

SAVUNDRA: He said he was a first-class organiser and had first-class connections in the Arab world.

BUZZARD: But the organising was in relation to these cargoes (of arms)?

SAVUNDRA: Organising in relation to everything connected with these highly delicate operations.

BUZZARD: Well the one thing you did know about Mr. Walker was that he had had absolutely no experience of insurance, wasn't it?

SAVUNDRA: That is so, sir . . .

BUZZARD: Why did you decide upon or advance Walker's name as managing director of a new insurance company?

SAVUNDRA: Well, I have felt, sir, that organisational ability is more important than technical know-how because the boffins of this world are liable to get bogged down in the boffining way much to the detriment of the organisation . . .

BUZZARD: Did you think a man who had engaged in that sort of traffic was a man who was likely to be honest and trustworthy?

SAVUNDRA: Emphatically yes, sir, because if you are dishonest in that sort of business the answer is a very short and sweet one, a six foot long wooden box.

BUZZARD: A good deal of double-crossing goes on in that sort of business, doesn't it?

SAVUNDRA: A lot of dying does too, sir.

Savundra spent twenty-eight hours in the witness box—seven and half court days. By the end of his evidence he looked pale and drawn and on one occasion he broke down under Buzzard's questioning. Buzzard had suggested that he and Walker would take what they wanted from F.A.M., even if the company was making a loss or if the result was that creditors would have to 'whistle for their money'.

'Bearing in mind, sir,' said Savundra, 'that the legal position was sound and that the definition of honesty in business is equated to legality, I did think it honest.'

'The kernel of the case is this, is it not? You thought that provided you could bring matters within the letter of the law you could not be touched?'

'I submit, sir, that we are all bound by the law and that is all there is to it.'

Buzzard moved to the subject of M.F.T. and began reeling off figures. It was at this point that Savundra broke down. He complained of feeling hazy and King-Hamilton suggested a ten-minute break. 'I don't think it would help, my lord,' said Savundra. 'If I took what I should take then I would not be answering questions at all.'

Sebag Shaw silenced him with a wave of the hand, and, shortly afterwards, he made to leave the court. He turned, walked a few paces, and then suddenly slumped down on the wooden steps of the witness box, burying his head in his hands, sobbing bitterly. From the other side of the court room, Pushpam, dressed in a brilliant orange sari, watched anxiously and people leant over the public gallery as a prison officer offered Savundra a red handkerchief and opened a glass phial. He inhaled deeply from the phial, took several pills, and then allowed himself to be led from the court.

It was Savundra's second last day giving evidence. He finished on the Monday—19th February—when he was undoubtedly very tired. 'It is reaching the point,' he said in the early afternoon, 'where I do not know whether today is yesterday or tomorrow. I am doing my best to keep up with your game of chess.' His replies to the final questions were almost inaudible. At the end of his examination Sebag Shaw said: 'The suggestion is that you embarked upon this F.A.M. enterprise and conducted its affairs for more than two years to provide yourself with extravagant living. Is that true?'

Savundra replied: 'I submit that I did everything in my power to replace the goose quill with the fountain pen, but was bludgeoned out of existence by the giants. I suppose I should have known better than to engage in war against the enormous forces ranged against me.'

So, at last, it was Walker's turn to give his version of events. Lyons began by dealing with what he called the 'slurs' cast on his client's character. Walker had his opportunity to deny that he had ever smuggled arms, or been chased by destroyers, to deny, in fact, just about everything Savundra had said about him.

He told the jury how he had met Savundra, been offered a job as his assistant, then on the F.A.M. board, 'because he wanted somebody he could rely upon', with a salary of £1,500 rising at the end of the year to £3,000.

He regarded Savundra as a brilliant and dynamic man, completely honourable and wholly honest. 'I did not lose confidence until after he had resigned from the company.' He believed Savundra to be very wealthy.

His counsel asked him: 'When he told you anything about himself or the company or when he advised any course of action, what was your reaction?'

'I accepted his views. He was always right.'

Walker was flattered when Savundra said in 1964 that he had recommended him for the job of London manager of Merchants and Finance Trust. He had never heard of the bank and told Savundra he had absolutely no knowledge of banking. Savundra said it did not matter. All he had to do was to follow instructions and 'merely be the London signatory'.

'Did he explain how the bank could help F.A.M.?'

'He said he proposed to transfer the capital assets and money of F.A.M. into it as this new bank would be in a position to provide new capital as and when we required it.'

Savundra told him he could borrow on the company's M.F.T. account. In 1965 he borrowed £9,000 for a house in St. Leonards, £30,000 for a house in Hampton Court and, he said, in all his borrowings from M.F.T. were about £55,000.

After Savundra's performance, Walker—a thin, balding, bookish man, speaking very softly—could hardly have created a more contrasting impression. He knew nothing about the forgeries, nothing about the real set-up of M.F.T., little about Savundra's past . . .

John Buzzard, however, was not convinced. He suggested that the evidence being given was 'a skilful mixture of truth and falsehood', and that Walker's only qualification for his job—as by his own admission he had known nothing of insurance or banking—was that he was a smooth, accomplished and convincing liar.

When Walker left the witness box, Mr. Buzzard began his closing address:

'It is perfectly clear, having heard the evidence and the cross-examination, that they are undoubtedly guilty of the main charge in this case—conspiracy to defraud.' He did make one concession. 'The jury will have to consider carefully the question of Walker's involvement in the uttering of a forged document [the £500,000 bond].'

Buzzard's speech was followed by those of the two leading defence counsel, Shaw and Lyons, Shaw saying that all the evidence gave the lie to Savundra being an evil genius and suggesting that Walker was the man responsible for M.F.T., Lyons saying roughly the opposite.

Then, on 4th March, 1968, almost two months and thirty-nine days after the beginning of the trial, the judge began his summing up. Turning to the jury, he opened, just as Pushpam took her seat, with this warning.

'One of the defendants is a coloured gentleman. You won't be biased on that count. In this country justice is colour-blind. It comes alike to all, regardless of colour, race, creed or nationality—one of the matters about which we are extremely proud.'

The jury shuffled doggedly backwards and forwards through their voluminous piles of paper as Judge King-Hamilton recapitulated the evidence.

The whole convoluted case, he said, through which shadowy companies in Liechtenstein and mysterious Middle East financiers flitted elusively, could be boiled down to a simple question: 'In doing what they did, were Savundra and Walker acting honestly, doing what they sincerely believed to be in the interests of F.A.M. and the policy-holders: or were they acting dishonestly, not in the interests of policy-holders, but fraudulently and in their own interests?

'At the end of the day certain issues stand out so clearly like signposts in a jungle; so clearly that you wonder how you ever thought there was a jungle in the first place.' The three vital issues were:

1) Was Merchants and Finance Trust really a merchant bank, and whatever it was, did Dr. Savundra and Mr. Walker have a part in its control?

2) Was there any concealment about the money of F.A.M. paid into M.F.T. accounts, and money drawn out from there, and if so, why?

3) Were the receipts for the deposits to M.F.T. genuine, and were the loan agreements from M.F.T. to the two defendants genuine?

On the charge of conspiracy to defraud, the judge said that whatever view the jury took, 'the circumstances which gave rise to the charge certainly cried out for investigation . . . two directors without consulting their board at all take the risk of depositing the company's money with an unknown merchant bank. The great bulk of the money is then drawn out and paid to the two directors. When you think of it, it is obvious numerous questions arise.'

There could be no doubt that Savundra was in control from the beginning even before he became a director. 'Was Walker his lieutenant?' asked the judge. 'Well, he was a director from the start, very soon becoming managing director and when Savundra became deputy chairman he shared Walker's rooms.'

'The general impression of the majority of the witnesses (which you may share—that is entirely a matter for you) is that Savundra has got the more dominating and forceful personality of the two.'

Walker may have played a subordinate role, but he had overall executive control of F.A.M. and supreme control, when, as not infrequently happened, Savundra was away. Perhaps, the judge went on, he was an equal personality to Savundra, but controlled his forcefulness more.

'He must at least have known and understood all that was going on.' It was no defence to say that he was completely dominated by Savundra's overwhelming personality, caught up in the vortex of

Savundra's business world, and submerged—unless he had been completely hypnotised by Savundra so as to act as an automaton. 'But that has not been suggested, and the evidence has not come within a thousand miles of it.'

Then, painstakingly, the judge began to lead the jury through the labyrinth of evidence, pausing and looking up at one moment to say: 'I have no head for figures.'

Judge King-Hamilton's summing-up lasted for two and a half days—almost eleven hours. Eventually, on Wednesday, 6th March, just after midday, the jury retired.

At 4.45 p.m., four and a half hours later, during which time a lunch of sandwiches and coffee had been served to them by the usher, they returned, and the foreman gave the verdict.

Savundra and Walker were convicted of plotting to defraud Fire, Auto and Marine policy-holders by misappropriating premiums; plotting to falsify the 1966 balance sheet; making a false entry in the 1965 balance sheet; and Savundra of uttering forged share certificates. Walker was found not guilty on this charge. On an earlier direction of the judge both men were found not guilty of conspiring to defraud potential policy-holders.

As the foreman pronounced him guilty four times, Savundra clutched the rail of the dock and closed his eyes. Pushpam, in the gallery, elegant in a turquoise and red sari, caught her breath and twisted the strap of her white bag in her fingers.

'My Lord,' said the foreman after announcing the verdicts, 'we have considered this very carefully and have deemed that Walker, during this period, was dominated by the influence of Dr. Savundra in all his actions.'

Walker, pale-faced, who had stood stiffly to attention two chair spaces away from Savundra while he heard himself pronounced guilty, repeatedly biting his lower lip, brightened slightly, and his wife, Carol, on the other side of the public seats to Pushpam, smiled in relief after having initially winced at the verdicts.

The two men stayed in court as the judge thanked the jury for their services and told them he would recommend their exemption from further jury service for life. Savundra, who had started the trial with so much flair and confidence, sat dejectedly, slumped in the dock, never looking up. Eventually a prison officer led him out and he shuffled downstairs to the cells. Walker followed, stepping briskly out of the dock and giving his wife a fleeting smile. Neither of them so much as glanced as one another before, during or after the verdicts.

The judge told the two wives that they could visit their husbands for fifteen minutes. Pushpam had told reporters earlier that she was 'not at all worried about the outcome of the case . . . I expect to go home with my husband tonight.' As Carol Walker left the court she said simply: 'I will stand by Stuart. I have always had faith in him. Whatever sentence he receives I will wait for him.'

The judge told the jury they could return to their places, if they wished, for the end of the case. When the court adjourned that evening they gave the court matron, who had treated them for minor ailments during the case, a bouquet and a two-pound box of chocolates 'from the girls and boys of Court One'.

CHAPTER TWENTY-TWO

Gone with the Wind

ON THE DAY AFTER the verdicts had been given, Thursday, 7th March, the court was re-convened to hear pleas of mitigation for the defendants before the passing of sentence.

For Savundra, Sebag Shaw, making one of his last appearances as a Queen's Counsel before himself becoming a judge, made no attempt to gloss over the magnitude of the F.A.M. disaster. 'Looking back at the wreckage of the insurance company, it is a shocking picture,' he told the judge. 'The sentence you will pass must be a salutary one—but there are limits even to a sentence of that kind.'

He went on to say that although F.A.M. had crashed with a total deficiency of £3,000,000 and that there were unsettled claims of more than £1,250,000, some of these losses were caused by the sudden crash and not as a direct result of his client's wrongdoing. 'The real fault of Dr. Savundra was that he devised a scheme by which he could anticipate profits before they came in.' He then pointed out that there was no evidence that any money had been salted away. All Savundra had got out of his fraud had been two years of extravagant living.

Nor did Sebag Shaw make any attempt to deny that Savundra had been the main architect of the fraud and Lyons, when he rose on behalf of Stuart Walker, hammered this point home. He stated unequivocally that his client had been Savundra's 'puppet'.

Walker, claimed Lyons, was corrupted and initiated to fraud by a slow and insidious campaign by Dr. Savundra, who was looking 'first for a front and then for a scapegoat'.

Speaking of the man who had 'masterminded F.A.M.', he paid Savundra a back-handed compliment:

'He is no ordinary mortal. And, if he is a crook, he is no ordinary crook. He is a man with a tremendous and fantastic personality, something of a genius with an uncanny knowledge of the law relating to companies in England, America and the Continent.

'I submit that Walker was innocently sucked into the vortex of Savundra's manipulations and into what, after three and a half years, turned out to be his phoney world of big finance.'

Earlier, Mr. Lyons had been given a piece of information which helped his plea on Walker's behalf. Detective Chief Inspector Overall had told the court that as a young man Walker had won the King's Commendation for bravery, for rescuing men overcome by dangerous gases while on salvage work.

Lyons asked Overall if Walker's failure to mention this to his own solicitor was in keeping with his character as a modest, as well as a brave man. Overall agreed.

When Judge King-Hamilton began addressing the court for the last time, he made it immediately clear that the sentences he would be passing were going to be severe. He offered three reasons for his decision:

Reason One: 'In the first place, when F.A.M. crashed there were nearly 400,000 persons who had bought premiums and who therefore believed themselves to be insured. Suddenly, to their dismay, they found they were not insured.

'For the most part they were persons who came from a modest-income group, and persons therefore to whom the finding of fresh premiums would cause considerable hardship. Over and above that I am told there were some 45,000 unsettled claims outstanding to the value of between £1,250,000 and £1,500,000.

'That state of affairs, and all the consequential anxiety and misery that must have flowed from it, is very largely, though not entirely, brought about by the dishonesty of you two.'

Reason Two: 'London is the insurance capital of the world. It is of the highest importance that the reputation and integrity of British insurance companies should not be devalued.

'Let it be clearly understood that if anyone who controls or is concerned in the operation of an insurance company is convicted of dishonesty in connection with that business, he will be severely dealt with by the courts.'

Reason Three: 'Both of you took part in a gigantic swindle. For two-and-a-half years in one way or another you helped yourselves either to cash, or to monies worth to the extent of over £600,000 of the company's monies which should have been available for paying claims.

'There came a time when you rationed the payment of claims, but there was no limit to the amount you drew from Merchants and Finance Trust, a completely bogus bank.'

King-Hamilton went on to say that M.F.T. had been used by Savundra and Walker for their own purposes so that the money put into it would not be available to their policy-holders. The two men listened to him impassively as he castigated their behaviour.

'You were as ruthless as you were unscrupulous. If three quarters of a million pounds had been taken in the course of armed robbery, the robbers would be sentenced to an exceedingly long term of imprisonment running into double figures.

'Well, you did not rob and you were not armed. But in effect you stole.

'Instead of arms you employed more subtle weapons—lies, forgeries and all the techniques of the confidence trickster.'

Judge King-Hamilton then turned to the different roles of the two men. Savundra got to his feet when his name was mentioned, but was told to sit down again.

'You were the moving spirit,' said King-Hamilton. 'I am quite certain it was your misguided genius which concocted the whole fraudulent scheme.

'I take into account your health and I have noted carefully the prison officer's medical report. I am satisfied that your condition is such that it will be well cared for by the prison medical authorities, as it has been since I withdrew bail.'

Savundra was then sentenced to eight years' imprisonment and fined £50,000 with an extra two years in jail if he failed to pay.

'I take into account,' said the judge, 'that there is litigation in which you are being sued for something over £400,000, and that a very large amount of the money you took from the insurance company has been spent. Nevertheless I think you should be fined.'

Savundra half rose as if to go down to the cells, but again the judge told him to sit down.

He turned to Walker: 'I take into account that you have no previous convictions, and also a commendation for bravery. You obviously played the lesser part of the two and had a smaller share of the money. Clearly you were under the influence of Savundra, but from your career you are a man of the world and not a child.'

Walker was then sentenced to five years and fined £3,000 with two years in default.

The clerk of the court asked both men if they had anything to say. With an almost imperceptible shake of the head, Walker indicated he had not. Savundra, however, rose to his feet. There was no trace of the former sparkling ebullience but there was still something drama-tic in his manner as he thanked the judge for the 'care and kindness' that had been shown to him during the trial.

Then he paused, as if at a loss for words, but summoning up all his energy he said very quietly: 'I can only say I did my best. It has all gone. If now it is judged that I have transgressed, so be it.' His voice faded away to a whisper as he spoke his last words in the room he had dominated for so many days.

As the court finally rose one figure seemed reluctant to leave, wan-dering slowly amongst the empty benches. In an emerald and gold sari, gold bangles jangling on her slim wrist, Pushpam Savundra had heard her husband sentenced with no outward sign of emotion. All she would say was: 'My plans are to carry on as usual. I shall stay in England with my five children. No, I do not intend to let my children see him while he is in prison.'

Carol Walker was unable to preserve the same calm. Outside the court she was seen weeping in an alcove. 'I did not think for one moment that Stuart would get five years. It's terrible,' she sobbed.

She was to find consolation from a totally unexpected direction. Three of the jury sought her out to tell her how 'surprised and sorry' they were at the severity of her husband's sentence. It was the general opinion of the whole jury, they said, that it had been altogether 'too steep'.

Later the jury, who had sat for forty-two days and who had developed a degree of intimacy through their shared experience, repeated their opinion to the Press and even assembled to be photo-graphed together. It was an unprecedented action and evoked con-siderable comment. The *Evening Standard* expressed what was the general opinion:

'In this case, the jury sat for forty-two days and had ample oppor-tuinity to form a view of the two defendants concerned. That they should have strong feelings about the sentences passed is inevitable. That they should voice these feelings is only natural. And many people will agree with their views.'

In the marathon trial a million and a half words had been taken down in shorthand but in the formidable mass of verbiage there was not a single clue to one of the most tantalising questions of all—how much money had Savundra and Walker really made and what had happened to it?

For a long time after the records of the trial had been consigned to the archives there was open speculation about a 'missing million' which, it was rumoured, Savundra had salted away in a Swiss banking account. If such a million ever existed the most intensive search by the liquidators failed to discover it.

There were questions, too, on how someone on legal aid could command the services of so distinguished a Q.C. as Sebag Shaw and arrive each morning at the court in a Rolls-Royce. In fact Savundra had engaged his counsel on a private basis and had only applied for legal aid after the trial had started, by which stage Sebag Shaw could scarcely have withdrawn even if he had felt inclined to. Savundra was able to show that everything, including the Rolls, belonged to his wife.

Finally the question was asked whether it was right that a criminal should be given the option of buying a shorter sentence. Should the Great Train Robbers, for example, have been able to earn earlier freedom in return for surrendering a portion of their money?

In the event the question was an academic one. On appeal the fine levied on Walker was remitted and Savundra never made any attempt to escape a further two years in jail by raising £50,000.

The trial may have ended but it was to be a long time before Savundra's name was out of the headlines. The prison gates had hardly closed behind him before the liquidator of his empire, Mr. Weiss, obtained a judge against him on behalf of Merchants and Finance Trust for £400,000.

Savundra appealed against the judgement to the Master of the Rolls, Lord Denning, on the grounds that the condition of the loan allowed him twenty years to pay. Denning would have none of it. 'That agreement,' he declared, 'is not worth the paper it is written on.'

Savundra appealed to the Lords. 'This is the court of last resort in this country,' he told the law lords. 'The stream of justice has been muddied in my case beyond all recognition by the virulent publicity accorded to me by those scurrilous rags parading as newspapers and those popinjays performing as television crusaders.'

The law lords were unimpressed and rejected his appeal.

The next day bankruptcy proceedings were started against him but they hardly got under way before they were interrupted by his appeal against sentence before Lord Justice Salmon.

Walker, whose appeal was heard at the same time, relied on trying to convince Lord Salmon that he had been a mere tool in Savundra's hands. 'He just put his signature to everything he was asked to and implicitly believed Dr. Savundra like a solicitor's articled clerk believes the Lord Chancellor,' Rudolph Lyons declared, and in the end the Justices quashed his financial penalty.

Savundra's counsel, Mr. Peter Pain, Q.C., who had replaced Sebag Shaw (now himself a judge), took a new tack. He claimed his client had had no chance of a fair trail because the air had been so poisoned by publicity beforehand. He went on to claim that in particular the Frost interview had turned proceedings into a farce. He also thought there was strong evidence that most of the missing money had not been hidden away but had 'gone with the wind'.

Lord Salmon quashed the appeal, but he did condemn the programme as 'deplorable' and declared: 'Trial by television will not be tolerated in a civilised country.

'This court hopes that no interview of this kind will ever again be televised,' he went on. He drew a sharp distinction between the Press coverage of the F.A.M. collapse and Frost's programme seven months later in February 1967. The Press Campaign, he said, came 'at a stage when there was no suggestion of criminal proceedings, so there was no question of contempt of court'.

The T.V. interview, however, came 'at a time when it must have been obvious to anyone that he was about to be arrested and tried on charges of gross fraud.

'It must not be supposed that proceedings to commit for contempt of court can be instituted only in respect of matters published after criminal proceedings have begun . . . No one should imagine himself safe from commital for contempt of court if knowing or having good reason to believe that criminal proceedings are imminent he chooses to publish matters calculated to prejudice a fair trial.

'On any view that television interview was deplorable. With no experience of television Savundra was faced with a skilled interviewer whose object was to establish his guilt before an audience of millions of people. None of the ordinary safeguards of a court of law were observed. They may seem prosaic to those engaged in the entertainment business, but they are the rocks on which all the rights of freedom from oppression and tyranny have been established in this country for centuries.'

If the television authorities produced another such interview, Lord Salmon concluded, they would do so at their peril. A television personality had never been censured in such harsh terms before.

At the time of the interview Frost had airily dismissed his critics by saying: 'I am not tough . . . I am never against anyone . . . This whole "trial by T.V." is a phrase made up by newspapers . . . It's a load of cobblers. People come of their own free will and are free to say what they like.'

While the appeal was being heard among the solemn trappings of the High Court, Frost was playing cricket in Maidstone—in a benefit match between a Surrey XI and a Kent XI. 'I have had a great day,' he said as he changed out of his flannels. 'I have scored twenty-five runs and made a catch behind the wicket.'

He may have been enthusiastic about his cricket but he was uncharacteristically silent when told about Lord Justice Salmon's remarks. 'I can't say anything about his comments until I have had time to sit down in some quiet corner and read what he has said,' he declared.

The result of his cogitations was a letter to *The Times*, in which he attacked Lord Justice Salmon for his criticism, saying his team had checked with the Board of Trade about the possibility of an impending prosecution and had been told: 'We have nothing against Dr. Savundra.'

Even so, it is hard not to accept the court's view that 'it was obvious to all that he was about to be arrested and tried on charges of fraud.'

Lord Justice Salmon had found it necessary, as a result, to define more clearly the balance between fair trial and free comment. His dictum about the perils to journalists who went on the air or into print 'having good reason to suspect proceedings were imminent' has since given many an editor a sleepless night.

With the dismissal of the appeals and the refusal of the court to grant permission for an appeal to the House of Lords the protracted case was finally closed but Savundra's bankruptcy proceedings were to drag on for another three years.

His attitude to the proceedings was quite simple. He refused to recognise that he was bankrupt largely on the grounds that he was not required by M.F.T. to repay his loans for twenty years. Having taken this standpoint he refused to co-operate in any way. Although he was aware that this could put him in contempt of court he gambled on the fact that the justices would be unlikely to order an extension of sentence on a man already serving ten years.

At his public examination in April 1969, he refused to take the oath. 'With the greatest respect,' he told Mr. Registrar Parbury, 'I cannot take part in these proceedings which are a gross and flagrant violation of certain international conventions.'

'All I need to know,' said the Registrar, 'is are you going to answer the questions?'

'All matters are subject to appeal by me,' replied Savundra obscurely.

'Answer my question,' said the Registrar. 'Are you going to answer my questions?'

I am trying to answer the questions.'

'You could answer "yes" or "no".'

'I regret the answer "yes" or "no" is impossible.'

In the face of this stonewalling Parbury gave up. 'I am going to assume that this bankrupt does not intend to answer questions put to him,' he snapped.

By a mixture of being ill at the right times and sudden changes of mind which heralded fleeting moments of co-operation, Savundra managed to stall matters for a year. Then, suddenly, he agreed to meet a senior examiner from the London Bankruptcy Court at Wormwood Scrubs.

There was still considerable conjecture about what was often referred to as 'Dr. Savundra's big secret'—the alleged missing million.

Now Savundra for the first time listed his expenditure between the years 1963 and 1968:

Loss on shareholding in F.A.M.—£217,813

Gifts to a property company which bought White Walls—£77,540.

Further expenditure on the house—£20,000

Household expenditure and personal expenses of himself, his wife and five children—£61,784

Losses on sale of powerboats—£35,000

Losses on Rolls-Royce cars—£9,000

Legals costs of trial—£20,000

Capital gains tax—£85,000

With equal care he listed his current assets as £16 in cash and jewellery worth £10.

Two months later he again appeared before a bankruptcy court where he reiterated to the Official Receiver, Mr. Norman Saddler—who had replaced Arthur Cheek—that reports of the missing million were 'complete fairy stories'.

'My life has always been fairly monastic,' he sighed. 'One cannot do very much with the ailments I have had.'

Saddler queried the word 'monastic'. Savundra insisted that he had lived for years on a diabetic diet, free of starch, sugar and salt. 'What else can you call it but monastic?' He hotly denied that he had been over lavish in his expenditure on his family but admitted that he had spent many thousands of pounds on power-boating.

He promised at the next hearing to disclose further details of how he had spent his money and give the court details of how he had used Swiss bank accounts.

When Savundra's case was again called, however, he had changed his mind. It was adjourned until May 1971, but by then he was ill in the prison hospital. Pushpam wrote to the Home Secretary asking for parole for her husband, whom she declared to be dying. At the same time a certificate from the prison medical officer informed the bankruptcy court that Savundra could not attend as he was suffering from 'chronic heart disease and diabetes'. The M.O. added: 'It is most unlikely that there will be any improvement in his medical condition in the foreseeable future.'

And that, as regards Savundra's bankruptcy, was that. It was quite obvious that he was never going to provide satisfactory answers. His many appearances in various courts had already lost the State a substantial sum. It would have been futile for the public examination to have continued.

CHAPTER TWENTY-THREE

The Howard Hughes of Wormwood Scrubs

PERHAPS IT WAS ONLY when he found himself squeezed into one of the narrow boxed-in double seats lining either side of the gangway in the Black Maria which was to take him to Wormwood Scrubs, that Savundra accepted for the first time that he had reached the point of no return.

He had been in tight spots before but this time there was no limousine to bear him off to a luxurious nursing home as a refuge, there was no Monsignor Asta to plead his cause in high places and no scapegoat to take his place on the hard bench, with only the defiant graffiti scrawled by previous passengers on the cubicle wall to look at.

Right up to the moment when the foreman of the jury had announced the unanimous decision that he was guilty, his optimism had refused to let him accept what everybody else must have known to be inevitable.

As soon as the prison gates closed behind him he was led to a bare cell where he was stripped naked, his expensive clothes packed away in a plastic bag and coarse prison garb issued in their place. But the formalities of transferring Dr. Emil Savundra, Ph.D., D.C.L., into prisoner number 9630 had hardly been completed before he demanded an interview with the Prison Governor.

Savundra's aim was to find out how soon he could be transfered to an open prison. Considering that the appeal against sentence which he had immediately lodged had not yet even been set down for hearing, the question was, to say the least, premature.

In pointing this out to him, the Governor also raised the matter of his health. At Wormwood Scrubs, he pointed out, the facilities for treatment were very much better than at an open prison so that there was little prospect of a transfer in any case.

'Have you ever heard of the miracle of Lourdes?' Savundra asked. The Governor admitted that he had.

'Well,' said Savundra with his most captivating smile, 'in another few months you will be hearing of the miracle of Wormwood Scrubs.'

Clearly he had no intention of allowing his heart condition to detain him in the grim Scrubs longer than was absolutely necessary, and he was relying, as he had so often in the past, on his condition improving as circumstances demanded.

While his appeal was pending he was allowed certain privileges not accorded to prisoners whose sentence had been confirmed. The main advantages were in the number of visits permitted, and in less restricted correspondence.

Pushpam remained firm in her determination not to subject her children to the stress of seeing their father in jail, but she herself made as many visits as could be arranged.

In his first letter to her he had complained chiefly about the uniform. 'The clothes are similar to an ordinary soldier's,' he wrote. 'It is a pity that I was an officer and did not have to rough it as much as the others.'

When she visited him he railed against his cramped cell and complained that the staple diet was corned beef—which, incidentally, it was not.

After she left the prison Pushpam talked about his plight to reporters.

'He seemed to be living in another world,' she told them. 'It breaks my heart to see him like that. Perhaps the best thing would be for him to die, rather than have this torture. I have never seen him so thin. There is something wrong with his eyes and his hands were shaking. He seems to have lost every scrap of gaiety.'

When it became known amongst the prison officers that Savundra was to be in their charge, it was generally considered that he might be in for a rough time at the hands of some of the other prisoners. Indeed, apart from the prisoners, there were warders who had been left holding worthless F.A.M. insurance policies.

In the event the fears did not materialise, although during the first few weeks the wits had considerable fun at his expense. One particular jingle, which used to be sung with great gusto, even the warders joining in, when Savundra put in one of his rare appearances from the hospital wing, went:

Oh, Doctor Savundra,
I know who you are;

And I know where I'd like you,
Under my car.

On the whole, however, the sight of his podgy, dark-skinned figure
shuffling along in his ill-fitting uniform and looking completely lost
elicited sympathy rather than taunts.

It has been said that a gullible man, spending a few days in prison,
would be easily convinced that it was populated almost entirely by
innocent men. It is certainly true that most first offenders spend much
of their time protesting their innocence to whoever will listen and in
this Savundra was no exception. The only way in which he differed
from most was in the intensity with which he held the belief.

Now that he had so much time on his hands to reflect on the chain
of events which had led to his present predicament, his ability to
delude even himself was given full play.

After all it was easy enough to believe that the money he had been
paid by the Chinese was only a fraction of what they owed the
Catholic Church, whose property they had confiscated, and was there
not now a fine convent in his native Ceylon as a monument of his
enterprise? And had he not anyway, at great risk to his own safety,
co-operated with the C.I.A. in seeing that no war-like materials
reached the enemy? Had he not been on the side of right and demonstrated his loyalty to his friend Nehru when he had helped to starve
the Goans into submission by not sending them rice, and would he not
now be recognised as the saviour of Ghana, had it not been for the
interference of the narrow-minded, unimaginative Geoffrey Bing
and being out-bribed by a deadbeat retired English general?

Thus, in his lonely cell, he dreamed the long hours away, reliving
his life through his own eyes. To a dazzled public he was the devil-
may-care millionaire playboy, lionized by society, whilst behind the
mask was the real Savundra, who had the confidence of the world's
most powerful men and was ever ready to employ his exceptional talents to strike a blow for the under-privileged and topple the ungodly
from their thrones.

There was sympathy, too, and some admiration for Pushpam, even
though her financial circumstances outwardly did not appear to be
too difficult. She put up a brave front. A doctor, visiting Wormwood
Scrubs shortly after Savundra's arrival, remembers her driving the
by-now famous Rolls-Royce through the gates and parking it in the
space marked 'For the Governor only', then, after carefully seeing

that all the car doors were locked, marching, her head held high, to the entrance for prisoners' visitors.

She made it clear that her relatives 'refuse to acknowledge my husband's misfortunes' but for her such a head-in-the-sand attitude was not so easy. She had to sell some of her jewellery and she was suddenly faced with dealing with situations she had never had to cope with during the whole of her married life. She described her predicament to a friendly journalist:

'I had never even paid a household bill before he was sentenced. He handled everything. My life followed the pattern of life in Ceylon twenty years ago. I did not do anything without asking his permission—even dine with a relative. I had been brought up to expect such a life—straight from the discipline of my father's house to my husband's in a marriage that was half-arranged.

'Since March I've had to learn to act alone—to make decisions and organise things I'd barely had contact with before. I had no friends of my own. Any entertaining we did at White Walls was for business, we didn't have a proper social life. And for relaxation my husband had his own hobbies. I never wanted to leave Ceylon in the first place. People of my class do not come from Ceylon to England to live.

'My main expenses are the children's school fees. I consider these above everything, for I want my children to have a profession. I don't want them to go into business.

'I knew nothing about my husband's business activities until I heard about them at the trial. I never offered opinions to him on those matters—but even if I'd known enough to do so, he wouldn't have taken any notice.'

It was impossible to shake Pushpam's faith in her husband. She was to defend him to the end. 'I'm nothing but proud of him,' she said. 'Like all brilliant, progressive men in history he has been persecuted.'

In spite of the optimism he had shown at his first meeting with the Governor, Savundra never left Wormwood Scrubs for the more congenial surroundings of an open prison. His health gave constant cause for anxiety so that, shortly after his appeal had been dismissed, he was transferred to the hospital wing and was so seldom seen by his fellow prisoners—including Walker, to whom he never spoke again—that he became known as 'The Howard Hughes of Wormwood Scrubs'.

There is no doubt that he was now seriously ill and indeed it was reported that he nearly died on three occasions.

One consequence of his chronic ill health was that he was not required to undertake any of the more tedious prison tasks like making toys or sewing mail bags. Instead, he was given the job of looking after the prison hospital accounts; a somewhat ironic position for the man who had once dealt in millions and at the same time described himself as 'the world's worst book-keeper'.

It might be thought that the nationwide publicity given to the F.A.M. scandal would have served as a warning to the public to entrust their insurance to nationally reputable firms.

In fact, there were a round dozen cut-price companies which crashed during the last four years of the nineteen-sixties. Some motorists were victims of as many as four of them. Much of the blame must lie with cynical brokers who redirected clients time after time to cut-price firms in order to collect higher commissions.

Savundra had himself once said: 'If we go down, we'll bring the whole bloody lot with us.'

It proved to be only too true. As the cut-price companies collapsed one after another, urgent measures were rushed through Parliament in an effort to block the holes Savundra had been the first to exploit.

The required capital figure of £50,000 for starting an insurance company was obviously inadequate. This sum was doubled in the 1967 Insurance Companies Act and in 1973 further raised to a realistic £250,000. Moreover, the Board of Trade were given new powers to keep an eye on the continued liquidity of a new company, and the ridiculous two-year rule by which new insurers were exempt from showing a solvency margin was scrapped.

Further, the Board of Trade were now empowered to investigate potential company owners as to their previous character, expertise and general knowledge of the business. Teeth were added to this safeguard in that the Board could refuse anyone the right to start an insurance business without being required to give a reason.

It is now generally recognised that there is no such thing as 'cheap' insurance. This was emphasised by the fact that the mammoth Vehicle and General Insurance Company, whose premiums were after all only marginally below the tariff rate themselves (and in whose conduct there was no question of fraud), eventually went down leaving 800,000 motorists uncovered—twice the number who suffered from F.A.M.

CHAPTER TWENTY-FOUR

End of the Road

SAVUNDRA STEPPED UNSTEADILY TO freedom on 4th October, 1974. He had served six years, seven months and three days of his ten-year sentence, having earned full remission. All the podginess had gone and he looked markedly older, but he was dressed as smartly as ever in a dark grey striped suit with a white shirt and red and black tie.

Pushpam was not at the prison gates to meet him. An acquaintance drove him back to the little white-painted house in Old Windsor. It was 7.30 in the morning and pouring with rain.

Once the door of the house had closed behind him Savundra refused to meet any reporters but he did give a brief interview to the B.B.C. To them he stressed that he had no money. 'My wife is sufficiently well endowed by God with the things of this world to make sure that I can, like a number of English aristocratic people, live off my wife.' Now all he wanted was privacy. 'I am living on borrowed time already. In prison my heart stopped beating on three occasions but each time the doctors brought me back to life.'

Certainly the days of opulent living were over. As Pushpam put it: 'We lived the life of the rich. We had the best. Servants did the work. But no longer. That is all gone.

'Everything we had has been sold—cars, pictures, silver. My children all worked in their holidays and at night to help make ends meet. Until we found a buyer I drove the Rolls to the launderette to do my washing. That amused people.'

Savundra had only one more comment to make. It was to say that he was not bitter against anyone except the judge and jury who had condemned him. He was going to take his case to the International Court of Human Rights in Strasbourg to clear his name.

231

All the time Savundra had been in prison, Gerhard Weiss had never given up his search for the 'missing million'. There was one moment when he thought he was getting close. He got a tip that Savundra had a bank account in a small town in the mountains above Geneva. Although private Swiss bank accounts are protected by a formidable barrier of secrecy, access is easier if there has been a conviction for large-scale internationally-reported crime. Weiss was able to get a judgement in the local court, after serving the necessary writ on Savundra. It was not defended.

A quaint ceremony now followed. The bailiff, who had seized the deed box, put it up for auction. Bidding was not keen and Weiss obtained it for ten francs which sufficed to pay the bailiff's fees.

The box contained almost £15,000 in securities, which must rate as a good bargain for ten francs, but was far below what the anxious creditors had been hoping for.

Weiss, however, had more success in another direction. There had been optimistic estimates of the amount owed to F.A.M. by brokers—some people putting it high as £1,500,000. In fact, the true figure was just a third of that. Altogether, from the company's creditors, he managed to rescue about £1,000,000. And at the end of 1977 he was able to pay out a dividend of 30 pence in the pound.

In the house at Old Windsor, Savundra, still only fifty-one years old, remained a recluse. All attempts by journalists to reach him were blocked. William Hickey of the *Express* at least got an indirect message. 'The *Express*? Tell those bastards to go to hell. I'm still trying to get my health back and that's all I've got to say. However much you pump me, I have nothing to say about my memoirs. Or anything.'

Apart from journalists, there were few visitors. Stuart de Quincey Walker, understandably, stayed away. The coldness was mutual. Walker, who all his life had been prone to grab the nettle of opportunity without giving much thought to the possibility that he might get stung, can be forgiven his disillusionment. After his release from prison he had quietly returned to his life-long love, the sea, one of the few tastes he had ever really had in common with Savundra.

But there were still a few who continued to hold some regard for Savundra. His personal secretary had said at the trial that she would work for him again, if he ever asked her, and Trevor Williams, his ex-management services manager, still says of his job: 'It was one of the best working relationships I've ever had.'

The former Ceylonese Premier. Sir Oliver Goonitelleke, who remembers Savundra from his early days in business, still calls him 'a good man'. 'You cannot but admire someone,' he says, 'who goes to jail and despite everything remains a character.' And Savundra had defenders in the Church, to which he had given life-long allegiance.

'I know Savundra as a good and devoted man,' a priest said of him. 'His family never go to bed until they have said their prayers and they attend church regularly.

'I hold Emil Savundra in the highest esteem and I do not believe that there is any evil in him. He always carries a picture of the Sacred Heart with him. He regarded it as immoral to make huge profits—he believed in sharing.'

No one, however, believed that Savundra would ever again figure in any large-scale financial operation. No one, that is, except Savundra himself. While leading the quiet life at Windsor, he was dreaming up a scheme which, had it come off, would have dwarfed all his previous enterprises.

It would have satisfied the three things he wanted to achieve most of all in his life: the aggrandisement of his family; the acquisition of a sum of money so vast as to make him one of the world's richest men; and a position of international significance.

The plan was nothing less than to sell to America the vast estates in north Ceylon which belonged to Pushpam's family. The object was to provide the American forces with territory near Trincomalee, where they could establish a strategically-placed nuclear base. Trincomalee, situated in the Bay of Bengal, had been the base of the British East Indies squadron in World War II and its geographical advantages to the Americans were obvious.

In return, Savundra was to acquire the sum of 200,000,000 dollars. But the deal would only go through if at the same time his wife was made Queen of north Ceylon.

That Pushpam should become Queen of Jaffna did not seem to him an outrageous idea at all. He had always maintained she was a direct descendant of the former royal dynasty of Jaffna. Savundra, after his discharge from prison, had developed a rediscovered pride in the land of his birth. Forgetting his once-fervent British nationalism, he commented: 'Don't forget that when you English were running around naked with blue paint on your faces our women were dressed in silks.'

He took this improbable venture seriously and went to the American Embassy about it. There is some evidence that the Embassy officials were considerate enough not to shatter too precipitately the delusions of a prematurely-aged and sick man.

The American Embassy did not have to be patient for very long. Four days before Christmas, 1976, and after only two years of freedom, Emil Savundra collapsed at the house in Ousely Road. An ambulance was summoned immediately but by the time it arrived at Old Windsor's King Edward VII Hospital, he was dead.

His heart, which had so often enabled him to postpone the judgements of his fellows, could no longer delay the higher judgement which, he believed, finally comes to all men.

Index

Compiled by Robert Urwin